STEP BY STEP THROUGH THE

NEW TESTAMENT

THOMAS D. LEA

TOM HUDSON

LifeWay Press®
Nashville, Tennessee

ISBN 978-0-8054-9946-9 • Item 001117273
Dewey decimal classification: 225 • Subject heading: BIBLE—NEW TESTAMENT

Cover photography: Ken Duncan, © 2012 Divine Guidance

To order additional copies of this resource, write to LifeWay Resources
Customer Service; One LifeWay Plaza; Nashville, TN 37234; fax 615-251-5933;
phone 800-458-2772; email orderentry@lifeway.com; or order online at LifeWay.com.

Printed in the United States of America

Groups Ministry Publishing • LifeWay Resources
One LifeWay Plaza • Nashville, TN 37234

Contents

The Authors 4

Introduction 5

UNIT 1   God and the New Covenant 7

UNIT 2   Introduction to the Gospels 25

UNIT 3   The Gospel of Matthew 42

UNIT 4   The Gospel of Mark 59

UNIT 5   The Gospel of Luke 74

UNIT 6   The Gospel of John 90

UNIT 7   The Book of Acts, Part 1 107

UNIT 8   The Book of Acts, Part 2 121

UNIT 9   The Writings of Paul, Part 1 137

UNIT 10   The Writings of Paul, Part 2 155

UNIT 11   The Writings of Paul, Part 3 172

UNIT 12   The General Letters 190

UNIT 13   The Book of Revelation 209

The Authors

THOMAS D. LEA wrote the content for *Step by Step Through the New Testament*. Thomas, dean of Southwestern Baptist Theological Seminary's school of theology, served as a professor of New Testament for 16 years. He pastored several churches, including Hunter Street Baptist Church, Birmingham, Alabama.

Thomas, a native of Houston, Mississippi, was a graduate of Mississippi State University and held a master of divinity and a doctor of theology from Southwestern.

Thomas was widely used as a conference leader and teacher at state and national conference centers, and he wrote for journals and denominational publications. He was the author of *How to Study Your Bible* and the coauthor of *MasterDesign: Your Calling as a Christian*.

TOM HUDSON is the author of the learning activities in *Step by Step Through the New Testament* and also for the companion study *Step by Step Through the Old Testament*. Tom is a former biblical-studies designer in the Adult Sunday School Ministry Department of LifeWay Christian Resources. He joined LifeWay in January 1986 after 21 years as the pastor of Oak Forest Baptist Church in Jackson, Mississippi. He also served as the pastor of First Southern Baptist Church in Anaconda, Montana, and the assistant pastor of Broadmoor Baptist Church in Jackson, Mississippi. While in Mississippi, he served in numerous positions in the Mississippi Baptist Convention.

Tom, a native of Jackson, Mississippi, is a graduate of Mississippi College and holds a master of divinity degree from Southwestern Baptist Theological Seminary and a doctor of ministry degree from New Orleans Baptist Theological Seminary.

Introduction

Step by Step Through the New Testament is an in-depth study designed to provide an overview of the characters and themes of the New Testament. This course has the following educational characteristics.

An In-Depth Study

- Participants interact with this self-paced workbook for 30 to 60 minutes each day and complete life-related learning activities.
- Participants meet for a 1½- to 2-hour small-group learning session each week.
- The course leader (or facilitator) guides group members to reflect on and discuss what they have studied during the week and then make practical application of the study to real life. This small group becomes a support group for participants as they help one another understand and apply the Scriptures to life.

Studying *Step by Step Through the New Testament*

Six Features in New Testament Study

During the next 13 weeks we will—
1. *examine* the nature of the New Testament;
2. *study* the world of the New Testament;
3. *investigate* the text of the New Testament;
4. *identify* the authors of the New Testament;
5. *explore* the contents of the New Testament;
6. *practice* principles of interpretation of the New Testament.

One Lesson at a Time

Step by Step Through the New Testament is different from most books in that it is not intended simply to be read from cover to cover. To get the most out of this course, you must take your time by studying only one day's lesson at a time. Do not try to study through several lessons in a single day. You need time to incorporate these thoughts into your understanding and practice. Do not skip any of the learning activities. These are designed to help you develop a framework for understanding and applying the New Testament.

Do All Learning Activities

 Learning activities will begin (like this paragraph) with a leaf indicating indented type. Follow the instructions given. After you have completed the activity, you will return to the content.

Normally you will be given answers at the bottom of the page, so you can check your own work. Write your own answer before reading mine. Sometimes your response to the activity will be your own response or opinion, and no right or wrong answer can be given. If you have difficulty with an activity or you question the answers given, write a note about your concern in the margin. Discuss it with your leader or small group.

Study with a Small Group

Once each week you should attend a small-group session designed to help you discuss the content you studied the previous week, share insights and testimonies, encourage one another, and pray together. Small groups should not have more than 10 members for maximum effectiveness. Larger groups will experience less closeness, less intimate sharing, more absenteeism, and more dropouts. If more than 10 people want to study the course, enlist additional leaders for each group of 6 to 10.

Enlist Your Friends

If you have already started studying *Step by Step Through the New Testament* alone, enlist a few friends to study through the course with you. You will discover that others can help you learn and apply the teachings of this course. You will miss much of the intended learning from this course apart from a small-group study.

Read the New Testament

As you study the New Testament step-by-step during these next 13 weeks, reading the New Testament itself will be most helpful. On each unit page you will find suggested New Testament readings for that week. By reading the passages indicated each week (averaging four chapters each day), you can complete the entire New Testament in 13 weeks.

Resources for *Step by Step Through the New Testament*

- Member book: *Step by Step Through the New Testament* (item 001117273)

- Leader guide: *Step by Step Through the New Testament Leader Guide* (item 005741125, available as a free PDF download from LifeWay.com)

To order additional copies of this resource, write to LifeWay Resources Customer Service; One LifeWay Plaza; Nashville, TN 37234; fax 615-251-5933; phone toll free 800-458-2772; email orderentry@lifeway.com; or order online at LifeWay.com.

Similar resources are available for *Step by Step Through the Old Testament* by Waylon Bailey and Tom Hudson:
- Member book: *Step by Step Through the Old Testament* (item 001116311)
- Leader guide: *Step by Step Through the Old Testament Leader Guide* (item 005741126, available as a free PDF download from LifeWay.com)

Unit **1**   *God and the New Covenant*

**Reading Through
the New Testament**

❑ Matthew 1–3
❑ Matthew 4–5
❑ Matthew 6–7
❑ Mark 1
❑ Luke 1–2
❑ Luke 3–4
❑ John 1

UNIT LEARNING GOAL: The study of this unit should help you understand the background of the events and writing of the New Testament. You will be able to:
- Describe the emphasis of pagan religions during the New Testament era.
- Recognize the vital role of the synagogue in Jewish religion.
- Define and describe writings not found in our Bible, such as the Apocrypha and Pseudepigrapha.
- List the main teachings of Jewish sects, such as Pharisees and Sadducees.
- Identify the criteria Christians used to determine the New Testament canon.
- Recall five principles of sound biblical interpretation.

PALESTINE IN THE TIME OF JESUS

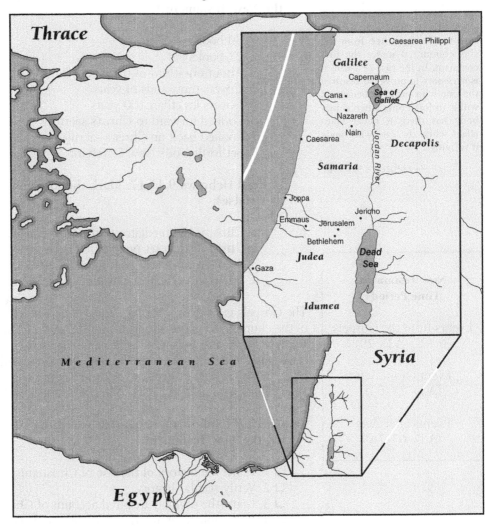

Day 1 New Testament Background

UNIT 1

The Nature of the New Testament

The 27 books of the New Testament present the life of Christ and His continuing work through His church. It is about one-third the length of the Old Testament. The Old Testament has 39 books. the events of the Old Testament covered thousands of years of divine history, but the events of the New Testament covered less than a century.

New Testament Means
New Covenant

The term *New Testament* means *New Covenant*, a contrast with the Old Covenant under which God dealt with Israel in anticipation of Christ's coming. The term "testament" usually refers to an agreement which goes into effect on the death of the one making the covenant. The death of Jesus put into effect the New Covenant (Heb. 9:15-17).

"For this reason Christ is the mediator of a new covenant, that those who are called may receive the promised eternal inheritance - now that he has died as a ransom to set them free from the sins committed under the first covenant. In the case of a will, it is necessary to prove the death of the one who made it, because a will is in force only when somebody has died; it never takes effect while the one who made it is living."

—Hebrews 9:15-17

A. In the blanks to the left of each of the following items write *OT* for those that describe the Old Testament and *NT* for those that describe the New Testament.[1]

____ 1. 39 books
____ 2. 27 books
____ 3. About one-third of the whole Bible
____ 4. Covers thousands of years
____ 5. Covers less than 100 years
____ 6. Looked forward to Christ's sacrifice
____ 7. Looked back on Christ's sacrifice
____ 8. Set forth God's New Covenant

B. Read Hebrews 9:15-17. Mark the following statements as *T* (true) or *F* (false):

____ 1. Christ is the mediator of the New Covenant.
____ 2. Christ died to set people free from their sins.
____ 3. A covenant or will is in force only after the person who made it dies.
____ 4. The death of Christ put the New Covenant into effect.

**New Testament
Time Periods**

Events from the Gospels
(6 B.C.–A.D. 29)

Events from Acts
(A.D. 29–63)

Events after Acts
(A.D. 63–76)

The Gospels refer to events of the earliest periods (6 B.C.-A.D. 29). The expansion of the church covers the period from A.D. 29 to 63 and includes the Books of Acts, Romans, First and Second Corinthians, Galatians, Ephesians, Philippians, Colossians, First and Second Thessalonians, Philemon, and James. The post-Acts period (A.D. 63-96) is seen in First and Second Timothy, Titus, Hebrews, First and Second Peter, First, Second, and Third John, Jude, and Revelation.

Check the following items that you think state a good reason for studying the New Testament.[2]

❑ 1. Learn the history of the rise of Christianity.
❑ 2. Verify secular history.
❑ 3. Learn the divinely inspired account of Christ's death and resurrection.
❑ 4. To be able to argue the Bible with other people.

---

1. Answers to A: You probably do not need to check your answers, but just in case: 1, 4, and 6 are OT; the rest are NT. Answers to B: Right! All of these are true.

❑ 5. Discover the beliefs and practices of Christians in the early churches.
❑ 6. Satisfy curiosity.
❑ 7. Grow in the grace and knowledge of the Lord Jesus Christ.

The New Testament World

The political world. Rome had grown from an obscure village on the Tiber River to become the ruling empire of the New Testament world. The Roman government controlled the Jewish state. What we learn about both Rome and the Jewish nation can make us more informed Bible students.

**Rome Founded
753 B.C.**

The Roman Empire. Founded in 753 B.C., Rome was initially a union of small villages in its immediate area. Although originally ruled by a king, it grew to become a well-organized republic by the fifth century B.C. Rome made alliances with neighboring towns and villages and fought grueling wars with the Etruscans and other neighboring tribes. In 146 B.C. Rome extended its power over Carthage in North Africa and over Macedonia and the Grecian peninsula. In 63 B.C. Pompey extended control to Judea.

**Rome Captured Palestine
63 B.C.**

The men who ruled Rome used the Roman army to conquer the known world. They also enforced their power at home. Augustus Caesar crushed his opponents in 30 B.C., and eventually became the first Roman emperor. He served in office (27 B.C. to A. D. 14) at the birth of Christ, revived the state religion of Rome, reorganized the government for efficiency, and built many splendid buildings. Some Romans worshiped him as "Lord and God," but there is no evidence that Augustus sought such worship.

**Roman Rulers During the
New Testament Period†**

1. Augustus Caesar
   (27 B.C.–A.D. 14)
2. Tiberius (A.D. 14–37)
3. Gaius (Caligula)
   (A.D. 37-41)
4. Claudius (A.D. 41–54)
5. Nero (A.D. 54–68)
6. Domitian
   (A.D. 81–96)

Augustus' adopted son, Tiberius, succeeded him and ruled from A.D. 14-37. He served during the time of Jesus' death. Gaius (Caligula), who was mentally unbalanced, ruled from A.D. 37 to 41 during Paul's early ministry, and Claudius, who ruled from A.D. 41 to 54, expelled Jews from Rome due to an outbreak of riots in Rome (Acts 18:2). He also made a determined effort to restore the Roman religion to its former place of importance.

The brutal and erratic Nero (A.D. 54–68) followed him. Nero carried out persecutions against Christians in Rome. Church tradition holds that Peter and Paul died in these persecutions. The emperor Domitian, who ruled from A.D. 81 to 96, insisted on being worshiped as "Lord and God." Many feel that his terrible persecutions against Christians are mentioned in Revelation (Rev. 2:13; 3:10).

**Senatorial Provinces—
Proconsuls**

As the Romans extended their power, they organized the conquered territories into two types of provinces. Relatively peaceful provinces were placed under the Roman Senate and had officers known as *proconsuls* (Acts 18:12). They were known as senatorial provinces. However, the emperor ruled directly over the more turbulent provinces. These imperial provinces had officers known as *procurators* (the term translated as "governor" refers to the procurator, see Matt. 27:11). Pontius Pilate is the best known of these procurators.

**Imperial Provinces—
Procurators**

Pax Romana

The Romans gave considerable liberty to the Roman rulers of the provinces, and in turn, the rulers usually did not interfere with the religious practices of the provinces. The reign of the Roman emperors of the New Testament period led to a time of peace known as the *Pax Romana*. The stability and unity of the civilized world under Rome made the spread of Christianity much easier.

---

2. Answers: Your response, but I hope you checked 1, 3, 5, 7.
†Butler, Trent, ed. *Holman Bible Dictionary* (Nashville: Holman Bible Publishers, 1991), 1208–9.

RESPONDING TO GOD'S WORD

While this unit is primarily an introduction to the New Testament, keep in mind that this material is directly related to your goal of more accurately understanding this part of God's Word. As I read the New Testament, I always ask the Lord to use His Word to work in my life in the two following ways. If this is your desire, check the boxes and make this your prayer to Him.

❏ Lord, as I study the New Testament, use the truth of Your Word to free me from all that would hinder Your work in my life (John 8:32).
❏ Lord, use Your Word in my life as "a lamp to my feet and a light for my path" so that You may lead and guide me to accomplish your will (Ps. 119:105).

Day 2 *The Social World*

UNIT 1

The Jewish State

Exiled to Babylon

42,000 returned

Many Jews were exiled to Babylon. Others escaped to Egypt (Jer. 41–43). Babylon fell to the Persian king Cyrus in 538 B.C. In his first year Cyrus issued a decree allowing all Jews to return to the Holy Land. He promised to pay for rebuilding the temple with money from the royal treasury (Ezra 6:1-5). A majority of the Jews preferred to remain in Babylon, but 42,000, mostly from Judah, Benjamin, and Levi, returned under the leadership of Sheshbazzar (Ezra 1:5-11,2:64). These who returned began to rebuild the temple (Ezra 3:8-13), but opposition delayed its completion for over 20 years (Ezra 4).

Ezra's Group

Nehemiah's Group

In 458 B.C. another delegation of Jews, headed by Ezra the scribe (Ezra 7:1-10), set out for Jerusalem. Some 13 years later Nehemiah joined them (Neh. 2:1-10). He mobilized the people to rebuild the demolished wall of Jerusalem (Neh. 6:15-16). Nehemiah, aided by Ezra the scribe, also instituted strict applications of Jewish laws (Neh. 8:1-8). These Jews were strongly devoted to the Old Testament law.

🌿 **Place the following events in chronological order by placing 1, 2, 3, 4, and 5 in the blanks on the left (1 = earliest; 5 = latest).[3]**

____ A. Ezra led a delegation of Jews from Babylon to Jerusalem.
____ B. Ezra and Nehemiah led in developing a group of Jews strongly devoted to the Old Testament law.
____ C. Cyrus of Persia conquered Babylon.
____ D. Sheshbazzar led 42,000 Jews back to the promised land.
____ E. Nehemiah mobilized the Jews to rebuild Jerusalem's wall.

Outside the Jewish State

Alexander the Great

Beginning with victories in 334 B.C., Alexander the Great of Macedonia spread Greek culture, or Hellenism, over much of the Middle East. By the time he died

---

3. Answers: A-3, B-5, C-1, D-2, E-4.

**Ptolemaic Rulers
from Egypt
(320–198 B.C.)**

prematurely in 323 B.C., Alexander's influence extended throughout the known world. After his death, four of his generals divided up his empire. Ptolemy gained control of Egypt and extended his influence into Palestine. Ptolemy's successors in Egypt ruled Palestine from 320–198 B.C. They were benevolent to the Jews and sponsored the translation of the Hebrew Old Testament into Greek. This translation, known as the Septuagint, was completed sometime during the reign of Ptolemy Philadelphus (285–246 B.C.). Jewish legend says that 72 scholars worked for 72 days on the project. The Roman numeral LXX is frequently used to represent the Septuagint (meaning 70 serving as the nearest round number to 72).

Septuagint (LXX)

**Seleucid Rulers from Syria
(198–168 B.C.)**

Eventually the rulers of Syria, know as the Seleucids, gained control of Palestine from Egypt (198–168 B.C.). Many of these rulers used the name Antiochus. Antiochus IV (175–163 B.C.), known as Epiphanes, attempted to force Hellenistic culture on the Jews. Antiochus invaded Jerusalem in 168 B.C., destroyed the city walls, and installed an image of Zeus in the Jewish temple. He inflicted the death penalty on those who possessed or read the Jewish Scriptures.

Mattathias

Devout Jews under the leadership of a village priest named Mattathias revolted in 167 B.C. Mattathias soon died, but leadership of the revolt passed quickly to a son of Mattathias, Judas. The family of Mattathias became known as the "Maccabees" from the nickname *Maccabeus* (the *Hammer*) given to Judas.

Judas Maccabeus

**Maccabean period
(167–142 B.C.)**

Judas led a struggle for freedom by waging successful guerrilla warfare. He ultimately recaptured the Temple and all Palestine and expelled Syrian troops from their citadel in Jerusalem (story is found in 1 Maccabees of the Apocrypha). After Judas' death in 160 B.C. the struggle continued under the leadership of his brothers, Jonathan and Simon. Simon won Jewish political freedom in 142 B.C.

**Hasmonean Dynasty
(142–63 B.C.)**

The history of the Maccabean rule (also know as the Hasmonean dynasty, named after Hasmon, an earlier relative) is a story of strife and discord caused by lust for power. The political aims of the Hasmoneans alienated many of the religious Jews. The descendants of the Hasmoneans became the *Sadducees* of the New Testament period. The successors of the devout Jews, who opposed the Hasmoneans (also known as the Hasidim, or "the holy ones"), became the *Pharisees.*

🌿 **Indicate the answer to the following questions by writing in the blank to the left *S* for Sadducees or *P* for Pharisees.**[4]

    ____ A. What group descended from devout Jews who were opposed to the political aims of the Maccabean rulers?
    ____ B. What group was known as the "Hasidim"?
    ____ C. What group was connected to the Hasmoneans?
    ____ D. What group was more politically oriented?
    ____ E. What group was more religiously oriented?

**Roman Period
63 B.C. Onward**

Herod the Great

After Pompey conquered Palestine in 63 B.C., the Romans allowed a native vassal ruler, Herod the Great, to control Palestine (37–4 B.C.). His father Antipater had built favor with the Romans, and he was able to manipulate Herod into power. Herod was an efficient ruler and a clever politician. He provided subsidies, including free grain and clothing, during times of famine. He began many building projects, the most notable of which was the beautification of the Jewish temple in Jerusalem. Although Herod occasionally attended Jewish services, he was never a godly Jew and was generally hated by devout Jews. Plagued by a sense of insecurity, he murdered

---

4. Answers: A-P, B-P, C-S, D-S, E-P.

any who opposed him, including some of his wives and children. The brutality toward children mentioned in Matthew 2:13-18 was characteristic of Herod.

Herod's Sons

Herod's sons lacked their father's ability and inherited only parts of his old kingdom. Archelaus (Matt.2:21-23) ruled Judea, Samaria, and Idumaea. Antipas (Mark 6:14-29) inherited the territories of Galilee and Perea. Herod Agrippa I, a grandson of Herod the Great, murdered James the Apostle and imprisoned Peter (Acts 12). Herod Agrippa II, son of Herod Agrippa I, heard Paul's defense (Acts 25; 26).

Archelaus lost his office due to misrule and was replaced with Roman governors, who ruled except for a brief time. One of them–Pontius Pilate–heard the Jewish charges against Jesus. Two other governors, Felix and Festus, sat in judgment on Jewish charges against Paul (Acts 23-26).

Roman Procurators (Governors)

Pontius Pilate
Felix
Festus

The Social World

Jewish society. Scholars estimate that 4,000,000 Jews lived in the Roman Empire during New Testament times. Only 700,000 lived in Palestine. Most of the Jews were "of the dispersion." They lived in cities throughout the Roman world such as Alexandria, Antioch, and Rome.

Multilingual

The common language of the people was Aramaic. The priestly language was Hebrew. Many spoke Greek. For example, Paul spoke three or more languages, and Jesus and His disciples spoke Hebrew, Aramaic, and possibly Greek.

A Wealthy Aristocracy

Judaism had a wealthy aristocracy. Many of these were Sadducees, virtual rulers of Judea. They controlled business linked with the temple such as revenues from the sale of sacrificial animals and the exchange of money. Some were also landowners who rented out farmland and received income from crops they raised.

Poor Majority

Most Palestinians were poor farmers, craftsmen, or businessmen. Slavery was not widely practiced among the Jews. Some of the disciples owned fishing businesses which provided them adequate support (Mark 1:16-20).

Jewish law made all persons equally responsible before God and all Jews morally equal in God's sight. It restrained the wealthy Jews from becoming too oppressive in their leadership. Jews regarded the wealthy as especially blessed by God, but in theory all persons could receive this blessing by good works and moral obedience.

Pagan society. Pagan society had clearly defined social classes. The upper class, consisting of landowners and businessmen, enjoyed a luxurious lifestyle. This luxury sapped the vitality of the upper class and discouraged the lower class.

The "Plebs"

The middle class was almost nonexistent. Wars led to the death of some middle class members, and slaves claimed the jobs of others. Many sank into the class of the "plebs," or the poor people, who quickly followed anyone who offered them food and amusements.

Slaves

Slaves represented the largest proportion of the Roman Empire. Less than half of the Roman world were freemen. Many of the slaves were well-trained professionals reduced to the position of slavery by war, debt, and birth, and not by ethnic differences. Slaves served as physicians, teachers, and skilled craftsmen, but the effect of slavery was a cancer on society. Masters depended on slaves for their labor and skill, thus often failing to develop their own ingenuity. Slaves fell into practices of fraud, deceit, and immorality. Living a moral life under this system was almost impossible.

The social conditions of unemployment, despair, and greed provided a fertile breeding ground for criminal minds and practices in the first century. Paul's picture of heathen life in Romans 1:18-32 is an accurate portrayal of the potential for evil inherent in the society.

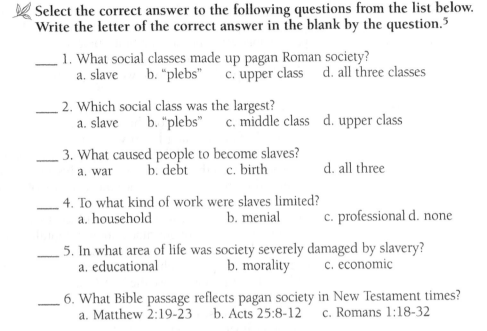

Select the correct answer to the following questions from the list below. Write the letter of the correct answer in the blank by the question.[5]

___ 1. What social classes made up pagan Roman society?
   a. slave   b. "plebs"   c. upper class   d. all three classes

___ 2. Which social class was the largest?
   a. slave   b. "plebs"   c. middle class   d. upper class

___ 3. What caused people to become slaves?
   a. war   b. debt   c. birth   d. all three

___ 4. To what kind of work were slaves limited?
   a. household   b. menial   c. professional   d. none

___ 5. In what area of life was society severely damaged by slavery?
   a. educational   b. morality   c. economic

___ 6. What Bible passage reflects pagan society in New Testament times?
   a. Matthew 2:19-23   b. Acts 25:8-12   c. Romans 1:18-32

RESPONDING TO GOD'S WORD

Read and meditate on Romans 1:18-32. List three characteristics of a world without Christ.

_____

Give thanks to God for the kindness and grace He has shown through giving us the Lord Jesus Christ as our Savior and Lord.

Day 3 *The Religious World*

UNIT 1

Pagan Religions

False Gods

In the ancient world people expressed their inherent religious nature through various religions that had arisen. In early Rome each family worshiped the gods of their own farm and home. These gods were a personification of the forces met in daily life. As Rome grew and conquered Greece, some of its deities were blended into Greek pantheon. Zeus and Hera, his wife, were the chief gods.

---

5. Answers:1-d, 2-a, 3-d, 4-d, 5-b. 6-c.

Emperor Worship

First-century Rome practiced emperor worship. At the death of Augustus, the Roman Senate bestowed divinity upon him. Caligula, Nero, and Domitian claimed deity for themselves. Emperor worship made support of the state a religious duty, and the refusal of Christians to practice it exposed them to persecution.

Mystery Religions

The Occult

The *mystery religions* of Eastern origin offered personal contact with a deity and a promise of personal immortality with an outlet for emotional experiences. Many people followed the superstitious practices of the *occult*. Formulas and rituals invoked the protection or service of spirits and demons. Horoscopes, astrology, and attempts to predict the future were frequently used in the New Testament world.

Gnostics

Educated people satisfied religious longings by turning to various philosophies. The Gnostics promised salvation through secret knowledge. They believed the supreme God could have nothing to do with tangible things. He produced a series of creations, each more worldly and less spiritual, the last of which created the world. Gnostics rejected the world as evil. Some became ascetics (strict self-denial). Others promoted immoral behavior since the activities of the body did not affect the soul.

Epicureans

The *Epicureans* (named after Epicurus, 4th century B.C.) taught that pleasure was the highest good. They sought moderation, tranquillity, and peace of mind. Some later followers became totally hedonistic, seeking an excess of pleasure. Paul probably referred to their philosophy in his statement, "If the dead are not raised, 'Let us eat and drink, for tomorrow we die.'" (1 Cor. 15-32).

Stoics

Other Philosophies

The *Stoics* emphasized virtue instead of pleasure. They stressed responsibility in the face of adversity. They emphasized a duty-bound acceptance of personal fate (Acts 17:18). The *Cynics* rejected all standards and conventions and tried to live with simple needs. The *Skeptics* gave up the hope for finding any absolute truth.

The Pagan World

- Family gods
- Greek Gods
- Emperor worship
- Mystery religions
- The occult
- Gnostic religion
- Epicureans
- Stoics
- Cynics
- Skeptics

🌿 **Match the items on the left with the descriptions on the right. Write the correct letters in the blanks.**[6]

___ 1. Worship of family gods that personified natural forces	A. Offered personal contact with a deity
___ 2. Worship of Greek gods	B. Zeus and Hera
___ 3. Worship of the emperor	C. Associated with astrology and foretelling the future
___ 4. Mystery religions	D. Gods of farm and home
___ 5. Worship of the occult	E. Support of the state as a religious duty
___ 6. Gnostic religion	F. Pleasure as the highest good
___ 7. Epicurean philosophy	G. Simplified life
___ 8. Stoic philosophy	H. No absolute truth
___ 9. Cynic philosophy	I. Salvation by knowledge
___ 10. Skeptic philosophy	J. Acceptance of personal fate

The Jewish World

First-century Judaism had several unique features. Although it originated among the Jews, it extended itself to many proselytes (one who converted to a religion). It emphasized monotheism. Followers did not even admit the existence of other gods. Judaism provided an ethical emphasis which was inherent in its religious worship. It was based on the sacred Scriptures that were a revelation from God.

---

6. Answers: 1-D, 2-B, 3-E, 4-A, 5-C, 6-I, 7-F, 8-J, 9-G, 10-H.

Denounced Idolatry

Theology of Judaism. The Jewish belief in one God led them to denounce idolatry. Jews based their beliefs on the concrete acts of God in history and not on mythology or speculation. The Old Testament emphasized the fate of the nation as a whole. The later captivity of the nation led to an interest in individual responsibility. The early books of the Old Testament did not place a significant emphasis on individual resurrection. However, some of the prophets and later apocryphal writings in the period between the Testaments indicated a more strongly stated belief in the doctrine of individual faith, individual living, and individual resurrection.

The Coming of Messiah

The Jews anticipated the coming of God's Deliverer, or Messiah. They believed that Messiah would deliver them from political oppression by destroying their enemies. The Jews were not prepared to accept a Messiah who would suffer for human beings or redeem them by His death. This led to a clash with the apostles who proclaimed that Jesus was God's Messiah sent to suffer for sins.

To review some facts about the Jewish world of New Testament times, fill in the blanks.[7]

1. The Jews emphasized_____and denounced idolatry.

2. Jewish beliefs were based on the _____ of God in history, not on mythology or speculation.

3. The Jews looked forward to the coming of a _____ who would be a political/military deliverer.

Chief Center of Worship

The temple. The Jewish temple was the chief center of worship in Jerusalem. Jesus and the apostles taught within its courts. In the late fifties A.D. some Jewish Christians still took Jewish vows in the temple precincts (Acts 21:23-26). Development of Gentile Christianity finally severed the connection of the temple with Christianity.

Purposes of the Synagogue

- A place for the study and teaching of the law.
- A place of instruction for children.
- A social center for fellowship

The synagogue. The destruction of the Jerusalem temple in 586 B.C. led to the rise of the synagogue. Jews driven from the Holy Land by the Assyrians and Babylonians eventually founded synagogues in major cities of the Roman Empire. Synagogues for foreign-born Jews also were founded in Jerusalem (Acts 6:9) Though synagogue worship influenced the worship of Christians, the stubborn rejection of Christ by Jews led to later and complete rupture between Christians and the synagogue.

Write the answers to the following questions.[8]

1. What major event led to the rise of synagogues among the Jews?

_____

2. Synagogues served what three purposes?

A. A place for _____

B. A place for _____

C. A place for _____

3. What led to a complete rupture between Christians and the synagogue?

_____

7. Answers: 1-Monotheism, 2-acts, 3-Messiah

The Jewish Supreme Court

The Sanhedrin. The Roman conquerors permitted the Jews to handle many of their own legal matters. Towns throughout Palestine had numerous local courts to deal with local issues. Jerusalem had the great Sanhedrin, the Jewish supreme court, which met daily in the Temple area except for Sabbath days and other holy days.

High Priest Presided

The high priest presided over the 70 other members of the court, who came from both the Pharisees and the Sadducees (John 11:47-53). In the New Testament the Sanhedrin had the name of the council, and the members of the Sanhedrin were the "rulers, elders, and scribes" (Acts 4:5). In the first century the Sanhedrin lacked the power of capital punishment and had to appeal to the Romans to execute Jesus after they found Him worthy of death (John 18:28-32).

The Jewish holy calendar. The Jewish religious year had seven festivals or feasts prescribed for annual worship. The first five appeared in the Mosaic law. The last two originated in the exile.

JEWISH FEASTS

1. Passover and the Feast of Unleavened Bread (a single feast, John 13:1)
2. Feast of Pentecost (Acts 2:1)
3. New Year (Rosh Hashanah)
4. Day of Atonement (Yom Kippur, Acts 27:9)
5. Feast of Tabernacles (John 7:2)
6. Feast of Dedication (Hanukkah, John 10:22)
7. Feast of Purim (or Lights)

RESPONDING TO GOD'S WORD

Reflect on the three purposes fulfilled by the synagogues.

How do the purposes fulfilled by the synagogue compare to those fulfilled by the local church? How do they differ?

_____

What other purposes(s) is being fulfilled through your church?

_____

Are you as involved in the life and work of your church as God wants you to be?

_____

---

8. Answers:1-Destruction of the temple in 586 B.C.; 2-A, teaching and studying the law; 2-B, instructing children about their ancestral faith; 2-C, weekly fellowship; 3-The rejection of Christ by the Jews.

Day 4 *The Scriptures*

UNIT 1

Jewish Literature

The Jewish people were a nation devoted to their divine book. They had the Jewish Old Testament in the original Hebrew and also in the Greek translation, called the Septuagint. The Jews also had access to the *Targums*, Aramaic translations of the Old Testament which added some material not found in the biblical text.

Apocrypha

The Jews were aware of other books not found in the canonical Old Testament. First among these books were the *Apocrypha*, a term that means *hidden* or *secret*. These are writings of history, fiction, and Jewish wisdom, usually accepted as authoritative by Roman Catholics today, but rejected by Protestants. Among the books in the Apocrypha are First and Second Esdras, Tobit, Judith, Wisdom of Solomon, Ecclesiasticus, Baruch, First and Second Maccabees, and additions to Esther and Daniel.

Pseudepigrapha

A second set of books not found in our Bible has the name *pseudepigrapha*. This word means "falsely attributed writings," and refers to books falsely claiming to be written by famous persons. Some of these books use the names of deceased Old Testament figures as authors in order to obtain authority. Other pseudepigraphical writings describe the coming of God's judgment and God's kingdom on earth with highly symbolic and visionary language. Among these writings are: First and Second Enoch, the Sibylline Oracles, the Testaments of the Twelve Patriarchs, the Assumption of Moses, Jubilees, Letter of Aristeas, and Third and Fourth Maccabees.

Dead Sea Scrolls

The Dead Sea Scrolls found in caves near the Dead Sea in the years following 1947 contain literature of the Jewish sect of the Essenes composed or copied from 200 B.C. until A.D. 70. Among the works found were the Damascus (or Zadokite) Document and commentaries on various Old Testament books. In addition, copies of each book of the Old Testament except Esther appear among the literature of the Essenes.

Match the following items on the left with the correct term on the right. Write the correct letters in the blanks.[9]

____ 1. Used names of Old Testament figures as authors

____ 2. Aramaic translations of the Old Testament with added material not in the Hebrew Scriptures

____ 3. Writings of history, fiction, and wisdom accepted as authoritative by Roman Catholics but not by protestants

____ 4. Includes all Old Testament books except Esther

____ 5. 1 and 2 Maccabees

____ 6. 1 and 2 Enoch

____ 7. Means *hidden* or *secret*

A. Targums

B. Apocrypha

C. Pseudepigrapha

D. Dead Sea Scrolls

---

9. Answers: 1-C, 2-A, 3-B, 4-D, 5-B, 6-C, 7-B.

The Sects of Judaism

Pharisees

In New Testament times the largest and most influential sect was the *Pharisees*. They originated shortly after the time of the Maccabees. By 135 B.C. they were well established. The Pharisees kept the law rigidly, believed in the existence of angels and spirits, and expected a resurrection of the body. Some were self-righteous, but many were men of integrity and honor. Modern orthodox Judaism follows the pattern of Pharisaic morality, ceremonialism, and legalism. Some early Christians came from a Pharisaic background (Acts 15:5). Those of the Pharisees who believed found in Jesus the fulfillment of their hopes.

Sadducees

In the New Testament period the *Sadducees* were fewer in number than the Pharisees, but they had greater political power. Most of the high priestly families in New Testament times were Sadducees. The Sadducees followed a literal interpretation of the Law or Torah, accepting only the first five books of the Bible. They rejected the oral tradition the Pharisees accepted. They denied the existence of angels and spirits and did not believe in personal immortality. Sadducees were ready to join in support of any government that could preserve their influence.

Essenes

Most scholars link the *Essenes* with the group who left the ruins at Qumran near the Dead Sea. They had theological beliefs similar to the Pharisees, but they followed Old Testament laws more strictly. They frequently avoided marriage and resembled the monastic groups of early Christianity.

Zealots

The *Zealots* were not a religious sect such as the Pharisees or the Essenes, but a group of fanatical nationalists who supported violence as a means of liberation from Rome. One of Jesus' disciples, Simon, had been a part of this group (Luke 6:15).

Herodians

The *Herodians* (Mark 3:6) were a small minority of important Jews who supported the Herodian dynasty and Roman rule. Their political views were the opposite of the Zealots. Not actually a religious sect, they came from the Sadducean priestly aristocracy. They considered it to be to their advantage to support Herod's rule.

✎ Check the correct answer for each of the following sentences.[10]

1. The largest and most influential Jewish sect was the
   ❑ a. Pharisees ❑ b. Sadducees ❑ c. Essenes ❑ d. Zealots ❑ e. Herodians

2. The sect with most political power was the
   ❑ a. Pharisees ❑ b. Sadducees ❑ c. Essenes ❑ d. Zealots ❑ e. Herodians

3. The sect that emphasized keeping the law rigidly was the
   ❑ a. Pharisees ❑ b. Sadducees ❑ c. Essenes ❑ d. Zealots ❑ e. Herodians

4. Most of the high priestly families belonged to the
   ❑ a. Pharisees ❑ b. Sadducees ❑ c. Essenes ❑ d. Zealots ❑ e. Herodians

5. A non-religious group was the
   ❑ a. Pharisees ❑ b. Sadducees ❑ c. Essenes ❑ d. Zealots ❑ e. Herodians

6. A small sect with opposite aims from the Zealots was the
   ❑ a. Pharisees ❑ b. Sadducees ❑ c. Essenes ❑ d. Zealots ❑ e. Herodians

7. A sect that believed in the resurrection was the
   ❑ a. Pharisees ❑ b. Sadducees ❑ c. Essenes ❑ d. Zealots ❑ e. Herodians

8. A group of fanatical nationalists was the
   ☐ a. Pharisees ☐ b. Sadducees ☐ c. Essenes ☐ d. Zealots ☐ e. Herodians

9. A sect that denied angels, spirits, and immortality was the
   ☐ a. Pharisees ☐ b. Sadducees ☐ c. Essenes ☐ d. Zealots ☐ e. Herodians

The First Christians' Bible

Old Testament Their Guide

Oral & Written Sources

What kind of Bible did the first Christians have? There was no New Testament, for God was in the process of producing the New Testament through human writers led by Holy Spirit. Early Christians used the Old Testament as their source of information about God. Notice how Peter relied on the Old Testament in his sermon at Pentecost (Acts 2:14-36). They also had oral and written sources about Christ's life and work (see Luke 1:1-4; 1 Cor. 15:1-4). Sometimes the early Christians depended on a direct revelation from God by a Christian prophet (Acts 11:28).

The Canon of the New Testament

Even after God moved on the early Christians to write the New Testament, centuries passed before all of the churches agreed to accept all the books of our New Testament as authoritative. Paul's writings and the Gospels quickly received acceptance by churches. Some books, such as Hebrews, required a longer time for acceptance because Christians were uncertain of their authorship. The apocalyptic style of the Book of Revelation made some of the churches slow to accept it as an inspired writing. Very brief books, such as Second and Third John, received recognition slowly. Many of the early churches hesitated to accept Second Peter as genuine because its style of writing raised questions about authorship by the Apostle Peter.

***Canon* Refers to Accepted Books**

Eventually Christians accepted the 27 books in our New Testament as inspired and authoritative. They used the term *canon* to describe the collection of books. The term *canon* originally referred to a measuring rod. It later came to refer to books that fit the "measuring rod," or standard, of the beliefs and practices of the early church. They became the canon or guide by which all other books were measured.

🌿 **Why was the word *canon* applied to the New Testament?**[11]

_____

_____

27 Canonical Books

A church council meeting at Carthage in A.D. 397 recognized 27 books as authoritative. Christians believe that God guided the churches in their selection.

What criteria did the churches use in determining the books of the canon? Early Christians regarded all canonical books as inspired, but they used some objective signs to guide them in their determination.
- First, they asked if an apostle, such as Paul or John, or an associate of an apostle, such as Mark or Luke, was the author of the book.
- Second, they accepted those books whose teachings agreed with apostolic doctrine.
- Third, they accepted those books which were morally edifying and which had widespread acceptance throughout the church.

Criteria for Acceptance

- Apostolic association
- Apostolic doctrine
- Morally edifying and accepted

---

10. Answers: 1-a, 2-b, 3-a or c, 4-b, 5-d, 6-e, 7-a, 8-d, 9-b.
11. Answer: Did you say that *canon* originally referred to a measuring rod and later came to designate the books accepted as inspired based on the beliefs and practices of the early church?

Some edifying non-apostolic books failed to receive acceptance into the canon. We consider the writings of many modern authors edifying, but we would not include them in Scripture. Early Christians had such books they rejected from the canon.

🌿 **Fill in the blanks in the following list of objective criteria that Christians used to determine the New Testament canon.**[12]

1. The book had to be written by an _____ or one associated with such a person.

2. The book had to agree with _____ _____.

3. The book had to be morally _____ and to have been widely

_____ throughout the church.

RESPONDING TO GOD'S WORD

Pray a prayer of thanksgiving to God for the way He has guided the writing and preservation of His inspired Word.

Plan now to develop a system for regularly reading God's Word, and prepare to discuss your plan in your group meeting this week.

Day 5 — *Understanding Our New Testament*

U N I T   1

Transmission and Translation of the New Testament

Manuscripts of the New Testament. Early Christians used papyrus, a writing material made from a plant. It was very durable in a dry climate and has survived centuries of storage in caves. As churches could afford better writing materials, they used vellum, calfskin, parchment, or sheepskin.

Early manuscripts of the New Testament were written in capital or uncial letters with little punctuation or paragraph indication. Later manuscripts appear in cursive letters. Chapter and verse divisions came into use after printed editions of the Bible became more common in the 16th century.

Versions

- John Wycliffe, 1382
- William Tyndale, 1525
- King James, 1611
- New American Standard, 1960
- New International, 1973

Versions of the New Testament. John Wycliffe produced an English translation of the New Testament from Latin in 1382. William Tyndale translated his English version from the Greek in 1525. The King James or Authorized Version appeared in 1611. Since the appearance of the King James, many excellent Greek manuscripts of the New Testament have been discovered. Scholars have also made great advances in understanding the principles of translation of New Testament Greek. Numerous versions in English continue to appear as a result of additional study. Among these are: Revised Standard Version (1946), New American Standard Bible (1960), New English Bible (1961), and the New International Version (1973).

---

12. Answers: 1- apostle; 2-apostolic doctrine; 3-edifying accepted.

🖎 **1. List two reasons for the publication of other English versions in addition to the King James Version.**[13]

A. _____

B. _____

2. List two versions of the Bible that have been published since the King James Version.

A. _____

B. _____

KEY PEOPLE OF THE NEW TESTAMENT

Name	Culture	Occupation	Activity
Matthew (Levi)	Jewish	Tax Collector	Apostle of Jesus, Author
(John) Mark	Jewish	Missionary	Disciple of Peter, Author
Luke	Greek	Physician	Wrote Luke and Acts
John	Jewish	Fisherman	Wrote Gospel, Letters, Revelation
Paul	Jewish	Tentmaker	Wrote Romans–Philemon
James	Jewish	Carpenter (?)	Brother of Jesus, Author
Peter	Jewish	Fisherman	Wrote 1–2 Peter
Jude	Jewish	Carpenter	Wrote Jude
Herod the Great	Idumean	King of Judea	Ruler of Judea at Jesus' Birth
Caiaphas	Jewish	High Priest	Presided over Jewish Trial
Pontius Pilate	Roman	Procurator	Presided over Roman Trial
Mary	Jewish	Homemaker	Mother of Jesus
Timothy	Jew/Greek	Missionary	Companion, Disciple of Paul

The writers of the New Testament. At least nine people served as writers of various books of the New Testament. The chart above includes most of their names and backgrounds. Eight of the writers generally are identified as the chart indicates. The authorship of Hebrews is uncertain. Some have suggested Paul as the writer of Hebrews, but most modern New Testament scholars do not favor him as the author. Paul authored 13 books; John wrote five; Luke and Peter each produced 2; and Matthew, Mark, James, Jude, and the author of Hebrews penned 1 each.

Contents and Interpretation of the New Testament.

Contents of the New Testament. Books of the New Testament can be grouped in at least two different ways. The chart on the following page presents a display of these two methods.

---

13. Answers: 1-Compare your answer with mine: A-Additional New Testament manuscripts have been discovered since the King James Version was published; B-Scholars have made advances in understanding the principles of translating New Testament Greek. 2-You could have listed *Revised Standard Version, New English Bible, New American Standard Bible, New International Version,* or others.

BOOKS OF THE NEW TESTAMENT

1. By Content and Author of Books

Historical Books	Paul's Letters	General Letters	Other
Matthew	Romans	Hebrews	Revelation
Mark	1 Corinthians	James	
Luke	2 Corinthians	1 Peter	
John	Galatians	2 Peter	
Acts	Ephesians	1 John	
	Philippians	2 John	
	Colossians	3 John	
	1 Thessalonians	Jude	
	2 Thessalonians		
	1 Timothy		
	2 Timothy		
	Titus		
	Philemon		

2. By Date of Events Covered in Books

6 B.C.-A.D. 29: Matthew, Mark, Luke, John

A.D. 29-63: Acts, Romans, 1 & 2 Corinthians, Galatians, Ephesians, Philippians, Colossians, 1 & 2 Thessalonians, Philemon, James.

A. D. 63-96: 1 & 2 Timothy, Titus, Hebrews, 1 & 2 Peter, 1, 2, & 3 John, Jude, Revelation.

We can divide the books of the New Testament by type of literature and by author. The four divisions would be: Historical Books, Paul's Letters, General Letters, and Revelation.

We also can divide the New Testament writings by date. Scholars differ in the exact dates which they assign to various books, but the dates indicated on the chart have wide acceptance.

Interpreting the New Testament. Some verses of the New Testament are easy to understand without lengthy discussion and argument. We can understand what Paul had in mind when he said, "Be kind and compassionate to one another, forgiving each other, just as in Christ God forgave you" (Eph. 4:32). Interpreting this verse is easy, while applying it may be hard, because we do not always like to forgive people who abuse or insult us.

However, many of the other verses of the New Testament require study, thought, discussion, and prayer before we can understand and apply them. For example, what did Paul have in mind when he said, "Greet one another with a holy kiss" (2 Cor. 13:12)? How long did Paul want us to pray when he said, "Pray continually" (1 Thess. 5:17)?

We need guidelines to direct us as we try to understand and apply Scripture. Using these guidelines will demand divine wisdom and informed human judgment. The following represent some sound principles of interpretation.

Normal Rules of Grammar   First, we need to interpret the Bible according to the normal rules of word meanings and grammar. We call this type of interpretation literal interpretation. The use of literal interpretation would help us see Jesus' death and resurrection as actual events in history and not as the triumph of courage and commitment over selfishness and vindictiveness.

Literal Interpretation

When we use literal interpretation, we know that many passages will contain some figurative elements. The psalmist used poetic language to describe God when he said that the Lord "will cover you with his feathers, and under his wings you will find refuge" (Ps. 91:4). We do not think that the psalmist views the Lord as a species of bird. We recognize that he is describing the tender, loving care of God by comparing it to the care of a hen for her chicks. Certain types of literature such as biblical poetry will contain more symbolic elements than the Gospels or Acts.

Knowledge of Setting

A second principle of interpretation is to discover the setting of a passage. The setting will include the purpose of the writer and the place and occasion for the writing. The setting also will include the context of the immediate circle of words. Understanding the setting of Paul's command in Philippians 4:4 to "Rejoice in the Lord always" can add depth to our understanding. Paul wrote these words from a Roman prison, not from the ease and relaxation of a seashore vacation.

Limits of Revelation

A third principle of interpretation is to accept the limits of God's revelation. God has not revealed an answer to every spiritual question we can ask. We must remember this when we are tempted to become too precise and exact in our interpretations. In matters of personal tragedy and difficulty it can be spiritual folly to use Scripture to prove God's reason for permitting a difficulty. Sometimes it is better to admit ignorance of God's complete purpose and claim His grace in the presence of our weakness. Paul practiced this as he faced his thorn in the flesh (2 Cor. 12:7-10).

Interpretation and Application

A fourth principle of understanding is to distinguish interpretation from application. A passage of Scripture can have only one meaning. If a passage could have several meanings, then opposing systems of theology could both be correct. For example, it cannot be true that we are saved by both faith in Christ and our own personal works. One of the claims is wrong. We are saved by faith.

Even though a passage can have but one meaning, we can find many moral lessons or applications from a single passage. All of these applications come from the single meaning. Paul's appeal to forgive others in Ephesians 4:32 encourages us to offer compassion and pardon to other believers because God has first treated us this way. A secretary can apply this to a testy fellow employee. A parent may use it in dealing with a rebellious child. A neighbor may use it in application to a neighbor who borrowed his lawn mower and returned it in several pieces.

Clearer Passages Dominate

A fifth guideline for interpreting Scripture is to interpret the difficult passage with the help of a clearer passage. Some passages may be stated so briefly that they are unclear. They require much study and reflection before application. For such passages seek a detailed statement from clearer passages of Scripture.

When Jesus said, "If you believe, you will receive whatever you ask for in prayer" (Matt. 21:22), He was not teaching that we can get anything we want for ourselves if only we have enough faith. Rather, He was indicating that faith is the channel by which we enter into partnership with God in getting His work done on the earth. Other passages help to interpret this verse. First John 3:22 stresses that an obedient life is a factor in answered prayer. We also learn that the will of God (1 John 5:14-15) is a vital ingredient in obtaining answers to prayer.

As we apply these guidelines to our study of the New Testament, we can prevent errors and promote a deeper grasp of God's message.

FIVE PRINCIPLES OF INTERPRETATION

1. Interpret the Bible literally.
2. Interpret Scripture in light of its setting.
3. Accept the limits of God's revelation.
4. Distinguish interpretation from application.
5. Interpret difficult texts with help from clearer texts.

🌿 **Place in the blank the number of the principle you feel would be most helpful in interpreting the following texts.**[14]

___ A. "Keep watch, because you do not know on what day your Lord will come" (Matt. 24:42).

___ B. "If you want to be perfect, go, sell your possessions and give to the poor" (Matt. 19:21).

___ C. "He must become greater; I must become less" (John 3:30).

___ D. "Continue to work out your salvation with fear and trembling" (Phil. 2:12).

___ E. "Each of you must put off falsehood and speak truthfully to his neighbor" (Eph. 4:25).

🌿 **SUMMARY REVIEW**

To review this unit, see if you can mentally answer the following questions. You may want to write the answers on a separate sheet of paper. Mark your level of performance on the left: circle *C* if you can answer correctly and circle *R* if you need to review.

C R 1. List two pagan religions existing during New Testament times, and give the major emphasis of each.

C R 2. What did the synagogue contribute to the Jewish religion?

C R 3. What were the Apocrypha and the Pseudepigrapha?

C R 4. What were the main teachings of the Pharisees and the Sadducees?

C R 5. What standards did the early Christians use to determine the New Testament canon?

C R 6. List three principles needed to properly interpret the Bible.

Review this weeks material to find the answers.

🌴 RESPONDING TO GOD'S WORD

Search your heart before God concerning your interpretation of His Word. Ask Him to override all prejudices in your life, ask Him to make you desire only to know what He is saying, and ask Him to make you willing to accept the meaning proper rules of interpretation indicate. Thank the Lord for the privilege of studying and interpreting His Word.

Set aside time daily for this study of the New Testament and for regularly reading God's Word.

---

14. Answers: More than one answer could be correct. My answers were: A-3, B-2, C-4, D-5, E-1.

Unit 2 — Introduction to the Gospels

Reading Through the New Testament

❑ Matthew 8–10
❑ Matthew 11–13
❑ Mark 2–3
❑ Mark 4–5
❑ Luke 5–7
❑ Luke 8–9
❑ John 2–3

UNIT LEARNING GOAL: The study of this unit should help you understand the background of the writing of the Gospels. You will be able to:

• Name the four Gospels in order of their appearance in the New Testament.
• Compare the size of Palestine to a state.
• List three characteristics of Jesus' teaching.
• Explain the term *kingdom of God*.
• Identify the years in which Jesus probably was born and crucified.
• Describe three major developments of Jesus' ministry.
• Identify two of the major events of Jesus' last week.

COMPARISON OF THE FOUR GOSPELS

Gospel	Characteristics	Birth & Early Life	Jesus' Early Ministry	Words & Works, Galilee & Judea	Jerusalem Journey	Final Weeks
Matthew	Jewish Readers in Mind / Emphasized Jesus' Teaching / Sermon on the Mount	1:1–2:23	3:1–7:29	8:1–18:35	19:1–20:34	21:1–28:20
Mark	Roman Audience in Mind / Emphasized Jesus' Actions and People's Emotional Response		1:1-45	2:1–9:50	10:1-52	11:1–16:20
Luke	Jesus' Compassion / Emphasized Holy Spirit's Work / Stressed Prayer / Women Featured	1:1–2:52	3:1–4:13	4:14–9:50	9:51–19:27	19:28–24:53
John	Emphasized Jesus' Miracles / Emphasized Jesus' Discourses / Jesus in Judea		1:19–3:36	4:1–2:50		13:1–21:25

Day 1 *Learning About Jesus*

UNIT 2

The Gospels

Josephus' Antiquities

Tacitus Annals

The Sources

The Gospels—Matthew, Mark, Luke, and John—are the chief sources for our information about Jesus. The other existing sources are so brief and incomplete that they do not give us a full picture of Jesus. These other sources confirm that Jesus lived, became a controversial public figure, and died in the times of Pontius Pilate. The Jewish historian Josephus made two references to Christ and described His life, mentioned His designation as the Christ, and spoke of the stoning of His brother James. The Roman writer Tacitus mentioned His death in the reign of Emperor Tiberius at the hands of Pontius Pilate.

Perhaps you have read that someone claimed to have found "the lost books of the Bible." Scholars have discovered collections of stories about Jesus and sayings which He supposedly gave. The Gospel of Thomas, discovered in Nag Hammadi, Egypt, about 1945, is one such collection. The so-called *Infancy Gospels* is another account. Anyone who reads these accounts will realize quickly that they are only a corruption of the canonical gospels or fantastic fictitious stories designed to satisfy human curiosity and spread some questionable ideas about Jesus. Although some of the statements are obviously influenced by Scripture, they add little to our biblical knowledge. However, the stories and sayings of the four canonical Gospels present a true picture of a Divine Redeemer. We will find their descriptions spiritually moving and fully reliable.

Unreliable Sources

- "Lost books"
- *Gospel of Thomas*
- *Infancy Gospels*
- Corrupted sources

Circle the most accurate statement from each of the following pairs.[1]

    1. A. Sources outside the Bible confirm that Jesus lived, was a controversial public figure, and died in the time of Pontius Pilate.
       B. Sources outside the Bible add much historically reliable information about the life, works, and teachings of Jesus.

    2. A. The only reliable sources that report Jesus outside the Bible are Josephus's *Antiquities* and Tacitus' *Annals*.
       B. The only reliable sources that report Jesus outside the Bible are Josephus's *Antiquities*, Tacitus's *Annals*, and *The Gospel of Thomas*.

    3. A. *Infancy Gospels* provide important information about Jesus' early life that was left out of the four Gospels.
       B. *Infancy Gospels* are fanciful stories that cater to natural curiosity about Jesus' early life.

The Geography of Jesus' Life

Lived in Palestine

Jesus spent most of His life in Palestine, a territory of no more than ten thousand square miles, about the size of the state of Vermont. When Jesus was an infant, Joseph took Him and Mary to Egypt to escape Herod's anger (Matt. 2:13-14). Jesus also visited Tyre and Sidon (Matt. 15:21). Whenever He crossed the Jordan River, He did not travel far into the trans-Jordanian country. Most of Jesus' travels were between Galilee and Jerusalem. Most of us find it hard to realize that the drama of the gospel story took place in such a small area.

---

1. Answers: 1-A, 2-A, 3-B.

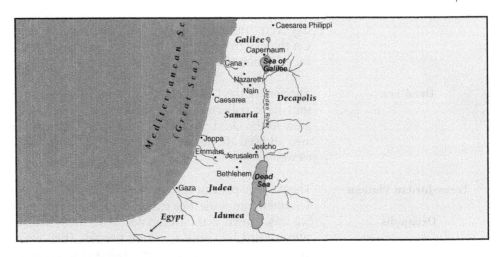

🍃 On the small map above, circle the names of as many places and geographical areas to which Jesus traveled during His earthly life as you can.[2]

East of the Mediterranean Sea

The land of Palestine is located on the western border of the Arabian desert. The western edge of Palestine, from Caesarea to Gaza, had a shoreline on the Mediterranean Sea of over 80 miles. From Mount Lebanon on the north to the southern end of the Dead Sea is a distance of about 175 miles. In the north the distance from the Mediterranean to the Sea of Galilee is 28 miles. In the south the distance from the Mediterranean to the Dead Sea is 54 miles. The Jordan River divides the land as it flows from north to south, arising near the foot of Mount Hermon and flowing into the Dead Sea. To the east of the Jordan River are the areas of Perea and the Decapolis.

Coastal Plain

The terrain of the land of Palestine changes quickly and provides a variety of climates and resources. The coastal plain starts in the desert of the south and ends at Mount Carmel in the north. Joppa (Acts 9:43) was a much-used harbor on the coast. The climate of the coastal plain was mild. The soil was fertile; agriculture flourished.

Hill Country

The hill country was rocky and barren. Its high elevation gave it a moderate climate. Most of the people raised grain and grapes and produced cattle. Jerusalem was located in the hill country, and most of Palestine's population lived in this section. Lakes, valleys, and plains provided opportunities for fishing and farming. Trade routes crisscrossed the area. Towns such as Nazareth, Cana, and Samaria were in the hill country.

Jordan Valley

The Jordan Valley is a part of a gigantic rift in the earth which begins in the Taurus mountains, continues through Palestine and Arabia, passes into the Red Sea, and ends in Africa. The Jordan River flows directly from the Sea of Galilee and ends at the Dead Sea which has no outlet. It flows through a river bed from one to two hundred feet wide. In rainy seasons sections of the gorge fill with muddy water. Once when I visited the area, floods had been so severe that roads along the side of the river had washed away. We had to delay our trip a day while the roads were being repaired.

Sea of Galilee

The Sea of Galilee is a body of water 13 miles long and 8 miles wide at its greatest expanse, and 682 feet below sea level. Sudden rushes of wind produce violent storms on the sea. Just to the west of this sea in Jesus'

---

2. Answers: You may not have known about some of these places. I have circled Jerusalem, Bethlehem, Emmaus, Egypt, Capernaum, Caesarea, Joppa, Nazareth, Nain, Cana, Caesarea Philippi, Jericho, Dead Sea, Judea, Samaria, Galilee (Sea of Galilee), and Decapolis. We will later encounter each of these places in Jesus' travels.

day were numerous towns and cities such as Capernaum, Cana, and Nazareth. On the eastern shore the banks are steep, and the country is wild (see Mark 5:13 for evidence of a steep bank on the eastern shore).

Dead Sea

The area of the Dead Sea functions as an evaporating basin in which minerals and salts have collected for centuries. The water is bitter to the taste. Nothing can grow in the Dead Sea itself, but in New Testament times the tropical climate of the area allowed the raising of fruits and crops which could not grow in the higher elevations.

Trans-Jordan Plateau

Decapolis

The eastern plateau across the Jordan stretches into the Arabian desert. In New Testament times the area east of the Jordan between the Sea of Galilee and the Dead Sea was known as the Decapolis (Mark 5:20) This was originally a federation of 10 cities settled by Greek-speaking people. They were not a single political unit, for in New Testament times several rulers controlled the area. Although some Hebrew people lived in the area, the majority of the population was Gentile. Jesus spent some time in the area (Mark 7:31) and was familiar with the language, customs, and beliefs of the people who lived there.

Mark the following statements *T* (true) or *F* (false).[3]

___ 1. The climate of the coastal plain was well suited to agricultural.
___ 2. Since little would grow in the hill country, most people raised cattle.
___ 3. The Sea of Galilee covers 682 square miles.
___ 4. The Sea of Galilee is protected by mountains and is a calm, placid body of water.
___ 5. Nothing would grow in the Dead Sea area.
___ 6. *Decapolis* refers to the area east of the Jordan and means *10 cities*.
___ 7. Most of the population of Palestine lived in the hill country.

Three Provinces

Galilee, Samaria, Judea

In New Testament times the area of Palestine included three provinces. In the north was Galilee, where a sizable Gentile population lived among the Jews. In the center was Samaria, containing a mixed-race population which viewed the Jews with contempt. In the south was Judea with a heavy Jewish majority and rigid Jewish customs and practices.

On the map on page 7 circle the names of Palestine's three provinces. Place a check here when you have done this: ❑

Most of Jesus' ministry was spent in rugged Galilee. He visited such cities as Nazareth, Cana, Nain, and Capernaum. In Judea Jesus confined His ministry to Jerusalem and such outlying villages as Bethany and Emmaus.

Locate these cities on the map on page 7. Place a check here when you have located each city: ❑

In the blank at the left of each city, place a *G* if that city is located in Galilee and a *J* if that city is located in Judea.[4]

___ 1. Cana   ___ 4. Jerusalem
___ 2. Capernaum   ___ 5. Nazareth
___ 3. Emmaus

---

3. Answers: 1-T, 2-F, 3-F(682 ft. below sea level), 4-F, 5-F, 6-T, 7-T.
4. Answers: 1-G, 2-G, 3-J, 4-J, 5-G.

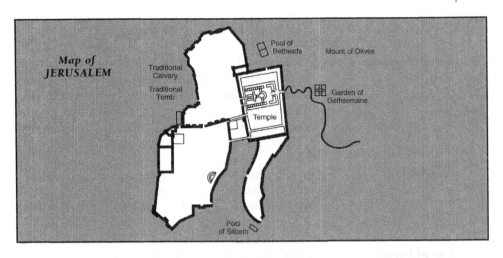

In Jerusalem locations such as the Pools of Siloam and Bethesda (John 9:7; 5:2), the Mount of Olives (Luke 22:39), and the Garden of Gethsemane (Matt. 26:36) are familiar names.

🌿 **Place a check beside each of the following locations in Jerusalem as you find it on the map above.**

❑ 1. Pool of Siloam   ❑ 5. Garden of Gethsemane
❑ 2. Pool of Bethesda   ❑ 6. Traditional Calvary
❑ 3. The Temple   ❑ 7. Traditional Tomb
❑ 4. Mount of Olives

RESPONDING TO GOD'S WORD

As Jesus lived and traveled in Palestine, He reflected the glory of the Father (John 1:14). Pray that God will help you reflect Christ in all the places you find yourself today.

Day 2 *The Teaching of Jesus*

U N I T   2

🌿 **Read Mark 8:1-3. In one sentence express one fact about Jesus' teaching that is implied in those verses.**

_____

_____

Did your answer reflect the idea that Jesus' teaching was so meaningful that people would leave their regular duties, and even go without food for up to three days to hear Him? Good!

Jesus was a master teacher. How else could He have kept a crowd so spellbound that they would go all day without food to listen to Him (Mark 6:34-36; 8:1-10)? What was unusual about Jesus' methods and manner?

The Method of Jesus' Teaching

Colorful Expressions

Often when I have sent a gift for a wedding, anniversary, or birthday, I have received an elegantly written thank-you note. Sometimes the note was scrawled by a forgetful child under threats from an insistent parent. Both recipients expressed gratitude in their own characteristic way, but the contrast between them was sharp. Jesus used sharp contrasts and strong statements. This was typical of the colorful expressions used by Jewish people in their daily language.

Authoritative

Jesus' attitude in teaching was authoritative (Mark 1:22). When He stated a truth, He proclaimed it on His own authority. (Observe His use of "I tell you" in the Sermon on the Mount, Matt. 5:22,28,32,39,44.) His teaching contained a directness and freshness which literally demanded attention from His listeners.

Use of Parables

Jesus' best known teaching device is the parable. His parables used illustrations from daily life to teach spiritual truths. The point of the parable often was clear to the audience without a need for additional interpretation. When Jesus told the parable of the two debtors in Luke 7:40-50, Jesus' host—Simon—understood that Jesus had rebuked his prideful, loveless attitude. To ask what the parable meant would resemble asking a masterful joke teller to explain his joke.

Picturesque Speech

Jesus also used pungent, picturesque speech. His teaching came with clearly contrasting shades of black and white. Sometimes He showed the ridiculous, humorous situations in daily life as when He spoke of taking a "plank out of your own eye" (Matt. 7:3-5). On other occasions He used deliberate exaggeration called hyperbole to communicate His point. For example, He never intended for anyone to pluck out a right eye or to cut off a right hand (Matt. 5:29-30). He taught that sin came from the inside, not the outside (Matt. 23:25-29). However, He wanted His listeners to be so determined in opposing sin that they would put righteousness ahead of the care of their bodies.

Arguments from Scripture

Jesus sometimes used argument in His teaching, but He normally argued on the basis of Scripture rather than from philosophy or abstract premises. In Matthew 22:23-45) Jesus based His arguments with the Pharisees and Sadducees on biblical statements. No opponents ever refuted His compelling logic.

Questions and Answers

Occasionally Jesus used questions and answers. His questions stimulated listeners, and they usually dealt with deep human problems or needs. Who can forget the pressing question contained in "What can a man give in exchange for his soul" (Matt. 16:26)? Not only did Jesus use questions, but He was eager to help His disciples learn more (Matt. 13:10ff.; Mark 4:10-20).

Object Lessons

Sometimes Jesus used object lessons. He used a child to illustrate childlike faith (Matt. 18:1-5), and He spoke about unselfish giving as a widow dropped two coins in the temple offering container (Mark 12:41-44). Jesus probably spoke the parable of the sower within viewing distance of a farmer sowing seed (Luke 8:4-15).

Frequent Repetition

Some of His teachings, such as His farewell discourses in John 13–16, were given only one time. Other teachings, such as those found in the Sermon on the Mount, may have been spoken on several occasions (for example, compare Matt. 5:11-12 with Luke 6:27-28; Matt. 5:38-42 with Luke 6:29-31; Matt. 5:43-48 with Luke 6:32-35). No doubt, Jesus' frequent repetition helped overcome some of the misunderstanding of His disciples. (Notice the three predictions of His death—Mark 8:31; 9:31;10:33-34).

🌿 **Match the following characteristics of Jesus' teaching with scriptural examples by drawing a line from the characteristic to the Scripture passage that illustrates it.[5]**

1. Authoritative	A. Matthew 7:3-5
2. Parables	B. Mark 1:22
3. Frequent repetition	C. Matthew 17:24-26
4. Hyperbole (exaggeration)	D. Luke 7:40-48
5. Arguments based on Scripture	E. Mark 8:31; 9:31
6. Questions and answers	F. Matthew 18:1-5
7. Object lessons	G. Matthew 5:21-22,27-30
8. Humor	H. Matthew 22:23-33

The Content of Jesus' Teaching

Moral and Theological Subjects

The Gospels contain records of both Jesus' teaching and action. Jesus spoke on many moral and theological subjects. In the Sermon on the Mount He discussed sexual morality (Matt. 5:27-32), love (Matt. 5:43-48), and prayer and forgiveness (Matt. 6:5-15). He often discussed the nature of God (John 4:21-24). He wanted His disciples to know His role in God's plan (John 12:27-36). He prepared His disciples to resist the persecution they would receive as His followers (John 16:1-4).

Organized Around His Own Person

Jesus never organized His teachings into a system. He organized the teaching around His own person. The value of His teaching stems from His position as God's Son and our Savior.

Kingdom of God

Many Christians have questions about Jesus' teaching concerning the Kingdom. What is the Kingdom? Is it simply the reign of Jesus over our lives? What about a future millennial reign? How do the Jews fit into Jesus' teaching about the Kingdom? Can we identify the Kingdom with the church? Usually our answers to these questions are only half complete. The kingdom of God is God's reign, but it can refer both to His present reign over us individually and also to His future reign over the world (Matt. 6:33; 13:31-32). Jesus reigns over individual Christians' lives today, but not yet over the world.

The Jews and the Kingdom

The Church and the Kingdom

The Jews will have a part in God's kingdom, but they must enter it on the basis of faith in Jesus as the Messiah (Matt. 21:43; John 8:24; Rom. 11:25-27). The kingdom of God is not identical with the church, but the action of the church helps to spread God's reign over the world (Matt. 28:18-20). The kingdom *was present* in the ministry of Jesus on earth (Matt. 12:28), *is now present* in God's reign over His people (Rom. 14:17), and *will be present* in a display of future greatness when Jesus comes again (Matt. 16:27-28).

Requirements for Entering the Kingdom

How can we participate in the kingdom of God? Jesus announced to Nicodemus that a first requirement was to be "born again" (John 3:3). The Bible mentions two conditions for entrance into the kingdom of God. First, we must repent. We must change our view of who Jesus is, and see Him as God's unique Son (Matt. 11:27). We must also turn from sin and obey as Jesus mentioned in Matthew 5:21-48. Second, we must exercise faith. Faith is not merely an optimistic outlook toward life, but it is complete and total trust in Jesus Christ alone for deliverance from sin (John 6:47). It is a surrendering of all that we are and have to Jesus (Mark 8:34-35) and a willingness to turn the control of our lives over to Jesus. Jesus used the attitude of a little child to teach the humility you and I need to come to Jesus (Mark 10:13-15). He also promised us life's greatest adventure if we come to Him

---

5. Answers: 1-B, 2-D, 3-E, 4-G, 5-H, 6-C, 7-F, 8-A.

in faith and repentance (John 10:10). You may have known for some time that you do not personally know Jesus as your Savior, or you may have just suddenly discovered it through this study. Make today a time of decision and response to Him.

RESPONDING TO GOD'S WORD

If you have never surrendered your life to Jesus as your Savior and Lord or if you are uncertain about your relationship with Him, settle this matter today. The following suggestions will help. Put a check in the box before each statement after you have read and completed each activity. (If you have already given your life to Jesus, review the Scriptures.)

❑ 1. Read Romans 3:23; in prayer confess to God that you are a sinner, that you have disobeyed His commands and have not lived up to the standards set by Jesus.

❑ 2. Read Romans 6:23 and 5:8; in prayer acknowledge that you deserve spiritual death, to be separated from God forever, because of your sins. Thank God that Jesus died for your sins.

❑ 3. Read 1 John 1:9. Confess your sins, and repent of them. Tell God you are willing to turn from your sins, claim His promise of forgiveness, and accept His cleansing from all unrighteousness.

❑ 4. Read Romans 10:13. Receive God's gift of eternal life by inviting Jesus to come into your life as your Lord and Savior.

❑ 5. Thank God for saving you and giving you eternal life.

❑ 6. Read Matthew 10:32-33. Share your decision for Jesus with your teacher or pastor. Publicly acknowledge your commitment to Him by making a profession of your faith in Jesus at the end of a worship service in your church and by being baptized (read Matt. 28:19).

Day 3   *The Periods of Jesus' Life*

UNIT 2

Most journeys are taken either by plane or by automobile. Both methods carry us to our destination, but each gives us a different perspective of the landscape.

In this section we will begin an overview of Jesus' life, looking at the big picture. In later units we will examine each Gospel in greater detail.

🌿 **Read John 20:30-31 and Mark 1:29-35. Beside each of the following statements put *M* if the statement is true of Mark's Gospel and *J* for John's Gospel.[6]**

_____ 1. This Gospel writer seems to have been quite conscious of the proper sequence of the events he reported.

_____ 2. This Gospel writer organized his material to aim for a specific response to Jesus.

---

6. Answers: 1-M; 2-J.

Four Gospels Are Different

All four Gospels give us an accurate picture of Jesus' life, but they do not always follow the same order. Sometimes the writer organized his material to aim for a specific response to Jesus. For example, John tells us that he included the incidents about Jesus which would lead us to believe in Him (John 20:30-31). On the other hand, notice the indications of time sequence Mark used in the paragraphs of Mark 1:29-39 (seen by "as soon as, that evening, in the morning").

Dates in Jesus' Life

Anno Domini

The Romans often calculated years by reckoning from the founding of the city of Rome in approximately 753 B.C. During the first half of the sixth century A.D. a monk named Dionysius proposed the reckoning of time from the point of Christ's birth. He used A.D. (Latin—*anno domini*, "in the year of our Lord") as an abbreviation for the Christian era. Dionysius erred by at least four years in his calendar, for he placed Jesus' birth after the death of Herod the Great. Matthew tells us that Jesus was born before Herod died (Matt. 2:1-18).

✎ **Mark the following statements *T* (true) or *F* (false).**[7]

    ___ 1. A. D. means After Death (of Jesus).
    ___ 2. A monk, Dionysius, proposed reckoning time from the birth of Christ.
    ___ 3. Herod the Great died before Jesus was born.
    ___ 4. Dionysius placed Christ's birth after Herod the Great's death.
    ___ 5. Dionysius' calendar is in error by around 40 years.
    ___ 6. Jesus was approximately 10 years old when Herod died.

Jesus' birth. The New Testament does not give us the precise date of Jesus' birth. It gives us an approximate age of Jesus when He began His ministry (Luke 3:23).

✎ **Read Luke 3:23 and write here Jesus' approximate age when He began His public ministry:_____.**[8]

Jesus Birth, 6 or 5 B.C.

The New Testament also indicates that Jesus' birth was near the date of a census by Augustus Caesar made when Quirinius was governor of Syria (Luke 2:2). Many scholars suggest a date of 6 or 5 B.C. It is unlikely that Jesus' birth was in December because the weather then would normally have been too cold for shepherds to keep their sheep in the fields at night (Luke 2:8).

Length of Jesus' Ministry?

Jesus' Ministry Begins A.D. 26

If we had only the Synoptic Gospels (the first three Gospels), we might conclude that Jesus had a ministry of one-year's length. However, John's Gospel mentions Jesus' involvement in at least three passovers (2:13; 6:4; 13:1). John also mentioned an unnamed feast in 5:1. Many scholars take the figure of "thirty" (Luke 3:23) as an approximate age and assume that Jesus could have been anywhere from two to three years older than 30. A common date for the beginning of Jesus' ministry is found by adding 32 to the date of His birth. This gives us a date of A.D. 26 or 27.

Jesus' Death, A.D. 29

Jesus' death. If the unnamed feast of John 5:1 is a passover, we can say that Jesus had a ministry of over three years stretching between four passovers. If the unnamed feast is not a passover, we can say that Jesus' ministry was between two and three years in length. A common date for Jesus death is A.D. 29.

---

7. Answers: 1-F, 2-T, 3-F, 4-T, 5-F, 6-F.
8. Answer: 30.

🌿 Write here the possible dates of Jesus' birth and death.[9]

_____ B.C. and A.D. _____.

Birth and Early Years

Matthew and Luke Are Sources

Both Matthew and Luke provide information about the birth and early life of Jesus and indicate that Mary gave birth to Jesus in the biological miracle of a virgin birth. Luke provides further details concerning the account of Jesus' birth and early years by including the story of the shepherd's visit to Bethlehem and the presentation of Jesus in the temple on the eighth day after His birth (Luke 2:8-38). Matthew outlines the story of the visit of the wise men (the magi) and the murderous outrage of Herod the Great in slaughtering the young children (Matt. 2:1-18). Only Luke provides authentic information about Jesus in His early years. Luke describes the visit of Jesus to the temple with His parents at age 12 (Luke 2:41-52).

Jesus' Early Years

🌿 Check the correct answer or answers for each of the following statements.[10]
1. The following Gospels give genealogies of Jesus:
   ❑ a. Matthew   ❑ b. Mark   ❑ c. Luke   ❑ d. John

2. This Gospel's genealogy contains the names of four Gentile women:
   ❑ a. Matthew   ❑ b. Mark   ❑ c. Luke   ❑ d. John

3. These Gospels present the virgin birth of Jesus:
   ❑ a. Matthew   ❑ b. Mark   ❑ c. Luke   ❑ d. John

4. This Gospel tells of the shepherd's visit to the manger and Jesus' presentation in the temple on His eighth day:
   ❑ a. Matthew   ❑ b. Mark   ❑ c. Luke   ❑ d. John

5. This Gospel tells of the visit of the wise men to Jesus and Herod having Bethlehem's children killed:
   ❑ a. Matthew   ❑ b. Mark   ❑ c. Luke   ❑ d. John

6. This Gospel tells of a boyhood experience of Jesus:
   ❑ a. Matthew   ❑ b. Mark   ❑ c. Luke   ❑ d. John

Jesus' Early Ministry

The Year of Obscurity

Jesus' first year of ministry began in Judea and ended with preaching and healing tours in Galilee. We often call this the year of obscurity because Jesus was largely out of public view in this year.

🌿 Fill in the blank.[11]

The first year of Jesus' ministry is often called the year of _____.

John's Gospel provides a picture of Jesus' many travels during this busy year. John described the call of the first disciples (John 1:35-51), the changing of water to wine (John 2:1-12), and the first cleansing of the temple (John 2:13-22). Notice the traveling Jesus did to perform these works. He talked with Nicodemus and the woman at the well as He traveled back through Samaria on the way to Galilee.

---

9. Answers: 6 to 5 B.C. and A.D. 29.
10. Answers: 1-a,c; 2-a; 3-a, c; 4-c; 5-a; 6-c.
11. Answer: obscurity.

Jesus' Galilean Activity

The Synoptic Gospels present signs of Jesus' activity in Galilee. Mark recorded a busy ministry in Galilee (Mark 1:21-34) when Jesus cast out demons, healed the sick, and taught about God. He also began some of His travels throughout Galilee in which He preached, taught, and performed many miracles (Mark 1:35-39).

🌿 **Check the following events that occurred in Jesus' first year of public ministry.[12]**

❑ 1. Calling the first disciples
❑ 2. Talking to Nicodemus about being born again
❑ 3. Rebuking a fruitless fig tree
❑ 4. Changing water into wine at a wedding feast
❑ 5. Praying in Gethsemane
❑ 6. Ministering primarily in Galilee

RESPONDING TO GOD'S WORD

Meditate on the information you have received today about the four Gospels. Check each box that becomes a part of your prayer today.

❑ Thank You, Lord, for the four Gospels, four different views of Jesus' life.
❑ Impress upon me the importance of these facts about Jesus' life, message, death, and resurrection. Apply the principles involved to my life.
❑ Help me follow Him as His life develops in the Gospel record.
❑ Show the power of Jesus' resurrection life in and through my life today.

Day 4 — *Developments in Jesus' Life*

UNIT 2

The first three Gospels contain a great deal in their presentation of material about Jesus. In addition, John's Gospel contains miracles and teaching sections the other Gospels lack.

The Year of Popularity

🌿 **To check your memory, fill in the blanks.[13]**

1. Jesus' first year of ministry is often called the year of _____.

2. Jesus' second year of ministry is often called the year of _____.

Centered in Capernaum

During the second year of Jesus' ministry, He made Capernaum His focus of ministry. Capernaum was a commercial town, located on the northwest shore of the Sea of Galilee. A tax collector had an office here (Mark 2:13-14). Jesus performed

---

12. Answers: You could have checked all except 3 and 5.
13. Answer: 1-obscurity; 2-popularity

Selected Apostles

miracles here, such as healing a Roman centurion's palsied servant (Matt. 8:5-13; Luke 7:1-10) and casting the demon from a demoniac (Mark 5:1-20; Matt. 8:28-34). Jesus also selected a smaller group of followers to carry out this work. He designated them as apostles and later instructed them to minister to the Jewish people (Matt. 10:1-4; Mark 3:13-19).

🖉 **What city was the primary focus of Jesus' work during His second year of public ministry?**[14] _____

Jesus made some trips to Jerusalem. John shows us a trip to an unnamed feast (John 5:1) along with the healing of a lame man at the pool of Bethesda (John 5:2-15). He also went to Jerusalem for a Feast of Tabernacles (John 7:2-13). Jesus also found opportunities for teaching and instructing His disciples. Matthew presents the Sermon on the Mount (Matt. 5–7), and two Gospels show a collection of parables (Matt. 13:1-52; Mark 4:1-34).

During this period the popularity of Jesus grew rapidly. On two occasions He fed several thousand people (Mark 6:30-44; 8:1-9). After feeding the five thousand, Jesus rejected the efforts of His audience to make Him into either a bread-king or a military leader (John 6:15). Some of those who had followed Him out of mere curiosity left when He made it clear that their relationship to Him would determine their readiness for eternity (John 6:35, 47, 52-66). Jesus' popularity declined when He refused to cater to their wrong ideas about a Messiah.

The Year of Rejection

🖉 **Now check your memory again. Fill in the blanks.**[15]

    1. Jesus' first year of ministry is often called the year of _____.

    2. Jesus' second year of ministry is often called the year of _____.

    3. Jesus' third year of ministry is often called the year of _____.

Travels Outside Galilee

During the final year of Jesus' time on earth He traveled and taught in several different areas. He traveled north of Galilee into regions near Tyre and Sidon (Matt. 15:21-28; Mark 7:24-30). He also went into an area of Gentile influence southeast of Galilee, the Decapolis (Mark 7:31). His exact routes and times are unknown because the records in the Gospels are brief.

Jesus spent more time with His disciples privately. He avoided the crowds and taught them more clearly (Mark 8:14-21; Mark 10:32-34).

🖉 **List two activities of Jesus that characterized His third year of public ministry.** [16]

    1. _____

    2. _____

---

14. Answer: Capernaum
15. Answer: 1-obscurity, 2-popularity, 3-rejection. See learning activity at the bottom of page 35, and the paragraph following.
16. Answer: Did you list His travels into an area of Gentile influence, the Decapolis, and His spending more private time with His disciples?

Peter's Confession

The most important evidence of Jesus' work with the disciples during this period was Peter's confession of Jesus as the Messiah (Matt. 16:13-20). Peter's confession showed that the disciples were willing to confess their loyalty to Jesus when many were turning from Him. After Peter made the confession, Jesus began to teach more clearly His coming death and resurrection (Mark 8:31; 9:31; 10:33-34).

🌿 Read Matthew 16:13-20. In one sentence give a reason why Peter's confession of Jesus as the Messiah (Christ) was so important.[17]

_____

RESPONDING TO GOD'S WORD

Check the statements that mirror your dedication to a quiet time.
❏ I feel spending time with Jesus is important.
❏ I feel spending time with Jesus daily might change my life.
❏ I will plan specific ways and times to meet with Him.

The best time for me to meet with the Lord regularly is _____.

Day 5   *Final Developments in Jesus' Life*

UNIT 2

Jesus' Final Week

🌿 Test your knowledge of the last week of Jesus' life. Match the days on the left with the correct events on the right. Write the correct letters in the blanks. Some days have more than one event.[18]

___1. Sunday   A. Preaching and teaching
___2. Monday   B. Debates and prophecy
___3. Tuesday   C. Cleansed temple
___4. Wednesday   D. Triumphal entry
                      E. Cursed fig tree

Now try matching this list.

___5. Thursday   F. Resurrection
___6. Friday   G. Arrest
___7. Saturday   H. Crucifixion
___8. Sunday   I. In tomb
                      J. Passover and last supper
                      K. Burial
                      L. Gethsemane

PALM SUNDAY

Jesus' final week of life on earth began with the triumphal entry into Jerusalem on Palm Sunday (Mark 11:1-11).

---

17. Answer: Your answer should include something about the disciples' loyalty in a time when people were falling away.
18. Answers: 1-D; 2-E, C; 3-A, B; 4-A; 5-G, J, L; 6-H, I, K; 7-I; 8-F.

Jesus presented Himself to the people as their Messiah, but the people misunderstood His role. They wanted a warrior king, while Jesus rode into Jerusalem on a donkey's colt. He did not bring the kingdom of God by force, but came to bring peace between man and God.

MONDAY

On Monday Jesus cursed the fig tree and again cleansed the Jerusalem temple (Mark 11:12-19). Jesus' action stiffened the determination of the Pharisees to get rid of Him.

TUESDAY

On Tuesday Jesus debated with the Pharisees and Sadducees and put them to shame (Mark 12:13-27). He also outlined a prophetic explanation to His disciples at the Mount of Olives (Mark 13). During this same time Judas made arrangements to betray Jesus to the Jewish leaders (Mark 14:10-11). While Jesus faithfully was following the will of God, Satan's influence for evil was also at work (Luke 22:3).

WEDNESDAY

The Gospels do not record any incident on Wednesday of Jesus' last week. We can assume that He was busy teaching and preaching as He followed God's will.

THURSDAY

On Thursday evening Jesus celebrated the Passover with His disciples (Mark 14:12-25). Afterward He went with them to the garden of Gethsemane, where He struggled in prayer to God (Mark 14:32-42). While there, Judas came with a band of soldiers to betray Him to the Jewish leaders (Mark 14:43-50).

Jesus' actions during this time encourage us in two ways. First, He never wavered from a commitment to do the will of God. Even when the horror of the cross was looming large in His mind, He could say, "Not what I will, but what you will" (Mark 13:36). Second, He was concerned about preserving His disciples during this time of crisis. He prayed for them as He was in the Garden of Gethsemane (John 17:9-19). He asked the Jewish leaders to let the disciples go free after they had arrested Him (John 18:8-9).

Jesus' Trial

Annas and Caiaphas

When the Jewish leaders had arrested Jesus, they tried to find Him guilty of breaking their laws. To accomplish this, they brought Him before some Jewish leaders including Annas, the former high priest, and Caiaphas, the current high priest (John 18:12-14). The Jewish leaders quickly tried to convene a meeting of the Sanhedrin, and Jesus later appeared before the entire body (Mark 15:1). The Jews collected some false witnesses whose accounts about Jesus could not agree (Matt. 26:59-61). Later Caiaphas succeeded in leading Jesus to claim that He would come again to earth as Son of man, a blasphemous statement to the Jews (Matt. 26:64-66).

Almost every feature of Jesus' trial was a perversion of Jewish justice. Jewish legal procedure demanded that a trial started during the daytime be adjourned before night if unfinished. Jesus' trial both started and went on all during the night. Jewish trial law also provided that no one could be convicted on his own testimony. That was the basis for Jewish conviction of Jesus, for Caiaphas accused Jesus on the basis of His response (Mark 14:60-64).

Read John 18:12-14, 19-24, 28-40; 19:1-16 to find the answers to the following questions.[19]

   1. Why did the Jewish leaders have to take Jesus to Pilate?

2. What Jewish law did the Jewish leaders claim Jesus had broken?

_____

3. What Roman law did the leaders claim Jesus had broken?

_____

FRIDAY

Jesus Before Pilate

After the Sanhedrin found Jesus guilty of blasphemy, they asked the Roman governor (Pontius Pilate) to crucify Him (John 18:28-32). The Jews could not carry out capital punishments without Roman approval. A Roman governor likely would not sentence someone to death for blasphemy, but he would fiercely oppose insurrection. The Jews accused Jesus of misleading the nation, forbidding the payment of taxes to Caesar, and claiming to be a king (Luke 23:2). Pilate found it hard to believe that these charges were valid (John 19:4). He weakly tried to release Jesus (John 19:12), but the Jewish leaders had stirred up the crowd to demand Jesus' crucifixion. When Pilate asked them which prisoner they wanted to have released, he probably hoped the crowd would call for Jesus' release. The crowd screamed out in unison for the release of Barabbas, a real rebel (Mark 15:11).Pilate reluctantly delivered Jesus to be prepared for crucifixion. He sentenced Jesus to a scourging, a beating which generally preceded crucifixion. The Roman soldiers mocked Jesus by twisting a crown of thorns and calling Him King of the Jews. The Roman leaders also compelled Jesus to bear the cross to Calvary. When His strength gave way, they pressed Simon into service (Matt. 27:27-32).

Scourging

Jesus' Death and Burial

The Romans used crucifixion as a brutal method of execution for slaves and criminals. The place of crucifixion was Golgotha, which means *Place of the Skull* (Matt. 27:33). The Roman execution squad nailed Jesus to the cross and placed Him between two thieves (Luke 23:32-33). Jesus hung on the cross for six hours, from around 9:00 a.m. until 3:00 p.m.

SEVEN LAST SAYINGS OF JESUS ON THE CROSS

"Father, forgive them" (Luke 23:34).
"With me in paradise" (Luke 23:43)
"Here is your son. … Here is your mother" (John 19:26-27).
"Why have you forsaken me?" (Matt. 27:46).
"I am thirsty" (John 19:28).
"It is finished" (John 19:30).
"Into your hands I commit" (Luke 23:46).

Crucifixion was more brutal than the gas chamber or the electric chair today because the victims died a slow, painful death. Nailing a victim to the cross did not injure any vital organs. A combination of pain, slow loss of blood, and heat exhaustion resulted in death.

The Resurrection and Ascension

Three Days

Jesus remained in the tomb Friday evening until Sunday morning. He was buried for a portion of three days. By Jewish standards this amounted to three days.

---

19. Answers: 1-see John 18:31; 2-see John 19:7; see John 18:30.

🌿 **Place a check in front any of the following statements that would help a person who questioned Jesus being in the tomb three days.**[20]

❏ 1. God chose to bring His Son into the world through the Jewish people.
❏ 2. God's inspired Word reflects the Jewish culture and standards.
❏ 3. By Jewish standards, any part of a day was reckoned as a whole day in describing duration of time.
❏ 4. By Jewish standards a day began at sundown.
❏ 5. Jesus was buried on Friday before sundown, which marked the beginning of Saturday, the Jewish Sabbath Day.
❏ 6. Christians observe Sunday rather than Saturday as a day of rest and worship.
❏ 7. Jesus was in the grave Saturday and part of Sunday, which began at sundown on Saturday.
❏ 8. By Jewish standards, Jesus was in the grave three days.

SUNDAY

Those who had buried Jesus in the tomb of Joseph of Arimathea were sure that He was dead (Luke 23:50-56). The Roman government had placed guards at the entrance of Jesus' tomb to prevent the theft of His body (Matt. 27:62-66). The women who came to the tomb early on Sunday morning found the tomb empty (Luke 24:1-3). The dramatic power of Jesus' resurrection so frightened the guards that they fainted with fear (Matt. 28:4).

🌿 **Cite three biblical evidences that Jesus actually died on the cross.**[21]

1._____

2._____

3._____

Resurrection Appearances

After the resurrection Jesus appeared to Peter, James, Paul, the apostles, and over 500 Christians in Galilee (1 Cor. 15:5-8; Matt. 28:16-20). He appeared early in the morning (John 20:11-18), at midday (Luke 24:13-35), in the evening (John 20:19-23), in an enclosed room (John 20:26), and along a seashore (John 21:1-14).

Birth of the Church

The birth of the church and the proclamation of the disciples are further evidences of the resurrection. Before the resurrection Jesus' followers were defeated, dejected, and bewildered. After the resurrection they glowed with confidence and were fearless before the might of Rome and the rage of the Jews (Acts 4:1-21). The resurrection of Jesus Christ is the best explanation for their pulsating power.

After a postresurrection ministry of 40 days, Jesus returned to heaven (Luke 24:50-53). No one has seen Him on earth since that time. His returning to heaven is a sign of the completion of His work and reflects the majesty which He is due (Heb. 1:3). In heaven today He prays for His people (Heb. 7:25; 1 John 2:1). From heaven He will one day return to reign on earth in glory (Acts 1:11).

🌿 **Mark the following statements *T* (true) or *F* (false).**[22]

____ 1. Jesus appeared to many people at different times and various places after His resurrection.
____ 2. The largest group to whom Jesus appeared was over 1,000.

---

20. Answers: You could have checked all except 6.
21. Answers: You may have mentioned that those who took Him down and buried Him were convinced He was dead; the Roman government was convinced He was dead because they sought to guard His body; the women who came to the tomb Sunday morning expected to find His body in the tomb.

___ 3. After His resurrection Jesus never appeared in the evening.
___ 4. An evidence of Jesus' resurrection was the amazing change in the disciples' attitude from cowering defeat to confident proclamation of the gospel.
___ 5. Jesus was on earth 40 days after His resurrection.

So What?

Someone may say, "This all sounds convincing and very nice. But so what?" The message of Jesus is not merely a nice, inspiring story. We must not merely honor Him as a marvelous example and as an incisive teacher and thinker. If He is the risen Lord and Savior, we must claim His forgiveness, experience His power, obey His Word, and proclaim His message.

Because Jesus died, you and I can have our sins forgiven. Because Jesus lives today, we can have His presence with us as we tell others about His amazing love, redeeming death, and saving life.

SUMMARY REVIEW

To review this unit, see if you can mentally answer the following questions. You may want to write the answers on a separate sheet of paper. Mark your level of performance on the left: circle *C* if you can answer correctly and circle *R* if you need to review.

C   R   1. Name the four Gospels in the order of their appearance in the New Testament.
C   R   2. What was the size of Palestine?
C   R   3. What were some characteristics of Jesus' teaching?
C   R   4. What does the term "kingdom of God" mean?
C   R   5. In what years was Jesus probably born and crucified?
C   R   6. List three of the major developments of Jesus' ministry.
C   R   7. List two of the major events of Jesus' last week.

Review this week's material to find the answers.

RESPONDING TO GOD'S WORD

Have you claimed Christ's forgiveness and experienced His power?

Are you proclaiming His message in various ways? Check each statement that is true for you.

❏ Talking about the Lord Jesus in daily conversation
❏ Witnessing to others about the Lord
❏ Sharing with my friends and family my faith in Jesus
❏ Demonstrating that I am proud to be Jesus' follower
❏ Praying for unsaved acquaintances
❏ Giving regularly to send the gospel to the ends of the earth

Thank God for the great salvation He has provided you in Christ. If you have not yet received Him, let today be your day of salvation.

---

22. Answers: 1-T, 2-F (500), 3-F, 4-T, 5-T.

Unit 3 The Gospel of Matthew

**Reading Through
the New Testament**

❑ Matthew 14–15
❑ Matthew 16–17
❑ Matthew 18–19
❑ Matthew 20–21
❑ Matthew 22–24
❑ Matthew 25–26
❑ Matthew 27–28

UNIT LEARNING GOAL: The study of this unit should help you understand the theme and purpose of Matthew's Gospel. You will be able to:
• Write two major characteristics of the Gospel of Matthew.
• Identify the chapters of Matthew in which we find the Sermon on the Mount.
• List one activity for each day of Jesus' last week.
• Cite at least two evidences for the resurrection of Jesus.

Author of Matthew: Levi Matthew, the tax collector (Matt. 9:9-13; Mark 2:13-17)

Date of Matthew: A.D. 60-70

Theme of Matthew: The Coming of God's Messiah

Outline of Matthew:
   I. Birth and Early Life of God's Messiah (1:1–2:23)
  II. Early Ministry of God's Messiah (3:1–7:29)
 III. Words and Works of God's Messiah in Galilee (8:1–18:35)
 IV. God's Messiah Travels to Jerusalem (19:1–20:34)
  V. Final Week, Crucifixion, and Resurrection of God's Messiah (21:1–28:20)

Importance of Matthew:
• Most quoted
• Most systematic
• Most clearly arranged
• Only source of some of Jesus' teachings

Special Characteristics of Matthew:
1. Highlights the teaching of Jesus (such as the Sermon on the Mount, Parables, and Olivet Discourse)
2. Evangelistic tool to reach unbelieving Jews
3. Emphasizes Jesus' miracles

Five Discourses in Matthew:
1. Sermon on the Mount (Chaps. 5–7)
2. Commission to the Twelve (Chap. 10)
3. Parables (Chap. 13)
4. Humility and Forgiveness (Chap. 18)
5. Olivet Discourse (Chaps. 24–25)

Day 1   *The Uniqueness of Matthew*

UNIT 3

Most Quoted

Importance of the Gospel

Since the second century Matthew has been the most quoted of the Gospels. It features a systematic arrangement of Jesus' teachings in such sections as the Sermon on the Mount and the parables. Matthew is listed first in New Testament writings, and for many centuries biblical scholars thought that it was the first Gospel to be written. Many biblical scholars today feel that Mark was the first written Gospel, but the quotable content and clear arrangement of Matthew's Gospel make it a favorite among many Christians.

Author of the Gospel

The Early Church Said Matthew

This Gospel makes no claim of authorship, but the early church almost unanimously attributed this Gospel to Matthew the tax collector. The book appeared early, and Christians quickly accepted it as a genuine book. Most Bible scholars feel that the man Matthew is the same as Levi (Matt. 9:9-13; Mark 2:13-17), the tax collector in Capernaum. His job would have made him an important person to the Romans but a despised figure to the Jews. His quick response to Jesus' call (Mark 2:14) indicated that he had listened to and thought about Jesus' public preaching. He demonstrated his eagerness to win his friends to Christ by hosting a meal for them in his home soon after he became a follower of Jesus. Jesus later chose him as one of the twelve apostles (Mark 3:13-19).

A Tax Collector

Matthew was not a prominent leader among the apostles. We know little about his life after his call by Jesus. That the church would so overwhelmingly designate this lesser known disciple as the author of the first Gospel is a strong argument for his authorship. The last appearance of his name in the Bible is in Acts 1:13.

The well-organized nature of Matthew agrees with the likely mentality of an orderly tax collector. This is the only Gospel that contains the story of Jesus' payment of the temple tax (Matt. 17:24-27). This too suggests that a tax collector had a role as author.

🖎 **Mark the following statements *T* (true) or *F* (false).**[1]

    ____ 1. Matthew was probably the first Gospel written.
    ____ 2. The Gospel of Matthew names Matthew as its author.
    ____ 3. Matthew was a fisherman before Jesus met him.
    ____ 4. Matthew was one of the stronger leaders among the disciples.
    ____ 5. Matthew's strong leadership is one reason for believing he wrote the Gospel of Matthew.

Date of the Gospel

Ascertaining when any of the Gospels were written is not easy, for they do not provide contemporary events with which to link them. Various scholars have dated this Gospel from as early as A.D. 50 to as late as A.D. 110.

---

1. Answers: I hope you marked all five statements false!

**Only Writer
to Use "Church"**

Matthew is the only Gospel writer to use the term "church" (Matt. 18:17). This suggests that he wrote when the doctrine of the church was becoming more important. He also writes with a Jewish style and interest. His frequent use of the Old Testament (Matt. 1:23; 2:6; 2:18), strong emphasis on ethics, and designation of God as "Father in heaven" (Matt. 5:16) represent features Jews would use.

🌿 **Check the following characteristics that are true of Matthew.[2]**

☐ 1. Matthew is the only Gospel writer to use the word *church*.
☐ 2. Matthew wrote in a poetical style.
☐ 3. Matthew reflects a Jewish style and interest.
☐ 4. Matthew quotes Greek philosophers.
☐ 5. Matthew emphasized ethics.
☐ 6. Matthew makes frequent use of the Old Testament.

Written After Mark's Gospel

These facts suggest a date later in the apostolic period after the church had developed, but before the destruction of Jerusalem in A.D. 70. After that time the prospects for converting Jews would not be bright. Matthew most likely was written after Mark's Gospel which would dictate a date between A.D. 60-70.

Theme and Purpose of the Gospel

**Teaching Manual
for Christians**

**Fulfillment of
Old Testament
Prophecies**

Matthew does not give us a specific statement about his purpose. Yet, we can learn his purpose by a careful reading of his Gospel. The systematic arrangement of the Gospel has made it useful in teaching. Jesus' claims as Messiah and His ethical and theological teaching are clearly presented. This makes the Gospel useful as a teaching manual for Christians. Matthew's Gospel shows Jesus in His Person and life as the fulfillment of Old Testament prophecies (Matt. 4:14-16).

🌿 **Use your Bible to illustrate how Matthew emphasized fulfillment of prophecy. Match the following references in Matthew on the left with the correct Old Testament prophecies on the right. Write the correct letters in the blanks.[3]**

____ 1. Matthew 2:5-8   A. Jeremiah 31:15
____ 2. Matthew 2:17-18   B. Micah 5:2
____ 3. Matthew 3:3   C. Isaiah 11:1-2
____ 4. Matthew 3:13-16   D. Isaiah 40:3

To Reach Unbelieving Jews

Various other facts about Jesus' life, including His birth, flight into Egypt, His introduction by John the Baptist, and His temptation experience with Satan, all suggest that Jesus is the Person for whom the prophets had longed. Matthew also emphasized the reality of Jesus' resurrection against any Jewish attempts to deny it (Matt. 27:62-66; 28:11-15). These features show a book that could be used as an evangelistic tool to reach unbelieving Jews.

🌿 **Mark the following statement *T* (true) or *F* (false).[4]**

____ 1. The theme of Matthew's Gospel is Jesus as the fulfillment of Old Testament prophecies.
____ 2. The purpose of Matthew's Gospel is to reach unbelieving Jews with the gospel.

---

2. Answers: If you checked all except 2 and 4, you are right.
3. Answers: 1-B, 2-A, 3-D, 4-C.
4. Answers: 1-T, 2-T.

RESPONDING TO GOD'S WORD

Jesus was the Master Teacher during His life on earth, and He is still the Master Teacher today.

Check the following statements which can become your prayer of dedication to God.

Lord, I plan daily to spend ❏ 15 minutes   ❏ 30 minutes   ❏ 1 hour studying Your teaching.

❏ I plan to put into practice what I learn from Your teaching.

Because You are the Master Teacher, I will strive to be a master learner:
❏ by studying personally as if You were using an audible voice.
❏ by studying obediently with a willing heart.
❏ by being willing to change whenever and whatever You direct.
❏ by trying to discover ways to present Your teachings to others.

Day 2   *Special Characteristics of Matthew*

UNIT 3

Matthew & the Synoptics

Matthew's view of Jesus' life has many similarities to the views of Mark and Luke. Since all three Gospels have a similar view of Jesus, we call them the "Synoptic Gospels" (from *syn* with or together and *opteo* to see). This means that they look at Christ in the same manner. Although they are similar, each Gospel gives a unique perspective on Jesus' life. John differs from the three other Gospels in that he omits much Synoptic material and also included some incidents omitted by them.

Emphasis on Miracles

Although the most outstanding feature of Matthew is his emphasis on Jesus' teaching (we will study this at length in days 3 and 4), another prominent feature is his emphasis on miracles. Often Matthew followed a teaching of Jesus with a description of His miracles (8:1-17). The finding of the coin in the mouth of the fish (17:24-27), the raising of the saints (27:51-31), and the action of the angel at Jesus' tomb (26:2-4) were indications of the miraculous power surrounding the life of Jesus. These miracles reminded the disciples of the power available to them as they went out to witness in His name (28:18-20). That same power is available for us today as we serve Him.

Matthew's Genealogy (1:1-17)

Through Joseph, His Foster Father

Direct Line of Descent

Matthew gives the descent of Jesus through Joseph. Even though Joseph was only the foster father of Jesus, not His birth father, Jews would want to know Jesus' genealogy through the father. Legal rights passed to a child from the father, even from a foster father. Matthew divided the genealogy into three groups of 14 generations. Therefore, Matthew's genealogy does not always mean a direct father-son relationship but rather indicates a direct line of descent. In 1:18 Matthew omitted the names of Ahaziah, Joash, and Amaziah after Jehoram (Joram). However, the names of these Old Testament rulers appear in 1 Chronicles 3:11-12, giving evidence that Matthew was speaking of a direct line of descent. Matthew traced the genealogy of Jesus back to Abraham and also called Jesus the son of David. These features would be of great interest to Jewish readers.

🌿 **Answer the following questions.**[5]

A. Why would Jews be interested in Jesus' genealogy through Joseph since Jesus was not really Joseph's son?

_____

B. Compare Matthew 1:8 with 1 Chronicles 3:11-12. Did Matthew's list omit any names? ❑ Yes ❑ No

C. What conclusion should be drawn about Matthew's genealogy? Check one:
   ❑ 1. It is unreliable.
   ❑ 2. Its purpose is to show the line of descent, not to give a complete record.
   ❑ 3. Parts of it must be lost.

D. Read Matthew 1:17. Now read the genealogy of Jesus in Matthew 1:1-16. In your Bible draw a line between the three sets of 14 "generations."

The Virgin Birth (1:18-25)

Engagement a Fixed Commitment

Joseph and Mary already were engaged when Mary became pregnant by the Holy Spirit. An engagement among the Jews was a fixed commitment to marriage, and breaking the engagement required a divorce. When Joseph learned of Mary's pregnancy, he made plans to terminate his engagement privately in order to avoid publicly embarrassing Mary.

🌿 **Read Matthew 1:18-25. Mark the following statements *T* (true) or *F* (false) in the blank to the left of each statement. In the blank after each statement, write the verse from Matthew 1 that supports your response.**[6]

____ 1. Mary and Joseph had not experienced a sexual union when she became pregnant by the Holy Spirit. v. ____

____ 2. Joseph's decision to divorce Mary quietly was motivated by his desire to hurt her. v. ____

____ 3. Joseph decided to name the child Jesus after a family member. v. ____

____ 4. "Immanuel" means "God with us." v. ____

____ 5. After Jesus was born, Joseph and Mary evidently had normal marital relations. v. ____

No Union

An angel came to Joseph in a dream and urged him to proceed with the marriage. Joseph learned that Mary had conceived the child by the Holy Spirit. Matthew pointed out that this was a fulfillment of Isaiah's prophecy in 7:14. Joseph's refraining from sexual relations with Mary "until she gave birth to a son" (1:25) suggests that Mary did not remain a perpetual virgin after giving birth to Jesus.

_____

5. Answers: A-Your answer should indicate the legal descent was reckoned through the father's lineage, even in the case of foster children. B-Yes. C-2. D. Did you draw lines after verses 6 and 11?
6. Answers: 1-T, v.18; 2-F, v.19; 3-F, v21; 4-T, v.23; 5-T, v.25.

**God Spoke
Through a Dream**

Matthew 13:55 mentions some of Mary's other children. Once in this section (1:20-24) and three times in chapter 2 (vv. 13, 19, 22) God spoke to Joseph through a dream. Joseph's obedience to each revelation in a dream showed his quick and ready willingness to do God's will. His actions provide an example for us to follow.

The Temptations of Jesus (4:1-11)

Satan Is an Accuser

The Hebrew term *Satan* is equivalent to the Greek term *Devil*. Both terms designate our opponent as an accuser. Satan delights in accusing us of disobedience and thereby lulling us into further compromise. Satan attempted to approach Jesus through normal avenues, but Jesus rejected each thrust.

🌿 **Read Matthew 4:1-11. Check the statements with which you agree.[7]**

    ❏ 1. Satan knows Scripture and seeks to lead people to misapply its teachings.
    ❏ 2. Knowledge of Scripture is a strong defense against temptations.
    ❏ 3. Christians who pray cannot be tempted.
    ❏ 4. Satan wants to lead people to do things his way rather than God's way.
    ❏ 5. Accomplishing God's purposes is more important than the methods used.
    ❏ 6. Satan knows our most vulnerable points and moments.
    ❏ 7. The issue at the root of most temptations if whether we will trust and obey God.

**Temptation Through
Normal Human Desire**

**Question of Obedience
to God**

Jesus had no sin, and Satan could not approach Him through a sinful nature. He could, however, approach Him through normal human desire. Jesus knew hunger. When He had been without food for 40 days, Satan's word to Jesus in Matthew 4:3 represented this kind of approach: "If you are the Son of God, tell these stones to become bread." Satan appealed to Jesus' natural hunger. Satan also raised a question concerning whether or not God genuinely would care for Jesus as He had promised. Satan's words might have led Jesus to take matters into His own hands and provide for His hunger in His own way. God intended that His Son trust Him to supply the food. Jesus' response to Satan pointed out that we need to obey God more than we need to eat food. Obedience to God was the issue in this temptation.

🌿 **Complete the following sentence.[8]**

In the temptation to turn the stones into bread, the issue was

_____ to God.

**Tempted to Put God
to the Test**

In the second temptation Satan prompted Jesus to make a presumptuous test of God's promise to care for Him. Satan even quoted a scriptural promise (Ps. 91:11) to prove that Jesus could rely on angelic assistance as He faced difficulty. Jesus' answer indicated that He did not need to put God to the test by leaping from the pinnacle of the temple. He already knew of God's loving care, and no daring leap into the air could prove God's care any more. Trust in God was the issue in this temptation.

🌿 **Complete the following sentence.[9]**

In the temptation to jump from the temple, the issue was _____ in God.

---

7. Answers: Hopefully, you checked all except 3 and 5.
8. Answer: Obedience.
9. Answer: Trust.

Direct Appeal for Compromise

Satan finally confronted Jesus with a direct appeal for compromise (4:9). He attempted to persuade Jesus that He could gain His destiny as Messiah without going to the cross. Jesus refused to surrender to Satan's temptation. He indicated that only God was worthy of worship. Satisfying personal ambition was the issue in this temptation.

🌿 **Complete the following sentence.**[10]

In the temptation to gain the world's kingdoms by worshiping Satan, the issue

was satisfying personal _____.

Jesus Answered from Scripture

Jesus' answers to Satan came from Scripture (Deut. 8:3; 6:16,13). His use of Scripture teaches us the importance of learning and obeying it as we serve God.

Scripture-Memory Helps

One of the blessings of my own Christian life has been Scripture memory. Much of the Scripture I now know and use I learned as a young Christian. If you have not made Scripture memory a regular practice in your Christian life, beginning Scripture memory now will be a source of deep enrichment and much spiritual help to you.

RESPONDING TO GOD'S WORD

🌴 **Read Psalm 119:6-11. Determine to develop a plan for memorizing verses of Scripture that especially speak to you. Spend a few moments in prayer asking God to help you hide His Word in your heart that you might not sin against Him.**

Put a check before each statement with which you agree and are willing to commit yourself.

❑ 1. I realize that it is Your will for me to learn Your Word (v. 7).
❑ 2. I also want to obey Your Word (v. 8).
❑ 3. I know that You want me to live according to Your Word (v. 9).
❑ 4. I can live a more pure life for Christ if I know Your Word (v. 9).
❑ 5. I sometimes am tempted to stray from living according to Your Word (v. 10).
❑ 6. I would not be so ashamed if I lived more according to Your Word (v. 6).
❑ 7. I want to meditate on and memorize (hide in my heart) Your Word (v. 11).
❑ 8. I am willing to spend the time necessary to learn and memorize Your Word.
❑ 9. I commit myself to hide in my heart Your Word. I commit myself to memorize at least one verse of Your Word: ❑ per week ❑ per month.

---

10. Answer: Ambition

Day 3 *The Sermon on the Mount (5–7)*

UNIT 3

The Teaching of Jesus

As has been mentioned, Matthew spotlighted the teaching of Jesus. He mentioned five sections of Jesus' teachings or discourses. Each passage presented a different aspect of Christ's life and person. The Sermon on the Mount in Matthew 5–7 showed the meaning of genuine righteousness. The commission to the 12 apostles in Matthew 10 led these disciples to expect both persecution and reward. The parables in Matthew 13 explained the meaning of the Kingdom. The discussion of humility and forgiveness in Matthew 18 showed the spiritual traits necessary for greatness in God's sight. The Olivet Discourse in Matthew 24–25 showed believers what they could expect both before and after Christ's return.

Prophet like Moses

In the Sermon on the Mount, Matthew presented Jesus as a prophet like Moses (Deut. 18:15), who went up into a mountain to receive and transmit a new law from God.

Principles of True Righteousness (5)

The Beatitudes

In Matthew 5:3-12 Jesus pronounced blessings on those who demonstrated certain types of spiritual attitudes. For example, Jesus pronounced a blessing to His followers who hungered and thirsted for righteousness like starving people. Palestine was a land where many people knew about hunger. Many of the people were poor. The land was dry and arid. Many knew about thirst. Jesus promised them a filling with righteousness if they desired righteousness this deeply.

Moral Implications of the Ten Commandments

Whereas God had given the Ten Commandments through Moses, Jesus brought out the deeper meanings and moral implications of the Ten Commandments for daily living (Matt. 5:19-48). He did not comment on the ceremonial laws of the Old Testament, but He spoke deeply about the spiritual dimensions of obedience to God in daily living.

Interpreting Old Testament Commands

In Matthew 5:17-48 Jesus contrasted His interpretation of the Old Testament with common misunderstandings of Jewish leaders of the day. Jewish leaders had taught that the command to love one's neighbor implied hatred for an enemy. Jews sometimes practiced this quite literally with many Gentiles. Jesus pointed out that the command to love (Lev. 19:18) demanded that we love our enemies, bless our accusers, and pray for our opponents who misuse and abuse us (Matt. 5:43-48).

A. **Read Matthew 5:17-48 and underline the phrases "you have heard that it was said" (or "it has been said") and "but I tell you." When you have done this, place a check here:** ❑

B. **Mark the following statements *T* (true) or *F* (false).**[11]

____ 1. Jesus did not believe the Old Testament.
____ 2. Jesus went beyond the letter of the law in interpreting the Old Testament commandments.
____ 3. Jesus pointed out the spiritual intent behind the Old Testament commandments.
____ 4. Jesus' teachings sometimes cut across the grain of human nature.
____ 5. Jesus' teachings are easily obeyed.
____ 6. People who claim their religion is the Sermon on the Mount may not be aware of what it demands.

Principles of True Worship (6)

In Matthew 6:1-8 Jesus taught principles to use in showing mercy, praying, and fasting.

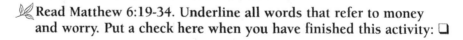 **Read Matthew 6:1-4. Check the sentence in each of the following pairs of statements that you feel is most accurate:**[12]

- ❑ A-1. Jesus wanted people to do their righteous acts in secret so no one would praise them.
- ❑ A-2. Jesus was concerned primarily about the motives with which people did righteous acts.

- ❑ B-1. Jesus said that people who did good in order to be praised would receive the reward they sought; praise of people.
- ❑ B-2. Jesus said that people who did good in order to be praised would receive no reward.

- ❑ C-1. Jesus' saying not to let the left hand know what the right hand did in giving means that we are not ever to sign pledge cards or to write the amounts of our gifts on offering envelopes.
- ❑ C-2. Jesus' saying not to let the left hand know what the right hand did in giving means that our giving should be rooted in obedience to God and love of people, not in a desire to be praised by people.

The Lord's Prayer

In the Lord's Prayer Jesus warned against the repetition of meaningless phrases. Jesus urged His listeners to begin their prayers with praise for God and a request for the triumph of His will. He urged them to ask God for their daily needs, the forgiveness of sins, and the strength to avoid temptation.

Greed and Anxiety

In 6:19-34 Jesus warned about greed and anxiety. He pointed out the corrupting effect of greed (6:24) and the futility of trying to solve life's problems by worry (6:27). Instead of concentrating on material aims in life, Jesus wanted His listeners to focus on doing God's will (6:33). While material needs in life are important, dedication and love to God should come first in every Christian's life. Jesus taught that if we put God first He will provide our needs in life.

Read Matthew 6:19-34. Underline all words that refer to money and worry. Put a check here when you have finished this activity: ❑

Principles of True Judgment (7)

A Judging Spirit

In Matthew 7 Jesus discussed the subject of judgment. Jesus prohibited a critical spirit that constantly finds fault with others. Nothing in Jesus' words prevents our making moral and spiritual judgments of others when those judgments are necessary (see Jesus' practice of this in Matt. 23:1-36). Jesus is warning against the fault-finding attitude of a moral Pharisee who constantly picks away at others.

God's Judgment

Jesus also warned of God's judgment. He taught that people must give obedience to God not by words alone but also by deeds (7:21-23). He promised divine judgment for those who willfully disobeyed God.

---

11. Answers: 1-F, 2-T, 3-T, 4-T, 5-F, 6-T.
12. Answers: A-2, B-1, C-2.

🌿 **Read Matthew 7:1-5 and check the correct answer for each of the following questions.**[13]

  1. Why did Jesus prohibit a critical spirit that constantly finds fault in others?
  ❑ a. You have faults of your own.
  ❑ b. You will be judged as you judge others.
  ❑ c. Both of the above.

  2. What did Jesus say to do about another person's faults?
  ❑ a. Ignore them   ❑ b. Rebuke them   ❑ c. Help them

  3. What is required before you can help someone else overcome a fault?
  ❑ a. Learn more about the fault.
  ❑ b. Get training in how to help people.
  ❑ c. Deal honestly and adequately with your own faults.

RESPONDING TO GOD'S WORD

🌴 **Read Matthew 7:24-27. In these verses what is the rock on which we are to build our lives? Check your answer.**[14]

❑ 1. Jesus Christ
❑ 2. Religious works
❑ 3. Hearing and obeying Jesus

Evaluate your interest in building your life on the rock of hearing and obeying God's Word by checking the statements that apply to you.

____ 1. I recognize Jesus' authority and know I ought to hear His Words.
____ 2. I know the storms of life will come. I need the support of God's Word.
____ 3. I am interested in hearing God's Word.
____ 4. I am interested in hearing God's Word, but many other things compete.
____ 5. I am eager to hear God's Word.
____ 6. I want my life to be stable and secure, built on God's Word.
____ 7. I want to be a wise person and build my life according to His directions.
____ 8. I will make time to hear God's Word.
____ 9. I am foolish to hear God's Word and not do it.
____10. I commit myself to obeying God's Word, and putting it into practice.

Pray that God will grant you determination and courage to hear and obey Him.

Day 4   *Jesus' Other Teaching*

UNIT 3

The Parables of the Kingdom (13:1-50)

Parables to Communicate

Jesus used parables to communicate the truth clearly to His disciples and to stimulate even His opponents to think seriously about His teaching. Unfortunately, the

---

13. Answers: 1-c, 2-c, 3-c.
14. Answer: In these verses, the answer is 3.

response of Jesus' Jewish hearers indicated dullness and stubbornness, just like that of many of the Jews who heard the prophets in the Old Testament.

Parable of the Kingdom

Parable of the Sower

In this chapter Jesus explained the progress of the kingdom of God. He compared the progress of the kingdom of God to the growth of a mustard seed (Matt. 13:31-32). Just as the seed started with a small beginning, the kingdom had started from a small beginning, but would someday extend to the ends of the earth. Jesus also compared the worth of the kingdom of God to the worth of a precious pearl. Jesus was saying (13:45-46) that the kingdom was of such worth that we should gladly give all to get it. The most familiar of these parables is the parable of the sower.

🌿 **Read the parable of the sower in Matthew 13:3-9, 14-23. Mark the following statements *T* (true) or *F* (false).**[15]

    ____ 1. Verses 14-15 best fit the seed on rocky places.
    ____ 2. Some seed was bad and thus produced no harvest.
    ____ 3. Some seed died because the sun was so hot.
    ____ 4. In the parable, thorns are evil companions.
    ____ 5. People who receive the seed produce the same amount of fruit.
    ____ 6. In the parable, the seed represented the Ten Commandments.

Different Responses to the Kingdom

Here Jesus was explaining why some of His listeners opposed Him. The various types of soil represented various attitudes of the human heart. Some who heard God's word would never understand it or receive it, because they would be deceived by Satan. Others would give in to compromise because of persecution. Others would have spiritual life choked from them because of preoccupation with worldly aims. Some who heard Jesus' message would receive the word seriously, deeply, and without reservation. In explaining this parable to the disciples, Jesus was saying that some of His opponents had "poor soil" in their hearts. They were determined not to listen to Jesus' message. Others had "good soil," hearts obedient to do Jesus' will. These would receive the word from Jesus and endure to reap eternal life. Jesus' words encourage us to apply His commands continually.

Peter's Great Confession (16:13-20)

Jesus Is the Messiah!

After the feeding of the five thousand was completed, Jesus found some of His popular support disappearing. The disciples, however, recognized Jesus as the Messiah when others turned against Him. When Jesus asked Peter, "Whom do you say that I am?" Peter answered that Jesus was the Messiah. Peter did not understand fully all that he was saying, or he would not have later responded with a rebuke for Jesus in 16:22. Nevertheless, Peter did have the right basic idea—Jesus was the Messiah!

Jesus' answer to Peter leaves some difficult questions for interpretation. What did He mean when He spoke of the rock on which He would build the church? Was Jesus pointing to Himself as the Rock? Was our Lord referring to Peter's confession or his faith as the rock? Or was Jesus saying that Peter himself (or better, his leadership) was the rock? While many scholars would disagree, I lean toward this as the most natural interpretation. Jesus' words to Peter spotlighted the leadership role Peter would have among the apostles. Jesus was not focusing on Peter as the sole founder of Christianity but as a prominent leader who, along with the other apostles, would greatly influence its development.

---

15. Answers: 1-F (it shows that willfully not understanding is intended); 2-F (the seed is the message of the kingdom); 3-F (same sun shone on all; problem was lack of the root of commitment); 4-F (worldly concerns); 5-F (100, 60, or 30 times what was sown); 6-F.

🌿 **Read Matthew 16:15-20 and answer the following questions.**[16]

Which interpretation of "rock" seems best to you? Check your answer:
❑ 1. Christ ❑ 2. Peter's confession ❑ 3. Peter's leadership

The Keys to the Kingdom

Another question involved the promise of the keys of the kingdom to Peter (Matt. 16:19). What power did this include? It doesn't mean Peter would sit at the entrance to heaven with a key to admit those who have met God's requirements. The power of "binding" and "loosing" has to do with the right to retain or forgive sins. The *decision* to retain or forgive sins belongs to God alone. However, Jesus gave Peter, as a spokesman for the apostles, the *authority to proclaim* forgiveness, to declare the terms of admission into God's kingdom by offering forgiveness of sins. We see later in Matthew (see 18:18) that this power belongs to all the apostles and indeed to all Christians (28:18-19). As Peter, the other apostles, and early Christians declared the forgiveness of sins through the gospel, they were loosing people from their sins, and providing them forgiveness. At no time did Peter (nor does any other human being) arbitrarily have the right to exclude someone from heaven.

🌿 **Write an explanation of "the keys of the kingdom of heaven."**[17]

_____

_____

Self-Denial and Cross Bearing (16:24)

Deny Self

To be properly related to Him in service, Jesus taught that we must deny self, take up the cross, and follow Him. Denying self means much more than simply denying ourselves an extra piece of cake for dessert or an extra hour of sleep in the morning. Jesus meant that we will need to deny *materialism,* the quest for wealth; *egotism,* the quest for self-satisfaction and special recognition; and *sensualism,* the quest for immoral and worldly living.

Take Up the Cross

When Jesus told His disciples to take up the cross, He was referring to the Roman practice of crucifixion. Here a condemned criminal carried a large, horizontal piece of wood, which was later attached to an upright pole. On the way to His death, He passed through jeering, cursing crowds. Carrying a cross exposed someone to the cruelty and hostility of an uncaring world.

Taking up the cross in this context involves more than merely facing life's hardships and sufferings. It is an exposing of ourselves to suffering for Him, an acceptance of the consequences of walking with Jesus. To follow Jesus means to listen to His voice, put Him first, and to be a doer of His Word, not just a hearer. Living the obedient Christian life is very difficult at times (Jesus compared it to a "narrow road," 7:14) and often involves great demands but provides eternal rewards.

Reconciliation and Forgiveness (18:15-35)

Wronged Person Initiates Reconciliation

Jesus taught that a wronged person must not demand apologies but offer forgiveness. When we are wronged, we should start the move toward reconciliation. Jesus mentioned four steps in solving these difficulties: (1) a private conference; (2) a conference with two or three witnesses present; (3) consideration of the problem

---

16. Answer: Your response.
17. Answer: Your answer probably expresses the idea that the keys were the authority to declare the terms of admission into the Kingdom, and that all Christians today have the keys.

by the entire church; (4) removing the stubborn party from the church. Jesus' hope was that individuals would settle their difficulties before taking all the steps.

> ## FOUR STEPS TO SOLVE RECONCILIATION PROBLEMS
>
> 1. A private conference
> 2. A conference with two or three witnesses
> 3. A conference with the entire church
> 4. Removal of the stubborn party from the church

Forgive

Peter's request to Jesus in 18:21 probably meant, "Lord, how many times do I need to forgive my brother when he sins against me?" Jesus' answer indicated that Christians were to forgive their offenders an unlimited number of times. The inference is that God treats sinners in the same way. This truth should not cause us to sin carelessly, but it should give us confidence for a renewed fellowship when we repent.

🌿 **Read Matthew 18:15-35. Fill in the blanks.**[18]

A. When an offender refuses reconciliation privately, we should hold

a conference with _____ or _____ present, then let the _____

consider the problem, and finally, remove the stubborn person. The aim

of these steps is _____ _____.

B. What was Jesus' message about forgiving (Matt. 18:21)?
  ❏ 1. Forgive seventy-seven times before breaking a relationship.
  ❏ 2. Forgive as often as necessary.
  ❏ 3. Forgive seventy-seven times before seeking revenge.

C. What message was Jesus probably giving in the parable of the unforgiving servant? Check your answer.
  ❏ 1. Forgiving other people saves us.
  ❏ 2. Saved people who don't forgive will be lost.
  ❏ 3. Forgiven people are to forgive others.

Jesus' Teaching on Divorce (19:1-12)

Jewish Bible scholars generally agreed that the law of Moses allowed divorce with the right to remarry (see Deut. 24:1-4). They differed on grounds for divorce. Hillel taught that if a wife did almost anything displeasing to her husband, he had grounds. The more conservative rabbi Shammai felt that immorality was the only proper reason for divorce. Jewish leaders tried to involve Jesus in this debate (v. 3).

God's Ideal: Married for Life

Jesus answered their question by indicating God's perfect will in all marriages—that a man and a woman remain married for a lifetime (19:6). He suggested that Moses allowed divorce as a concession to human wickedness, but the allowance was not a part of God's will from the beginning. Jesus then declared that the only valid ground for divorce was "marital unfaithfulness" (19:9), or sexual immorality. Some Christians also feel from Paul's words in 1 Corinthians 7:12-16 that desertion possibly constitutes another valid basis for divorce and remarriage.

---

18. Answers: A. 2-3 witnesses, church, ultimate reconciliation. B-2, C-3.

Jesus did not command divorce but stated grounds under which one may consider it. However, God's people must seek to meet the divine standards in 19:4-6.

RESPONDING TO GOD'S WORD

Search your heart to see if you are holding hard feelings toward a person who has caused you harm of some kind. Reflecting on Matthew 18:15-35, put a check beside the action you will take:

❏ I will confess my unforgiving spirit as sin.
❏ I will seek reconciliation first by apologizing for my unforgiving spirit.
❏ Second, I will explain how I perceived the action that hurt me and freely offer forgiveness.
❏ Third, I will acknowledge that as a Christian I want a wholesome relationship with the person.
❏ Finally, I will pray for God to help me and the person to be reconciled.

Day 5   *Jesus' Final Week (21–26:46)*

UNIT 3

Events of the Final Week (21–28)

PALM SUNDAY

Triumphal Entry

On Sunday Jesus came to Jerusalem in the triumphal entry (21:1-11). He entered on a donkey in fulfillment of Zechariah 9:9, and presented Himself to the Jews as a Messiah who came in a meek and lowly manner. The enthusiastic response of the Jews indicated that they accepted Him as a Messiah, but many still viewed Jesus as a political Messiah. They accepted Jesus but on their own terms.

Check the following statements with which you agree.[19]

❏ 1. Jesus chose to ride into Jerusalem because He was weary.
❏ 2. Jesus knew Zechariah 9:9.
❏ 3. Jesus entered Jerusalem as He did in order to signal His true identity.
❏ 4. The people's response indicates that they understood Jesus' signal.
❏ 5. The people's response indicates that they did not understand Jesus' signal.

TUESDAY

Debate with Religious Leaders

Tuesday of Jesus' final week was a day of controversy. The chief priests and elders of the people questioned Jesus' authority to cleanse the temple (21:23-27). On this same day the Pharisees asked Jesus the legality of paying taxes to Caesar (Matt. 22:15-22). Jews hated the payment of the poll tax, for they regarded the use of a coin with Caesar's image on it as a similar to idolatry. They also resented having to acknowledge any power over their nation other than that of God. Jesus would make enemies if He answered their question about payment of taxes either yes or no. A yes answer would bring opposition from religiously fervent Jews, who objected to payment of taxes to Rome. A no answer would bring Roman opposition down on Jesus as a rebel. Jesus answered in an ingenious fashion that both

---

19. Answers: Hopefully you checked 2 and 3; you may have checked either 4 or 5 because, though the people recognized Jesus as the Messiah, they apparently missed the message that His meek and lowly manner was conveying.

Caesar and God should be given what was theirs, what belonged to each. The Pharisees could only marvel at the wisdom of Jesus' response. Elsewhere in the New Testament, we learn that Christians are encouraged to offer their governments the payment of taxes, obedience and respect (Rom. 13:7), and to pray for officials (1 Tim. 2:1-2).

🌿 **Read Matthew 22:15-22 and check the correct answer or answers to the following questions.**[20]

1. Why did the Jews hate the required Roman poll tax?
   ❏ a. The coin with Caesar's image was like idolatry to them.
   ❏ b. They could not afford the payment.
   ❏ c. They resented acknowledging any power over their nation other than God's.

2. Whom would Jesus have offended had He said yes to the question in v. 17?
   ❏ a. The Jews   ❏ b. The Romans

3. Had Jesus answered no, whom would He have offended?
   ❏ a. The Jews   ❏ b. The Romans

4. Which of the following is an accurate summary of Jesus' answer?
   ❏ a. Yes and no   ❏ b. Maybe one or the other   ❏ c. No answer

Questions About Resurrection

Also, on Tuesday Jesus answered questions from the Sadducees about the resurrection of the dead (Matt. 22:23-33) and questions from a lawyer about the greatest commandment (Matt. 22:34-40). He gave a lengthy denunciation of the hypocrisy of the Pharisees (Matt. 23:1-39).

Olivet Discourse

One of the lengthy discourses of Jesus on this day was the Olivet Discourse given on the Mount of Olives (Matt. 24–25). Jesus used the picture of the destruction of Jerusalem in A.D. 70 as a description of God's punishment on evil during the tribulation period preceding the return of Christ. In A.D. 70 Roman armies destroyed Jerusalem. The temple of God was defiled by the presence of pagan Roman soldiers in those sections of the temple reserved for the priests. Jesus used this national tragedy to give a picture of what God would do in the last times as He faced and overcame evil. Paul described this outbreak of evil in the great tribulation in 2 Thessalonians 2:3-12.

Jesus' Return

In Jesus' discourse His return would follow the period of tribulation (Matt. 24:29-31). Jesus warned that those who saw the destruction during the tribulation should recognize that His return was not far away (Matt. 24:32-25). Jesus stated that He did not know the exact time of His return, but He urged believers to live in such a way that they would be ready whenever it occurred (Matt. 24:37-44).

Jesus concluded His presentation on the Mount of Olives by presenting a vivid picture of the final judgment (25:31-46). This final judgment will be universal, for all nations are involved in it (Matt. 25:32). The Lord will judge the nations for the works they have performed or omitted (Matt. 25:34-46). We understand that these works are the result of (or indicate a lack of) a living faith and are not the basis of our salvation (Eph. 2:8-10). As Paul indicated in Romans 2:6, the Lord will judge people on the basis of their deeds. These deeds will be the sign and evidence of genuine faith or will indicate the lack thereof.

---

2. 0Answers: 1-a and c (and b would be true of many); 2-a; 3-b; 4-perhaps a is the best answer, b is close, c is wrong.

🌿 **Read Matthew 25:31-46. Mark the statements *T* (true)or *F* (false).**[21]

    ___ 1. Jesus' parable should be understood as teaching that eternal salvation is earned by works.

    ___ 2. Jesus' parable described how people who are saved by faith in Christ relate to people.

    ___ 3. Jesus' parable clearly teaches that every person is facing either eternal punishment or eternal life.

    ___ 4. Jesus' parable teaches that Christians are to do good for people in whom they recognize Christ.

    ___ 5. Jesus' parable applies to all people everywhere.

WEDNESDAY

THURSDAY

Though the Gospels do not record any incident on Wednesday of Jesus' last week, we can assume that He was busy teaching and preaching as He followed God's will. On Thursday we see Jesus observing the Passover with His disciples (Matt. 26:17-30) and praying in the garden of Gethsemane (Matt. 26:36-46).

The Crucifixion of Jesus (27:32-56)

FRIDAY

Jesus carried the horizontal beam of His cross to the place of crucifixion. Generally, the upright beam of the cross was left in place, standing erectly in the ground. The horizontal beam was lashed to the upright beam. The scourging of Jesus left Him weak and exhausted. The Romans forced Simon to assist Jesus in carrying the cross to the place of execution (Matt. 27:32). The crucifixion lasted about six hours after starting around 9:00 a.m. At noon darkness settled over Jerusalem (Matt. 27:45). At 3:00 p.m. Jesus cried out, "My God, my God, why have you forsaken me?" (Matt. 27:46). Other signs accompanying His crucifixion were the earthquake, the splitting of the veil of the temple, and the appearance of saints who were taken from their graves (Matt. 27:51-52).

🌿 **Read Matthew 27:32-36, 45-53 and check the correct answer for each of the following questions.**[22]

1. Around what time was Jesus crucified?
   - ❏ a. 6:00 a.m.
   - ❏ b. 9:00 a.m.
   - ❏ c. Noon
2. How long was Jesus on the cross before He died?
   - ❏ a. Six hours
   - ❏ b. Nine hours
   - ❏ c. No one knows.
3. How long was darkness over the land?
   - ❏ a. A few minutes
   - ❏ b. An hour
   - ❏ c. Three hours
4. What events occurred when Jesus died?
   - ❏ a. An earthquake
   - ❏ b. Temple curtain torn from top to bottom
   - ❏ c. Soldiers fainted.
   - ❏ d. Many who had died were raised to life.

Jesus' Resurrection (28:1-15)

SUNDAY

Postresurrection Appearances

The postresurrection appearances of Jesus occurred with different people, times, and places. If the appearances were limited to a few people in the murky light of sunrise or sunset, some might feel that they had been mistaken. However, the number and variety of post-resurrection appearances is a proof of their reality. The repeated sightings of Jesus took place over a period of 40 days and then suddenly stopped when Jesus ascended to heaven. We will see Jesus again only when He returns to take His people to be with Him (John 14:1-6). This hope of seeing Jesus again fills us with a desire to live a sober, righteous, and godly life (Titus 2:11-13).

---

21. Answers: 1-F, 2-T, 3-T, 4-F, 5-T.
22. Answers: 1-b, 2-a, 3-c, 4-a,b,d.

🌿 **Read Matthew 28:1-20 and match the answers on the right with the questions on the left.**[23]

____ 1. What was the basis of the women's message to the disciples about Jesus' resurrection?

____ 2. How did the tale about Jesus' body being stolen by His disciples get started?

____ 3. Where did Jesus tell His disciples to meet Him?

____ 4. What three things did Jesus tell His followers to do?

____ 5. What promise did Jesus make to His followers to encourage them to do the three things He commanded?

A. Galilee

B. To be with them

C. The angel's announcement and a personal experience with the risen Lord

D. The chief priests bribed some of the guards who were at the tomb to say this.

E. Make disciples, baptize them, teach them to obey His commands

🌿 **SUMMARY REVIEW**

To review this unit, see if you can mentally answer the following questions. You may want to write the answers on a separate sheet of paper. Mark your level of performance on the left: circle *C* if you can answer correctly and circle *R* if you need to review.

C R 1. What is the theme and purpose of Matthew's Gospel?

C R 2. What are two characteristics of the Gospel of Matthew?

C R 3. In what chapters of Matthew is the Sermon on the Mount found?

C R 4. Name one activity for each day of Jesus' last week.

C R 5. Give at least two evidences for the resurrection of Jesus.

RESPONDING TO GOD'S WORD

🌴 Reflect on the ways you are obeying Jesus' command in Matthew 28:19-20. Describe below how you are making disciples of all nations.

_____

_____

Describe below how you are assisting in seeing that disciples are baptized.

_____

_____

Describe below how you are currently helping to teach them.

_____

Can you think of other ways in which you could obey that command? Ask God's guidance and help in carrying out this command.

---

23. Answers: 1-C, 2-D, 3-A, 4-E, 5-B.

Unit 4 The Gospel of Mark

Reading Through the New Testament

❑ Mark 6
❑ Mark 7–8
❑ Mark 9
❑ Mark 10–11
❑ Mark 12
❑ Mark 13–14
❑ Mark 15–16

UNIT LEARNING GOAL: The study of this unit should help you understand the unique features of Mark's gospel. You will be able to:
- Distinguish Mark's major emphasis from Matthew.
- Cite at least two characteristics of Mark's Gospel.
- Write the outline of Jesus' ministry in Mark
- Write your interpretation of what constitutes the unpardonable sin.

Author of Mark: John Mark, coworker of Paul (Col. 4:10-11)

Date of Mark: Late 50s

Theme of Mark: The Ministry of God's Servant

Outline

Outline of Mark:
  I. Jesus' Early Ministry (1:1-45)
 II. Jesus' Ministry in Galilee (2:1–9:50)
III. Jesus' Journey to Jerusalem (10:1-52)
 IV. Jesus' Final Week, Crucifixion, and Resurrection (11:1–16:20)

Special Characteristics of Mark:
1. Shortest of the Gospels
2. Written for Roman Readers
3. Focuses on Actions of Jesus
4. Stresses Servanthood of Jesus
5. Records More Miracles
6. Records Emotional Reactions
7. Stresses Obedience to the Gospel

Day 1 Learning About Mark

UNIT 4

John Mark

Author of the Gospel

The early church viewed the Gospel of Mark as the writing of John Mark, Paul's companion for a part of his first missionary journey. Such early Christian leaders as Papias, Irenaeus, and Clement of Alexandria all believed that Mark wrote the second Gospel. Papias indicated that Mark had not heard the Lord nor followed Him personally, but the teaching and instruction of Peter provided Mark with an authoritative source of information about the Lord.

✍ **How do we know that John Mark, Paul's companion for part of his first missionary journey, wrote the Gospel of Mark? Check your answers.[1]**

❏ 1. The Gospel of Mark says that John Mark is the author.
❏ 2. Some well-known, early Christian leaders stated that John Mark is the author.
❏ 3. The Book of 1 Peter says that John Mark wrote the Gospel of Mark.

John Mark grew up in a Christian home with his mother Mary as his most important spiritual influence (see Acts 12:12). His home being large enough to host a sizable Christian prayer meeting and the servant girl being mentioned indicates some wealth in his family. On the first missionary journey Mark left Paul and Barnabas at Perga in Asia Minor (Acts 13:13) and returned to Jerusalem. Paul's refusal to let Mark accompany him and Barnabas on the second journey led to a separation between Paul and Barnabas (Acts 15:37-40). Barnabas' loyalty to Mark could be based partly on blood relationship. They were cousins (Col. 4:10). Paul and Mark eventually were reconciled and worked together (Col. 4:10). Peter's reference to Mark in 1 Peter 5:13 as "my son" may indicate that Mark and Peter worked together in Rome. Despite his early failure and rejection Mark found a useful place in Christian service. His endurance in serving God can give us encouragement as we face defeat and opposition.

Date

Mark the First Gospel?

Mark lacks specific reference to a date of writing just as Matthew does. Mark's prophecy about the destruction of the temple (13:2,14) dates the Gospel before A.D. 70. Opinions in the early church differed over whether Mark wrote it before or after Peter's death in the mid-sixties.

Many New Testament scholars feel that Mark was the first Gospel to be written. Matthew includes about one-half of the verses in Mark. Also, neither Matthew nor Luke ever differ from the sequence of events of Jesus' life which Mark follows. Matthew and Luke often repeat the exact words of Mark (see Mark 2:20; Matt. 9:15; Luke 5:34-35). These facts have led New Testament scholars to conclude that Matthew and Luke had access to Mark's Gospel when they wrote.

Late 50s

Acts ends with Paul in prison in Rome, a date in the early sixties. Luke would have been written still earlier. If Luke (and Matthew) used Mark in his writing. Mark probably wrote his Gospel sometime in the late fifties.

---

1. Answer: 2.

1. Which of the Gospel's probably was the first one written?[2] _____

2. What two Gospels repeat parts of Mark word-for-word?_____

and _____.

3. Write here the possible date for Mark: _____

Theme and Purpose

Mark, like Matthew, does not give a specific statement of its purpose. However, we can learn about his purpose by observing what Mark included in his Gospel.

Emphasis on the Gospel

Several statements in Mark's Gospel clearly showed the importance of preaching and believing the gospel (10:29; 13:9-10). Mark's emphasis on the good news of salvation in Christ provided strong encouragement to the church to continue preaching the truth.

Emphasis on Jesus' Deity

Mark strongly emphasized that Jesus was the Son of God. His opening words clearly stated this (1:1). God the Father witnessed the same truth at Jesus' baptism (1:11). The Roman centurion who watched Jesus die shared the same witness (15:39).

Emphasis on Jesus' Servanthood

Mark also presented Jesus as God's servant who committed Himself to go all the way to the cross (10:45). Jesus' ministry as a servant led to our redemption.

Check the following statements that reflect the theme and purpose of Mark's Gospel.[3]

❑ 1. To convince Jews that Jesus is the Christ
❑ 2. To show the importance of preaching and believing the gospel
❑ 3. To present Jesus as the Son of God
❑ 4. To present Jesus' commitment to dying for our redemption

To Encourage Persecuted Church

The Gospel of Mark shows the importance of Jesus as God's son and servant. It emphasizes the importance of preaching the gospel. Mark wanted to encourage a persecuted church to preach the gospel of Jesus' sacrificial death in order to bring salvation to the world. This is still God's command for our church today.

For Roman Readers

Several features of Mark's Gospel suggest that he wrote for Roman readers. He occasionally explained Greek expressions by their Latin equivalents. He also translated some Aramaic expressions which the Roman readers likely would not understand (5:41; 7:34). Many New Testament scholars feel that Mark aimed his Gospel toward Christians who were living in Rome.

Jesus' Emotional Responses

Mark also demonstrated an open, candid insight into the thoughts of the people he mentioned. In 3:5 he mentioned Jesus' anger and deep distress at the stubborn cruelty of the Pharisees. Jesus' reaction was not a sinful, selfish attitude but a response mixed with grief and indignation for the Pharisees' disregard of the man with the withered hand. Although other Gospels mention the miracle, only Mark mentions Jesus' emotional response on this occasion. Mark also mentioned the response of Jesus' family to the Lord's incessant work (3:21). The family felt that Jesus was "out of his mind." Mark showed his truthful portrayals of events with his candid statements.

---

2. Answers: 1-Mark; 2-Matthew and Luke; 3-the late 50s.
3. Answers: You could have checked 2, 3, and 4.

> ## RESPONDING TO GOD'S WORD
>
> 🌴 Mark evidently spent most of his life serving the Lord. He wrote his Gospel to help others receive the salvation God provided through His Son. Pray for God to help you understand how He wants to use you to help others receive Christ's salvation.

Day 2 *Outline of Mark*

U N I T 4

Most scholars feel that Mark provided a framework (or outline) from which Matthew and Luke were later written. Read slowly and carefully through the outline of Mark below, noting the major points (with Roman numerals), and doing each learning activity.

I. Jesus' Early Ministry (1:1-45)
A. Jesus' Baptism and Temptation (1:1-13)
B. Calling of First Disciples (1:14-20)
C. Miracles to Help the Sick (1:21-45)

🌿 **Check the correct answer(s) for each of the following questions.[4]**

1. Jesus' early ministry stressed
   ☐ a. His baptism   ☐ b. His first disciples   ☐ c. His miracles

2. Jesus' temptation seemed to indicate that
   ☐ a. His Father appointed Him to it
   ☐ b. Satan desired it
   ☐ c. Angels assisted Him in it

3. Jesus' eagerness to heal meant
   ☐ a. Peter's mother-in-law was about to die
   ☐ b. He wanted publicity
   ☐ c. He was filled with compassion
   ☐ d. He had come to destroy people with demons

II. Jesus' Ministry in Galilee (2:1–9:50)
A. Exciting Days of Ministry (2:1–3:35)
B. Jesus' Parables (4:1-34)
C. Jesus' Demonstrating God's Power (4:3–5:43)
D. Success and Opposition (6:1–8:26)
E. Jesus Teaches His Disciples (8:27–9:50)

III. Jesus' Journey to Jerusalem (10:1-52)
A. Jesus' Teaching on Divorce (10:1-12)
B. Little Children and Jesus (10:13-16)
C. The Kingdom and Sacrifice (10:17-31)
D. Jesus Predicts His Death (10:32-34)
E. The Desire to Be First (10:35-44)
F. Blind Bartimaeus of Jericho (10:46-52)

---

4. Answers: 1-a,b,c, 2-a,b,c, 3-c.

🌿 Mark the following statements *T* (true) or *F* (false).[5]

___ 1. Jesus' parables taught about the kingdom of God.
___ 2. Jesus' nature miracles demonstrated God's power.
___ 3. Jesus' ministry in Galilee demonstrated great success and no opposition.
___ 4. Jesus' discussion of who was greatest was an example of His teaching the disciples.

Jesus' Final Week (11–16)

PALM SUNDAY

MONDAY

TUESDAY

THURSDAY

FRIDAY

SUNDAY

IV. Jesus' Final Week, Crucifixion, and Resurrection (11:1–16:20)
   A. Jesus' Final Week (11:1–14:42)
     1. The Triumphal Entry (11:1-11)
     2. Jesus Curses Fig Tree, Cleanses the Temple (11:12-19)
     3. The Fig Tree and Faith (11:20-26)
     4. Jesus Questioned (11:27–12:34)
     5. Jesus' Teaching About the Christ, and the teachers of the Law (12:35-40)
     6. The Widow's Offering (12:41-44)
     7. Jesus' Olivet Discourse (13:1-37)
     8. Jesus Anointed at Bethany (14:1-11)
     9. The Lord's Supper (14:12-26)
    10. Peter's Denial Predicted (14:27-31)
    11. Gethsemane (14:32-42)

   B. Jesus' Crucifixion (14:43–15:47)
     1. Jesus Arrested (14:43-52)
     2. Trial Before High Priest and Sanhedrin (14:53-65)
     3. Peter's Denials (14:66-72)
     4. Trial Before Pilate (15:1-15)
     5. Jesus Flogged and Mocked (15:16-20)
     6. Crucifixion of Jesus (15:21-47)

   C. Jesus' Resurrection (16:1-20)
     1. Women's Early Visit (16:1-8)
     2. Jesus Appeared to Mary Magdalene (16:9-11)
     3. Jesus Appeared to Two in the Country (16:12-13)
     4. Jesus Appeared to the Eleven (16:14)
     5. Jesus' Great Commission (16:15-18)
     6. Jesus' Ascension (16:19-20)

🌿 **Fill in the blanks of Mark's outline below.**[6]

   I. Jesus' E_____ M_____(1:1-45)

   II. Jesus' M_____ in G_____(2:1–9:50)

   III. Jesus' J_____ to J_____ (10:1-52)

   IV. Jesus' F_____ W_____, C_____, and R_____
     (11:1—16:20)

---

5. Answers: 1-T, 2-T, 3-F, 4-T.
6. Answers: 1-Early Ministry, II-Ministry in Galilee, III-Journey to Jerusalem, IV-Final Week, Crucifixion, Resurrection.

RESPONDING TO GOD'S WORD

Jesus was the Master Teacher and also the Master Servant during His life on earth.

Read Mark 10:45. Put a check by the commitments that apply:

❑ I plan consciously and regularly to ask God for a servant's heart.
❑ I plan to look for ways to serve others.

I will strive to be a Master Servant by:
❑ serving personally, even if my hands get dirty
❑ serving diligently and faithfully
❑ serving obediently with a willing heart
❑ serving heartily as if I were serving the Lord
❑ trying to discover winsome ways to serve that will make others want to know and accept my Lord

---

Day 3   A Busy Beginning

UNIT 4

Reading Mark's Gospel is like reading a pictorial history of Jesus' life. Mark uses vivid words, phrases, and descriptions to take us quickly through the life of Jesus, God's Son and our Savior.

The First Disciples (1:16-20)

Andrew and Peter

James and John

When we read the story of Jesus' call of Andrew and Peter, we might ask, "Would I follow a stranger as quickly as they did?" However, Jesus was not really a stranger to these disciples. He already had met Andrew and Peter (and perhaps John, see John 1:35-42). They had listened to Jesus and had considered His claims. When Jesus called them to be His disciples, they already were convinced that making disciples out of men was more important than looking for fish. Peter, Andrew, James, and John left their fishing business to follow Jesus.

Read John 1:35-42 and Mark 1:16-20. Mark the following statements *T* (true) or *F* (false).[7]

_____ 1. Mark 1:16-20 shows that Jesus called total strangers to follow Him as disciples.
_____ 2. Peter, Andrew, James, and John left their fishing business to follow Jesus.
_____ 3. Jesus would never disrupt people's lives today as He did those of His first disciples.

Helping the Hurting (1:21-45)

Control over Demonic Power

This section shows Jesus beginning His Galilean ministry with a full two days of teaching, healing, and exorcism. The demon that controlled the man in verses 23-24 saw in Jesus a threat to his existence. Many Jews attempted to perform exorcisms

---

7. Answers: 1-F, 2-T, 3-F.

by repeating the name of Jehovah in a series of formulas. Jesus spoke only a few words and showed His absolute control over the demonic power in the man. The people were both astonished and alarmed at Jesus' power, and the report of his power and authority spread throughout the entire region.

Sunset (v. 32) signaled the end of the Sabbath. With the passing of the Sabbath it was once again permissible by Jewish law for Jesus to heal. Throngs of people came to Jesus' residence, and He healed many of them. Mark's words in verse 34 distinguish between general sickness and demon possession. Jesus' time alone with His Father and His compassionate healing of a leper conclude these two busy days.

Exciting Days of Ministry (2:1–3:35)

Mark included several incidents showing a powerful ministry but demonstrating the development of opposition to Jesus. Some of these incidents do not appear in chronological order in the other Gospels. Perhaps Mark has grouped these incidents together as a topical collection to show how hostility toward Jesus began.

🌿 **Read Mark 2:1-12. Answer the following questions.**[8]

1. What offended some teachers of the law?

   _____

2. What did Jesus' healing the paralyzed man show?

   _____

Paralytic Carried by Four

In 2:1-12 Jesus offered forgiveness to a paralyzed man as a response to the faith of both the man and those who carried him. They showed their faith by breaking through the roof. Jesus' pronouncement of pardon showed that we can be completely whole only when His grace overcomes the decay and separation sin has caused.

The scribes were both right and wrong. They were right in recognizing that a mere man could not forgive sin. They were wrong in refusing to see Jesus as God's Son. Jesus' healing of the man proved that He had the power to forgive sin.

🌿 **Read Mark 2:13-17 and answer the following questions.**[9]

1. What offended teachers of the law and Pharisees?

   _____

2. What did Jesus' answer in verse 17 show? _____

Call of Levi

Jesus' association with the tax-collector Matthew (2:13-17) and his friends puzzled the scribes and Pharisees. They asked Jesus why He spent time with such outcasts. Jesus' answer indicated that Christianity provides the power of God to overcome the effects of sin in people's lives and make them whole.

Many Jews had turned the practice of fasting into a traditional act lacking spiritual earnestness (2:18-22). Jesus indicated that fasting was to serve as a means of showing

---

8. Answers: 1-Jesus' claim to forgive sins, an authority that belonged only to God; 2-that Jesus had authority to forgive sins.
9. Answers: 1-Jesus' associating with known sinners; 2-that Jesus came to save sinners.

earnestness and commitment in days of trial. He compared the new faith (Christian faith) to new wineskins which could expand with the pressure of new wine. Judaism resembled old, brittle wineskins that would break under the pressure of new wine. Jesus warned that they must not take the old forms of Judaism such as routine fasting, and impose it on the throbbing life of Spirit-filled Christianity.

🌿 **Mark the following statements *T* (true) or *F* (false).**[10]

____ 1. The Pharisees were offended by the disciples plucking grain (working) on the Sabbath.

____ 2. Jesus taught that meeting human needs is more important than keeping religious rituals.

Jesus, Lord of the Sabbath

The Jews held Jesus accountable for the actions of His disciples (2:23-28). Their picking and threshing of the grain constituted work on the Sabbath and was a sin in the eyes of the Pharisees. Jesus' answer suggested that the prohibition of all work on the Sabbath was a mere human interpretation of what God had spoken. God always had intended that meeting a human need, such as hunger, be more important than refraining from any activity on the Sabbath.

Sabbath for Rest and Worship

Jesus also reminded His hearers that the Sabbath was a time for man to experience rest and worship of his God. The Jews wrongly had turned it into another day in which God supposedly tested man's obedience to various arbitrary laws.

Always Lawful to Do Good

Jesus also clashed with the Jewish leaders when He healed a man with a deformed hand on the Sabbath (3:1-6). Jews prohibited unnecessary healing and health care on the Sabbath, viewing it as work. Jesus stirred up the contempt and murderous hatred of the Pharisees and Herodians when He said that it was always lawful to do good and save life, even on the Sabbath.

The Unpardonable Sin (3:20-30)

🌿 **Read Mark 3:20-30 and put a check here when you have done so:** ❑

Jesus healed a demon-possessed man, blind and speechless (Matt. 12:22-24). The people were amazed at Jesus' display of power, but the Pharisees claimed that Jesus was demon possessed and cast out the demon by demonic power. Jesus stated three things in His response. First, He showed that it was illogical to accuse Him of using demonic power to cast out Satan. If He used demonic power, then Satan fought against Satan, and his kingdom would be destroyed by internal division. Second, He explained what He really had done. He was stronger than Satan and had restrained him while He freed a demon-possessed man from satanic control. Third, He warned His listeners against committing blasphemy against the Holy Spirit.

🌿 **Fill in the blanks.**[11]

Jesus answered the charge of having an evil spirit with these facts.

1. To think that Satan was driving out Satan is _____.

2. He explained that He was stronger than _____.

3. He warned of the danger of blasphemy against the _____ _____.

---

10. Answers: 1-T; 2-T.
11. Answers: 1-illogical, 2-Satan, 3-Holy Spirit.

Some people fear they have committed the unpardonable sin. They may have sinned, but their demonstration of concern is good evidence that they have not committed the unpardonable sin. If they had done this, they would fear no guilt. Notice that Jesus did not say that the Pharisees had committed the unpardonable sin. Rather, He indicated that they were treading on the edge of it.

RESPONDING TO GOD'S WORD

Spend a few moments meditating on this thought: the opposite attitude to that of one who is in danger of committing the unpardonable or eternal sin is a tenderness and sensitivity toward God. Write a short description of your present attitude toward God.

_____

_____

Ask God to help you continue/develop an attitude characterized by tenderness of heart and a sensitive spirit.

Day 4   *Important Events of Mark*

UNIT 4

Feeding the Five Thousand (6:30-44)

Read Mark 6:30-46 and John 6:24-35,49-56,66. Put a check here when you have read these verses: ❏

Only Miracle Recorded in All Four Gospels

This is the only miracle of Jesus that all four Gospel writers record. It must have made a tremendous impression on them!

Jesus performed this miracle near the season of the Passover (John 6:4). He had originally intended to take His disciples aside for a time of rest, but a crowd followed them to a remote area on the shore of the Sea of Galilee. Jesus spent all day teaching the crowd. At the end of the day He commanded the disciples to feed the crowds (Mark 6:37). The disciples answered that feeding the crowd would require bread costing 200 denarii. A denarious was the average pay for a day's labor. A person would need to work eight months to get 200 denarii!

The disciples brought to Jesus a boy with five barley loaves and two fish. Jesus directed the disciples to seat people in groups on the green grass (Mark 6:39), took the food, blessed it, and gave it to His disciples to distribute. The loaves and fish multiplied until there was enough for all with twelve baskets full of leftovers.

Fill in the blanks in these three statements that reflect important features of the miracle of feeding the five thousand.[12]

1. This miracle led some Jews to show _____

2. Following this miracle many followers of Jesus _____

3. This miracle taught that Jesus could provide spiritual _____

Questions About Cleanness (7:1-23)

A delegation of Pharisees and scribes from Jerusalem hounded Jesus as He traveled throughout Galilee preaching. In this section they criticized Jesus' disciples for breaking rabbinic tradition by eating with ceremonially unclean hands. Their charge did not involve the sanitary practices of the disciples but a violation of religious practice, which was serious sin to the Pharisees.

🌿 **Read Mark 7:1-4. Mark the following statements *T* (true) or *F* (false).**[13]

　　　___ 1. This passage indicates that the Pharisees had discovered the value of sanitation in the prevention of disease.

　　　___ 2. The Pharisee's religious life was governed by many, many traditions of the elders.

　　　___ 3. The Pharisees and teachers of the law were critical of Jesus' disciples because they willfully broke the law of Moses.

　　　___ 4. The Pharisees and teachers of the law were critical of Jesus' disciples because they did not observe the traditions handed down from the elders.

Practice of Corban

Jesus responded to the Pharisees, "You nullify the word of God by your tradition" (Mark 7:13). As an example of their violation of God's laws, He cited the practice of Corban. By abusing an ancient tradition of dedicating gifts to God, a son who wanted to avoid giving some type of support to his needy parents might dedicate it to God by declaring it as Corban. He could retain possession, use the object for himself, and then give it to God at his death. The parents would go without support while their greedy son indulged his selfish living. To Jesus obeying God was more important than following human tradition. To the Pharisees obeying rabbinic tradition was as important as obeying Scripture.

🌿 **Read Mark 7:14-23 and check the correct ending to the statements.**[14]

1. Jesus said concerning the idea of unclean foods that
   - ❏ a. no food could spiritually defile a person
   - ❏ b. only certain foods could spiritually defile a person
   - ❏ c. all foods declared unclean in the Old Testament could defile a person

2. Jesus explained that because food passed through the body
   - ❏ a. it affected the whole body
   - ❏ b. you are what you eat
   - ❏ c. it had no spiritual effect at all on the body

3. Jesus taught that spiritual defilement
   - ❏ a. came from associating with worldly people
   - ❏ b. came from a person's own heart
   - ❏ c. was a matter of heredity

4. From Jesus' teaching it is safe to assume that
   - ❏ a. all people are capable of being spiritually defiled
   - ❏ b. Christians are safe from spiritual defilement
   - ❏ c. neither of the above

---

12. Answers: 1-messianic fervor. 2-left him. 3-strength.
13. Answers: 1-F, 2-T, 3-F, 4-T.
14. Answers: 1-a, 2-c, 3-b, 4-a.

Jesus explained (7:14-23) that eating food did not really harm a person spiritually. We receive spiritual harm when we indulge evil thoughts within such as greed, lust, and pride. Jesus' strong words abolished the distinction between clean and unclean foods (7:19).

Jesus' words teach us that human rituals are not as important as doing God's will. We human beings often place more emphasis on following our traditions than in obeying God.

The Rich Young Man (10:17-22)

🕮 **Read Mark 10:17-22 and check your answer to each of the following questions.[15]**

    1. Which word do you think describes the rich man's purpose in coming to Jesus?
    ❏ a. To seek
    ❏ b. To flatter
    ❏ c. To deceive

    2. What did the Commandments that Jesus cited encompass?
    ❏ a. Relationship with God
    ❏ b. Relationships with others
    ❏ c. Both

    3. What was Jesus' response to the man's claim to have kept those Commandments from his youth?
    ❏ a. Skepticism
    ❏ b. Disgust
    ❏ c. Love

    4. Why did Jesus tell the rich man to sell all and give away the proceeds?
    ❏ a. Jesus knew this would be the hardest demand He could make.
    ❏ b. The man's spiritual failing was materialism (greed, covetousness).
    ❏ c. Jesus wants all His followers to be poor.

    5. Why did the rich man go away sad?
    ❏ a. He loved his wealth more than God.
    ❏ b. Jesus did not give him an acceptable answer.
    ❏ c. He did not understand what Jesus was saying.

Only God Is Good

The rich young man seemed to feel that he could win eternal life by some heroic deed. Jesus responded to the young man's address of "Good teacher" by affirming that only God was good. He wanted to lead the young man to see that if Jesus were truly good, He also was divine.

The Tenth Commandment

Jesus repeated to the young man all of the Ten Commandments except the tenth commandment, "Thou shalt not covet." The ruler's ready response that he had kept all of these commands makes us suspicious of his genuine obedience. The one thing Jesus prescribed for him to do directly hit the problem of covetousness. When the young man refused to turn from his riches, he went away sadly. He had not repented of his greed. He had nice thoughts about Jesus, but he refused to turn from his covetous, greedy ways and truly follow Jesus.

---

15. Answers: 1-your response. I checked a; 2-b; 3-c; 4-b; 5-a.

The Desire for Greatness of James and John (10:35-45)

James and John, along with their mother (Matt. 20:20), came to Jesus to ask for favored positions in the Kingdom. Jesus answered that His disciples were destined for suffering and martyrdom. James and John, hardly recognizing what they were promising, said that they were ready to pass through anything that Jesus would face.

Genuine Greatness

🌿 **Read Mark 10:35-40 and in the following pairs of sentences check the sentence that is more correct.**[16]

____A1. James and John thought they were better than the other disciples.
____A2. James and John wanted the highest places of honor and authority in Jesus' kingdom.
____B1. Jesus used the term *baptism* to describe His exaltation and glory.
____B2. Jesus used the term *baptism* to describe His coming suffering and death.
____C1. Jesus did not grant James and John's request because He did not have that privilege.
____C2. Jesus did not grant James and John's request because of their proud ambition.

When the other disciples learned what James and John had done, they became indignant. They were jealous for their own position and fearful that James and John might steal an advantage over them.

Jesus' Definition of Greatness

Jesus' answer to His self-seeking disciples leaves us much to ponder about ourselves. He contrasted the squabble for power by Gentile rulers with the submission to service and sacrifice which should characterize Christians. Christians were not to show their greatness by flaunting their authority over others. Genuine greatness came from demonstrating love through serving others. A Christian becomes great by serving others, not by exercising power.

Jesus' Life Demonstrated Service

Jesus' own life showed that He came to serve. He voluntarily concealed His glory as God's Son and became a servant of God who went to the disgraceful death of the cross (Phil. 2:6-8). Jesus' death was a ransom. By the payment of His life He delivered us from sin. Because He laid down His life for us, we ought to sacrifice in service for Christian brothers and sisters (1 John 3:16).

RESPONDING TO GOD'S WORD

🌴 Jesus was the Master Servant during His life on earth. Complete the servant exercise below. Check when you have completed each activity.
❑ I have reread Mark 10:45.

I have asked God to show me how I can be more like Christ in relating to:
❑ people in my family
❑ people on the job
❑ people at my church
❑ I have waited quietly for Him to bring people and thoughts to my mind.
❑ As He has brought specific sins to mind, I have confessed each one.
❑ I have asked God to help me become more of a servant for Him this week.

---

16. Answers: A2, B2, C1.

Day 5 — *Jesus' Final Week*

UNIT 4

Events of the Final Week (11:1–14-42)

🌿 Scan Mark 11:1-33 and check the sections that Matthew includes (Matt. 21).[17]

❑ 1. The triumphal entry
❑ 2. Jesus cleanses the temple.
❑ 3. Jesus curses the fig tree.
❑ 4. Jesus' authority Is questioned.

Mark followed the same pattern in describing Jesus' last week as did Matthew. The triumphal entry on Sunday preceded the cursing of the fig tree and the cleansing of the temple on Monday. On Tuesday the chief priests and elders questioned Jesus' authority to cleanse the temple, and the Pharisees and Herodians asked Him about paying taxes to Caesar. Also, on Tuesday one of the scribes came to Jesus with a question about which was the greatest commandment. This scribe asked the question sincerely (12:28, 34). His open attitude is a contrast to the deceitful attacks other Jewish leaders made against Jesus.

The Greatest Commandment

Jesus answered that we are to love the Lord our God with completeness. Because God is unique, we are to love Him with all our beings. We are to seek God for His own sake, and we are to have pleasure in doing His will. This commitment to God leads to a similar commitment to human beings. The two commitments stand together. A complete love for God finds its expression in a selfless concern for another person. Our chief aim in life is not to get riches or fame. Our chief aim is to love God completely and serve with unselfish zeal those whom He has created.

🌿 **Read Mark 14:12-25 and check here when you are finished:** ❑

On the night of Jesus' betrayal, Jesus and His disciples observed the Jewish Passover celebration (14:12-25).

🌿 **Match the following items on the left with the item on the right that they represent. Write the correct letters in the blanks.**[18]

___ 1. Passover	A. Jesus' body
___ 2. Lord's Supper	B. Deliverance from slavery in Egypt
___ 3. Bread	C. Jesus' blood
___ 4. Wine	D. Redemption from sin

The Lord's Supper

The Passover reminded the Jews of God's deliverance of Israel from slavery in Egypt. Jesus instituted the Lord's Supper, to celebrate the redemption of God's people from slavery to sin. Jesus' shed blood was the price of that redemption.

The bread of the Lord's Supper represents Jesus' body that was given for sinners. The cup of wine represents the blood of Jesus that was shed for sin. The new covenant that Jesus began was based on His shed blood and not on the blood of animal sacrifices.

---

17. Answer: All four.
18. Answers: 1-B, 2-D, 3-A, 4-C.

A Reminder of Jesus' Death

When we celebrate the Lord's Supper, we remind ourselves of two features of Jesus' death. First, we reflect on the fact of His death. We can take His death for granted and neglect to praise Him for His sacrifice which delivers us from sin.

Second, the death of Jesus reminds us that He is coming again (Mark 14:25; 1 Cor. 11:26). The Lord's Supper has a backward emphasis when we focus back on Jesus' death. It also has a forward emphasis when we anticipate His return.

🌿 **Read Mark 14:32-41. Mark the statements *T* (true) or *F* (false).**[19]

    ___ 1. Because Jesus was the Son of God, facing the cross was not difficult for Him.

    ___ 2. Jesus did not want to die on the cross.

    ___ 3. Jesus was determined to do whatever God wanted Him to do.

    ___ 4. Jesus indicated to His disciples that prayer would not help prepare them for temptations.

    ___ 5. Jesus knew Judas' betrayal before it happened.

The Trial of Jesus (14:43–15:20)

The deceitfulness of Judas in the arrest of Jesus appears clearly. Judas led the soldiers to the garden of Gethsemane where he knew the soldiers could arrest Jesus without causing a public uproar. After Judas had identified Jesus to the soldiers by kissing Him, they stepped forward to take Him away. Peter drew a weapon to defend Jesus against capture. He even cut off the ear of a servant (John 18:10).

Jesus' response to Peter showed His confidence in God in this moment of deep danger. Rebuking Peter (Matt. 26:52-53) and healing the ear (Luke 22:51), He expressed confidence that He could even then call for legions of angels to come to His rescue. Jesus chose to do the will of God rather than struggle to protect Himself. When you and I face instances of danger, we can trust that this same God will not leave us nor forsake us (Heb. 13:5).

The disciples showed their fear by fleeing as a group (Mark 14:50). The young man who fled naked when some laid hands on him may have been Mark (Mark 14:51-52). Not wearing an undergarment suggests that he had dressed hastily.

🌿 **Read Mark 14:53-54,66-72 and check the correct ending for each of the following statements.**[20]

    1. Peter's going into the courtyard of the High Priest was
        ❑ a. an act of courage
        ❑ b. a foolish act
        ❑ c. a way of showing off

    2. The servant girl identified Peter as a follower of Jesus because
        ❑ a. he looked out of place
        ❑ b. she evidently had seen him with Jesus
        ❑ c. she did not know him

    3. People near Peter, having heard him deny being one of Jesus' followers, accused him of being one because
        ❑ a. he had a Galilean accent
        ❑ b. his denial had seemed forced
        ❑ c. he was obviously tense and ill at ease

---

19. Answers: 1-F, 2-T, 3-T, 4-F, 5-T.

4. The reason Peter denied Jesus was
❑ a. his shallow commitment to Him
❑ b. his fear
❑ c. his confusion

5. When Peter heard the rooster crow a second time, he wept because
❑ a. he was exhausted from being up all night
❑ b. he realized the day of Jesus' death was at hand
❑ c. he had failed His Lord

Peter's Denial

Peter's denial of Jesus showed his own fear and wavering commitment (14:53-72). One of the servant girls of the high priest accused him of being a follower of Jesus, and he denied the charge. Some of those standing by the fire to warm themselves took up the charge and indicated that even his speech indicated that he was from Galilee. This time Peter profanely denied the charge. After his third denial, he heard the crowing of the rooster and remembered Jesus' prediction (Mark 14:72).

Peter's failure should not blind us to the marvelous comeback he made in the Book of Acts. Peter found grace in God's forgiveness for even a willful sin and became a leader among the Christians in the first century. Even though we may stumble and falter, God can forgive us and give us an opportunity for added usefulness.

Mark's account of Jesus' trial contains both a Jewish phase and a Roman phase. The Jewish phase contains an appearance before the high priest and the Sanhedrin. The Roman phase contains an appearance before Pilate (14:41–15:20).

The Ending of Mark's Gospel

The best manuscripts of the Greek New Testament place the end of Mark's Gospel at 16:8. In later manuscripts verses 9-20 appear that leads many to conclude that these verses were added at a later time.

🌿 SUMMARY REVIEW

To review this unit, see if you can mentally answer the following questions. You may want to write the answers on a separate sheet of paper. Mark your level of performance on the left: circle *C* if you can answer correctly and circle *R* if you need to review.

C R 1. Comparing Matthew and Mark, which is more systematic? shows more activity? more interested in Jesus' teaching? more interested in Jesus' servanthood?

C R 2. What are two characteristics of Mark's Gospel?

C R 3. Give the general outline of Jesus' ministry in Mark.

C R 4. What constitutes the unpardonable sin? Can a Christian commit it?

Review this week's material to find the answers.

RESPONDING TO GOD'S WORD

Meditate on the truth that Jesus Christ is alive, that He loves you, that He wants the best and most fulfilling life possible for you. Spend a few moments praising Him.

---

20. Answers: 1-a, 2-b, 3-a, 4-b (or a or c), 5-c.

Unit 5 — The Gospel of Luke

Reading Through the New Testament

❑ Luke 10–11
❑ Luke 12–13
❑ Luke 14–15
❑ Luke 16–17
❑ Luke 18–19
❑ Luke 20–22
❑ Luke 23–24

UNIT LEARNING GOAL: The study of this unit will help you understand the contribution of Luke to our knowledge of the life and ministry of Jesus. You will be able to:

- Describe Luke the person and relate him to the New Testament Books he wrote under the inspiration of the Holy Spirit
- Identify the audience to which Luke addressed his Gospel
- List facts about the birth of Jesus that only Luke recorded
- Explain why the genealogies in Matthew and Luke are different
- Interpret the teaching of Jesus about material possessions and our responsibility for the needy
- Describe how God feels toward sinners
- List two facts about the crucifixion Luke alone recorded

Author of Luke: Luke, a Gentile Physician and companion of Paul. The material in Luke's Gospel and Acts together make Luke the largest contributor to the New Testament.

Date of Luke: Late 50s (probably after Mark) or early 60s

Theme of Luke: The Seeking Savior

Outline

Outline of Luke:
I. Birth and Childhood of Jesus (1:1–2:52)
II. Jesus' Early Ministry and Preaching (3:1–4:13)
III. Galilean Ministry of Jesus (4:14–9:50)
IV. Final Journey to Jerusalem (9:51–19:27)
V. Final Week, Crucifixion, Resurrection, and Ascension (19:28–24:53)

Luke's Hymns of Praise

- The Magnificat of Mary (1:46-55)

- The Benedictus of Zechariah (1:68-79)

- The Gloria in Excelsis of the Angels (2:14)

- The Nunc Dimittis of Simeon (2:29-32)

Special Characteristics of Luke:
1. Longest Gospel, only Gospel not written by an eyewitness of Jesus' life
2. Written to reach and encourage Gentile Christians
3. Shows interest in the poor and needy
4. Vivid picture of Christ
5. Emphasizes Jesus' prayer life
6. Emphasizes the role of the Holy Spirit
7. Emphasizes hymns of praise

Special Parables of Luke:
1. Parable of the Good Samaritan (chap. 10)
2. Parable of the Rich Fool (chap. 12)
3. Parable of Watchfulness (chap. 12)
4. Parable of Fig Tree (chap. 13)
5. Story of Wedding Guest (chap. 14)
6. Parable of Lost Sheep, Lost Coin, Lost (Prodigal) Son (chap. 15)
7. Story of the Shrewd Manager (chap. 16)
8. Story of the Rich Man and Lazarus (chap. 16)
9. Parable of the Persistent Widow (chap. 18)
10. Parable of the Pharisee and Publican (chap. 18)

Day 1   A Reliable Witness to Jesus

UNIT 5

Importance of the Gospel

The Book of Luke gives many evidences of the historical reliability of the events of Jesus' life. From the day He was born until He ascended to heaven, Jesus lived before many witnesses. They saw and observed His commitment to do the will of God. They saw the death of Jesus, and observed that His death was not a secret, shadowy event. It took place before a multitude of Jewish and Roman witnesses. Later Jesus appeared to His disciples in both small and large groups to provide proof that He had conquered death and completed the payment for sin.

Longest Book in the New Testament

Luke's Gospel is the longest book in the New Testament. Luke is the author of the third Gospel and the Acts. These two books together make Luke the largest contributor to the New Testament. Luke was also the first historian of the church. No other Gospel anchored itself so firmly in the secular events of the time. (See Luke 3:1-2.) In his two writings Luke set out the historical development of Christianity, first in the ministry of Christ and then in the outreach of the church.

People-Centered

Luke wrote with the compassionate heart of a pastor-teacher. His opening verses radiated concern for the Christian growth of his friend Theophilus (Luke 1:1-4). Luke also emphasized the spread of the gospel to outcasts. He showed Jesus' acceptance of immoral people (Luke 7:36-50) and ministry to poor people (Luke 14:12-14). He also emphasized that the gospel reached out to Gentiles (Luke 2:32; 3:6; 4:25-27; 7:9; 4:24-27).

Exclusive Parables

The parables of Jesus recorded only in Luke (for example, Luke 15) are among the most beloved of His parables. Luke's Gospel shows the tender, compassionate Savior who came to seek and to save the lost (Luke 19:10).

Check the statements that reflect the importance of Luke's Gospel.[1]

> ❑ 1. Luke was the first Gospel written.
> ❑ 2. Luke contributed more content to the New Testament than any other writer.
> ❑ 3. Luke was the first church historian.
> ❑ 4. The Gospel of Luke emphasizes the spread of the gospel to outcasts.
> ❑ 5. The Gospel of Luke emphasizes that the gospel reaches out to Gentiles.
> ❑ 6. The Gospel of Luke focuses more on Jesus' actions than His teachings.
> ❑ 7. The parables in the Gospel of Luke are among the most beloved.

Author of the Gospel

Although the third Gospel was written anonymously, leaders in the early church affirmed Luke as the author of the Gospel. Irenaeus is one of the early writers who stated that Luke was the author.

Acts Is Key

We also can determine the author of the Gospel by reference to the Book of Acts. For a fuller presentation read the discussion of the authorship of Acts. Both writings

---

1. Answers: You could have checked all except 1 and 6.

have a dedication to Theophilus (Luke 1:3; Acts 1:1). They have a similar interest and style. Acts 1:1 makes reference to an earlier writing which most likely is Luke's Gospel. The same person probably wrote both books.

Companion of Paul

The author of Acts was a companion of Paul. Acts contains three sections in which the writer puts himself among Paul's companions by using a "we" (Acts 16:10-17; 20:5–21:18; 27:1–28:16). Most of Paul's close associates are named in Acts in the third person (see Acts 10:4-5), and this eliminates considering them as possible authors. Luke himself was with Paul during his Roman imprisonment (Col. 4:14) and seems best to fit the requirements for authorship. Since Luke wrote Acts, we can state that he also wrote the Gospel of Luke.

A. Check your response to this statement: Since evidence in the Book of Acts points to Luke as its author, we may safely conclude that Luke also wrote the third Gospel.[2]

❏ Agree   ❏ Disagree

B. Read Colossians 4:10-14 and answer the following questions.

1. What was Luke's profession? _____

2. Since those named in verses 10-13 are Jews and Demas and Nympha are

    Gentiles, was Luke a Jewish Christian or a Gentile Christian? _____

Date

Luke was not a witness to the events of Jesus' life.

A. Read Luke 1:1-4 and list the sources Luke used in writing the Gospel of Luke.[3]

1._____

2._____

B. Check the correct answer.
Luke's information about the spread of Christianity and the development of the early church probably came largely from:

❏ The Old Testament   ❏ John
❏ Paul   ❏ James

Slightly Later than Mark

Luke relied on the words of eyewitnesses and some written sources (1:1-4). Since Luke wrote Acts after Paul had been in Rome for two years (around A.D. 63, see introduction to Acts, Unit 7, Day 1), Luke wrote the Gospel at an even earlier time. If we assume that Luke used or had seen Mark when he wrote, we would want to date Luke slightly later than Mark. A date in the late fifties or early sixties is possible.

---

2. Answers: A.-I hope you checked "agree." B-1-A physician; 2-probably a Gentile.
3. Answers: A-1-written accounts; 2-eyewitness' accounts; B-Paul.

Written in Caesarea or Rome

Luke may have written his Gospel in Caesarea during Paul's imprisonment (Acts 24:27; 27:1), or in Rome while he stayed with Paul during the imprisonment there (Acts 28:30-31).

Theme and Purpose

To Strengthen Faith

To Reach Gentiles

Luke stated his purpose in the opening words to the Gospel, known as the prologue. He wanted to set out an orderly account that would help his friend, Theophilus have an assurance about Christian belief and doctrine (Luke 1:1-4). Theses words suggest that Luke had two chief goals. First, he wanted to set out an accurate account both in the facts which he recorded and in the truths which he explained. Second, he wanted to strengthen the faith of his Gentile Christian friends. We also understand that he hoped his message about Christ would lead many unsaved Gentiles to a commitment to Christ.

RESPONDING TO GOD'S WORD

As Luke taught about the Holy Spirit, he emphasized that both Mary (1:35) and Zechariah (1:67) were filled with the Holy Spirit. He also emphasized the joy Jesus exhibited in the Holy Spirit (Luke 10:21). Acts 2:38 stresses that the Holy Spirit is given to all believers.

Put a check by the statements you make to God in prayer.

❑ I need to be filled with the Holy Spirit too.
❑ I confess that without Your help I cannot live the Christian life in an acceptable way.
❑ I ask You to cleanse me and fill me with Your Spirit.
❑ I pledge to walk in the Spirit by faith today.

Day 2   *Unique Facts About Jesus' Birth*

UNIT 5

Luke used the term "most excellent" when he addressed Theophilus (Luke 1:3). Paul had used this same term when he spoke to the Roman governors Felix (Acts 24:3) and Festus (Acts 26:25). Theophilus was probably a Gentile Christian who may have helped Luke finance the distribution of his Gospel. If so, Luke wrote with a general purpose of reaching Gentiles with a message of salvation.

Our reading of Luke's Gospel can confirm our confidence in the events of Jesus' life. Luke has taken great care to present enough information to give us a firm basis for our faith. Nowhere is this more evidenced than in the events surrounding Jesus' birth.

🌿 Read Luke 1:5-25 and write the verse that supplies each of the following bits of information.[4]

___ 1. Zechariah and Elizabeth's lifestyle
___ 2. the age of Zechariah and Elizabeth
___ 3. Zechariah's profession
___ 4. the name of the angel who spoke to Zechariah
___ 5. why Zechariah questioned the angel's message
___ 6. Zechariah's punishment for not believing the message
___ 7. the first thing that happened to confirm the angel's message

The Birth of John the Baptist (1:5-25,57-80)

Zechariah's Vision

Zechariah, the father of John the Baptist and an older village priest, served two separate weeks out of the year in the Jerusalem temple. As a Levite he was a member of the order of Abijah (see 1 Chron.. 24:7-18). While serving in Jerusalem, the priests cast lots to determine who among then would burn incense. Once selected to do this, a priest usually never received another chance to burn the incense in his lifetime. This practice allowed many priests to experience this special privilege. The angel Gabriel appeared to Zechariah during this once-in-a-lifetime experience and announced that he and his wife Elizabeth would have a son. When Zechariah responded with disbelief, the angel left him speechless until the birth of his son.

John's Birth

When John was born nine months later, the family gathered for a ceremony of circumcision and naming on the eighth day after birth. Friends and relatives suggested the name of Zechariah, but both parents insisted on the name John, which means *the Lord is gracious*. The speechlessness of Zechariah was removed after this event when he sang a song of praise often called "The Benedictus."

The Announcement of Jesus' Birth (1:26-56)

🌿 Read Luke 1:26-38 and answer the following questions.[5]

1. What was the angel's name who appeared to Mary? _____

2. Did Mary's question express doubt?   ❑ Yes   ❑ No

3. Who was to be the child's father? _____

4. What was Mary's response? _____

5. How much older than Jesus was John the Baptist? _____

Gabriel's Announcement

Luke showed Mary's involvement in the birth events. Gabriel announced to Mary that she would give birth to Jesus, the Son of God and heir of David's throne. When Mary inquired how she, a single person, would do this, Gabriel announced that the power of the Holy Spirit would cause her to conceive. The disclosure Gabriel made could have frightened and overwhelmed Mary, who was likely a teenage girl. Her response, "May it be to me as you have said" (1:38), challenges us with a magnificent display of faith.

---

4. Answers: 1-6, 2-7, 3-5, 4-19, 5-18, 6-20, 7-24.
5. Compare your answers with mine: 1-Gabriel; 2-No; she asked how. 3-God; 4-willing acceptance (faith); 5-six months..

Mary's Visit to Elizabeth

The Magnificat

After Gabriel left, Mary visited her cousin Elizabeth to share about the visit. Elizabeth pronounced a blessing from God on Mary. Elizabeth's words led Mary to speak the words of praise in 1:46-55 that we call the Magnificat. Mary's words show her humble background (v. 48) and her deep love for God. Her words of praise remind us of the words of praise of Hannah in 1 Samuel 2:1-10.

The Birth of Jesus (2:1-20)

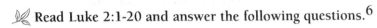 Read Luke 2:1-20 and answer the following questions.[6]

   1. How did Luke relate the birth of Christ to secular historical events?

   _____

   2. What do you find significant in the angels' announcing Jesus' birth to shepherds?

   _____

Luke located the time of Jesus' birth during a census in the administration of the Roman governor of Syria, Quirinius. Joseph and Mary returned to their ancestral town to enroll in the census. At that time, Mary gave birth to Jesus and put him in a manger, a feeding trough for animals. The actual location of the manger may have been a cave in the hillsides used to shelter animals at night.

To Shepherds Near Bethlehem

Angels announced Jesus' birth to shepherds near Bethlehem (2:8-20). The shepherds provided the appropriate audience to view someone who came in the manner of the earlier shepherd king, David. Because Joseph, Mary , and Jesus were still in the area of the manger, the arrival of the shepherds probably was shortly after Jesus' birth. All of these events, left Mary with much to ponder (2:19).

The Childhood of Christ (2:41-52)

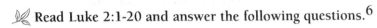 Read Luke 2:41-52; place a check here when you finish: ❑

Only Luke has given us accurate information about the childhood of Jesus. After Jesus' lifetime some Christians wrote fictitious gospels know as the *Infancy Gospels* to satisfy natural human curiosity about Jesus' childhood. The facts in these gospels do not give an accurate picture of Jesus.

Bar Mitzvah

At the age of 13 Jewish boys took part in their *bar mitzvah* and became full members of Judaism. Joseph and Mary probably took Jesus to the temple at age 12 to acquaint Him with the surroundings and festivals held there. Also, this would prepare Him for the *bar mitzvah* on the next year.

In My Father's House

After Joseph and Mary discovered that Jesus was missing, they returned to Jerusalem to search for Him. They found Him in the Jerusalem Temple discussing with the leading teachers among the Jews. Jesus' answer to His parents' question about His disappearance was "Didn't you know that I had to be in my Father's house?" (v.49). Jesus, even as a young boy, had an awareness of His special calling from God.

---

6. Answers: 1-He gave the historical background in verses 1-3; 2-Your response; you may have mentioned their humble station, the fact that Jesus came as the Good Shepherd.

🌿 **Check the statements with which you agree.[7]**

❑ 1. Nonbiblical sources give more accurate information on the childhood of Jesus than do the four Gospels.

❑ 2. Jesus' parents probably took Jesus to the temple for his *bar mitzvah* on this visit to Jerusalem.

❑ 3. Those who heard Jesus' questions and answers in the temple were amazed at His understanding.

❑ 4. Jesus' staying behind in the temple when his parents left Jerusalem was an act of rebellion.

❑ 5. Jesus no longer had to be obedient to his parents.

❑ 6. Jesus grew intellectually, physically, spiritually, and socially.

Luke concluded this section with the summary that Jesus grew intellectually (in wisdom), physically (in stature), spiritually (in favor with God), and socially (in favor with man). His pattern for growth provides an example we should imitate.

RESPONDING TO GOD'S WORD

🌴 **Think about the singing of praise to God which is emphasized in Luke. Singing is a means of reminder and of worship. Through it we can commit and recommit our lives to Him. Place a check beside the statements you can use to worship the Lord today.**

❑ "My soul glorifies the Lord" (1:46).
❑ "My spirit rejoices in God my Savior" (1:47).
❑ "Praise be to the Lord, the God of Israel" (1:68).
❑ "[God gives] His people the knowledge of salvation through the forgiveness of their sins" (1:77).
❑ "Glory to God in the highest" (2:14).
❑ "Lord … dismiss your servant in peace. For my eyes have seen your salvation" (2:29-30).

Day 3   *Early Experiences in Luke*

UNIT 5

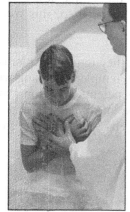

Immersed like Jesus

The Baptism of Jesus (3:21-22)

All four Gospels make reference to Jesus' baptism. Luke's statement that the Spirit descended on Jesus in the bodily form of a dove indicates an appearance that could be seen. The dove symbolizes the coming of the Holy Spirit into the life of Jesus.

For Christians, baptism represents a turning from sin and a uniting with Christ in His death, burial, and resurrection. For Jesus, it meant something different, for He had no sin to confess. In baptism Jesus the Son submitted Himself to the will of God. The Father assured Jesus through the voice and the vision. The Holy Spirit anointed Jesus to fulfill His God-given task.

---

7. Answers: Hopefully you checked 3 and 6.

Luke's Genealogy (3:23-38)

The genealogies in Matthew and Luke are different. Luke's genealogy is longer than that of Matthew. Matthew traced the genealogy of Jesus back to Abraham, but Luke traced Jesus' ancestors back to Adam. Matthew began with Abraham and worked forward to Joseph. Luke began with Joseph and worked backward to Adam. Only Luke's Gospel listed the ancestors of Jesus from Abraham to Adam.

Jewish people would be interested in Jesus' connection with their forefather Abraham. Matthew, the gospel written for Jews, has given this information. Luke wrote his Gospel for all the world, both Jews and Gentile. It is fitting that Luke's genealogy would go back to Adam.

Jesus at Simon's House (7:36-50)

Each Gospel contains the story of the anointing of Jesus by a woman (see Mark 14:3-9). Luke's incident took place earlier in Jesus' ministry and described an anointing by a sinful woman who was worshiping Jesus. The other three Gospels told of an event during Jesus' last week of life. There the woman who anointed Jesus' feet was Mary of Bethany (John 12:1-8).

A Pharisee named Simon had invited Jesus to a meal in his home. A woman of the street, probably a prostitute, learned of the meal and entered Simon's house. Frequently, uninvited people came to a dinner party and stood to watch what was happening. The guests at such meals were not seated at a table but were leaning on the left arm with the head toward the table and the body stretched away from it. The woman could approach Jesus' feet without any difficulty.

The woman intended to anoint Jesus' feet with an expensive perfumed oil only, but her tears fell on Jesus' feet. She wiped them with her hair, an unusual act, for Jewish women did not unbind their hair in public. Simon noted to himself that Jesus was not a prophet because a prophet would know the kind of woman who was touching Him, and would, he thought, avoid her.

> **Read Luke 7:40-50 and check the correct ending for each of the following statements.[8]**
>
> 1. Jesus told Simon the Pharisee a story in order to
>   ❏ a. instruct him   ❏ b. entertain him   ❏ c. embarrass him
>
> 2. Jesus' story and question pointed out that
>   ❏ a. we should forgive one another
>   ❏ b. borrowing is unwise
>   ❏ c. the more we are forgiven, the more we love the forgiver
>
> 3. In His explanation to Simon, Jesus
>   ❏ a. said that the woman was more moral than Simon
>   ❏ b. contrasted the behavior of the woman with that of Simon
>   ❏ c. showed anger
>
> 4. Jesus said that the woman was saved by her
>   ❏ a. loving more   ❏ b. kindness to Him   ❏ c. faith

---

8. Answers: 1-a, 2-c, 3-b, 4-c.

Parable of God's Forgiveness

Jesus knew Simon's thoughts and told a parable of God's forgiveness. Jesus used the parable to contrast the behavior of Simon and the woman toward Him. Simon had not given Him the common courtesies of hospitality, but the woman had performed the humble act of kissing Jesus' feet and anointing them with oil. Jesus declared that her love was a sign of her forgiveness. Her faith had brought her to salvation.

Relating to the Lowly and the Outcast

One of the glorious features of our Savior is His ability to relate to the lowly and the outcast. Simon, rich and proud, was the religious man whom we would expect to show genuine love for Jesus. We expect little from the immoral woman. Jesus' message had made an impact on the woman, and she found forgiveness. All who come to Jesus—from backgrounds of wickedness, self-centeredness, failure, or smug self-righteousness—can find His mercy.

RESPONDING TO GOD'S WORD

Spend two minutes (time yourself) meditating on how you do/ do not demonstrate your love to Him who has forgiven your sins. List what you have concluded.

_____

_____

_____

Day 4

Teaching and Parables on the Way to Jerusalem (9:51–19:27)

UNIT 5

The Good Samaritan (10:25-37)

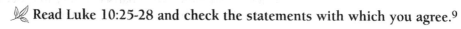 **Read Luke 10:25-28 and check the statements with which you agree.**[9]

❑ 1. The question of the teacher of the law was sincere.
❑ 2. Jesus often answered a question with a question in order to evade the issue.

What was Jesus teaching by His use of this story? Jesus' answer to the learned Jew's first question presented the evidences of eternal life. The lawyer was not interested in genuine learning but in argument. His second question tried to involve Jesus in an argument over whether he was obligated to show love to some undesirable neighbor or to an enemy.

Compassion to Anyone in Need

Jesus' use of the parable really did not answer the lawyer's question, but told him to whom he should be a neighbor. Jesus asked the man to show a willingness to demonstrate neighborly compassion to anyone in need.

---

9. Answers: I hope you checked neither. The teacher was testing Jesus. Jesus' questions were usually designed to probe a person and to help that person think.

In Jesus' story both the priest and the Levite would have caused themselves great inconvenience if they had stopped to help the wounded man. If the man had been dead, their touching him would have cost them temple privileges and would have given them the responsibility for burial of the corpse. The mention of the Samaritan would cause great shock to a Jewish audience. Jews and Samaritans had bitter hatred for one another. The Samaritan not only stopped to investigate, but he took every step possible to show love to the needy man.

Love Overcoming Prejudice

When Jesus asked His questioner, "Which of these three do you think was a neighbor to the man?" the lawyer could not even speak the word "Samaritan." He could only say, "The one who had mercy on him."

Jesus' words warn us that we must not quibble over legal technicalities to avoid responsibility to those in need. As Jesus' followers we must stand ready to offer help to those who, like the wounded man, are physically beaten or are beaten down by sin, defeat, sickness, or evil.

The Rich Fool (12:13-21)

🌿 **Read Luke 12:13-21. Check the statement in each of the following pairs that you feel to be most accurate.[10]**

- ❏ A1. Jesus is keenly aware of the tendency toward and danger of greed.
- ❏ A2. Jesus was against owning property.
- ❏ B1. Many people today, including many who attend church regularly, believe that getting ahead materially is the main thing.
- ❏ B2. People who attend church regularly do not show evidence of being interested in material things.
- ❏ C1. Jesus warned against becoming wealthy.
- ❏ C2. Jesus warned against valuing material things over spiritual things.
- ❏ D1. Jesus called the man a fool, because he invested his life only in that which he would have to leave at death.
- ❏ D2. Jesus called the man a fool because he was mean.
- ❏ E1. Being rich toward God has nothing to do with money but only with how we treat other people.
- ❏ E2. Being rich toward God includes the proportion of our income we give to God.

Right Use of Possessions

A statement from the crowd provided Jesus with the opening to teach about the right use of material possessions. The hearer demanded that Jesus persuade a brother to surrender some inheritance to him. Jesus responded with a warning about material possessions. Jesus was concerned about the attitudes of those involved, not with who got the inheritance.

Jesus warned that life does not consist of merely possessing things. He drove His idea into their minds with a parable. A wealthy farmer with a good harvest decided to take care of his storage problems by building bigger barns. The farmer's concerns were only with himself. He had no interest in God's will or in helping others.

God could call the man "Fool" because the man assumed that he controlled the future. He did not consider that all that was important to him could vanish in a moment. Jesus wanted His hearers to develop wealth toward God by obedience and deeds of service. Jesus' words are appropriate for those of us who live in a time of affluence. We need to use our wealth or influence to serve others and bring honor to God.

---

10. Answers: A,1; B,1; C,2; D,1; E,2.

The Parable of the Lost (Prodigal) Son (15:11-24)

Father's Love to Sinners

Jesus' chief theme in this parable is the love of the Father to sinners. This is an important source of appeal to the lost as we share the gospel.

🌿 **Read Luke 15:11-24 and check the correct answer or answers for each of the following questions.**[11]

1. Why does God let people turn from Him to go their own way?
   - ❑ a. He has given humans freedom of choice.
   - ❑ b. He wants to be a Father, not a jailer.
   - ❑ c. He wants loving obedience, not forced labor.
2. How does God feel about people who turn from Him to go their own way?
   - ❑ a. He is indifferent to them.
   - ❑ b. He loves them and longs for them to return to Him.
   - ❑ c. Neither of the above.
3. What did the lost son have to do in order to be received by his father?
   - ❑ a. Repent (change his mind) and trust (have faith) that his father would receive him.
   - ❑ b. Make arrangements to pay back his inheritance to his father.
   - ❑ c. Work as a slave for his father.
4. What do lost people have to do in order to be received by the Father in heaven?
   - ❑ a. Repent of their sins and place their faith in Jesus Christ.
   - ❑ b. Live a good life to make up for their sins.
   - ❑ c. Devote themselves to religious activities.
5. What kind of life can a person experience living in fellowship with the Heavenly Father?
   - ❑ a. Restricted and confined
   - ❑ b. Abundant and joyful
   - ❑ c. Meaningful and fulfilling

The younger son who asked for his inheritance normally would receive a third of the estate. The remaining two-thirds would go to the firstborn. For an heir to receive the usage of the money while the father was still alive was unusual.

In this instance when the lost son received his inheritance, he squandered it. He ran out of money and into famine at the same time. He took the most degrading job a Jew could assume, caring for swine. The prodigal's sense of misery and need led him to repentance. He made no claim on his father, he only asked for mercy.

The Father's Love

The father's response overwhelmed the son. The father saw him a long distance off and ran to meet him. Running was not normal for an aged oriental man, but the father's love overpowered his dignity. Before the son could blurt out his confession, the father commanded that he receive the best robe, a ring of authority, shoes denoting that he was a freeman, and food to begin a time of celebration.

Two features stand out in the parable. First, the love of the Father for us even when we sin constantly overwhelms and encourages us. When we feel that we are undeserving and unable to receive blessings from God, He overwhelms us with His generosity. Second, we find true pleasure only in returning to the Father. Living away from the Father in disobedience brings no lasting sense of joy. Joy comes in living daily in the will of the Father.

---

11. Answers:1-a,b,c; 2-b; 3-a; 4-a; 5-b,c.

The Rich Man and Lazarus (16:19-31)

✒ **Read Luke 16:19-31 and check here when you have finished:** ❏

Rich Man Lived for Himself

In this parable Jesus urged His listeners to repent of their smug living and help others by generous sharing. He pictured a rich man who lived a life of comfortable ease. He lived for himself. Lazarus was a poor beggar who lay at the gate of the rich man and wanted to be fed. The name Lazarus means "God is (his) help." We are to understand that the name implied that Lazarus was a devoted servant of God. This Lazarus is not related to the one Jesus raised from the dead (John 11:38-44).

Lazarus a Faithful Servant

Because Lazarus was a faithful servant of God, angels took him to "Abraham's side" (v. 22). This is a symbolic expression, showing the joy and delight of God's people in the life beyond.

The rich man went to a place of torment. He showed his haughty attitude by asking Abraham to have Lazarus do a favor for him. Abraham's answer showed that in the eternal realm a different set of values ruled. Both Lazarus and the rich man were receiving the justice of God for their response to Him.

Abraham's answer (v. 26) indicated that the chasm between the rich man and Lazarus was impassable. In the life beyond we cannot cross between the resting place of the righteous and that of the wicked.

Rich Man's Five Brothers

The rich man showed interest in others by asking that Lazarus go on an errand to warn his five brothers of what lay ahead for them. Abraham answered that the Bible would give the rich man's brothers all the warning that they needed. Even the appearance of someone risen from the dead will not bring repentance to those who reject Scripture.

This parable is more important for us to use as a warning against abusing wealth than to tell us what the life beyond has in store. Jesus wants us to use our resources to help others for His glory.

✒ **Mark the following statements *T* (true) or *F* (false).[12]**

    ____ 1. Lazarus was saved because he was poor.
    ____ 2. The rich man was lost because he was rich.
    ____ 3. The heart that willfully rejects Scripture can explain away the miraculous.
    ____ 4. The purpose of this parable is to explain heaven and hell.
    ____ 5. The purpose of this parable is to warn against selfish indifference to other people.

The Persistent Widow (18:1-8)

✒ **Read Luke 18:1-8 and check here when you have done so:** ❏

Persisting in Prayer

Jesus presented this parable to encourage His people to persist in prayer. His brief parable had two characters—a powerful judge, who cared not for God or for people, and a poor, defenseless widow, who wanted justice from the judge.

The widow had two assets on her side. Her cause was right; she wanted justice and not vengeance. Also, she was persistent. The judge finally responded to her request. His motive was to avoid having to face the pressure of her repeated requests.

---

12. Answers: 1-F, 2-F, 3-T, 4-F, 5-T.

God Will Respond

The application of this parable is not that we should "pester" God as the widow did the judge. The application rather moves from the less to the greater. If a poor, defenseless widow with nothing on her side except justice and persistence could finally overcome the reluctance of a wicked judge, how much more can the children of God expect their Heavenly Father to respond to their repeated pleas?

This parable provides an incentive for us to persevere in our praying for any request which God shows to be His will. Wherever we find a violation of God's will, we must persist in coming to God until He provides the answer.

🌿 **Check each of the following statements with which you do not agree.**[13]

❑ 1. Jesus taught that God was like an unjust judge.
❑ 2. We must pray and pray before God will hear us.
❑ 3. Prayer seldom can overcome God's reluctance.
❑ 4. God always delays answers to prayers.
❑ 5. God answers prayers so that we will quit bothering Him.

RESPONDING TO GOD'S WORD

List here ways that you respond to other person's needs.

_____

_____

If you feel your list is inadequate in light of God's Word, ask God to show you specific needs of specific persons to which you can respond.

Day 5   Jesus' Final Week (19:28–22:53)

UNIT 5

🌿 **Write here a brief explanation of how comparing the accounts in the Gospels can be helpful.**[14]

_____

_____

TUESDAY

Time of the End

Jerusalem Surrounded by Armies

On Tuesday Jesus faced the disciples' question about the time of the end (21:5-9). Luke presented a discussion similar to Matthew and Mark's. However, Luke referred (21:20) to Jerusalem's being surrounded with armies in that future day. Luke's description of Jerusalem's violent end made a specific reference to the destruction of Jerusalem in A.D. 70. When this prophecy was fulfilled, Jerusalem was surrounded with armies. Only Luke gave this precise prophecy.

---

13. Answers: Surely you marked all of these as statements with which you do not agree!
14. Compare your answer with mine: Some Gospels include details that others omit; comparing them gives a more complete picture of events and teachings.

THURSDAY

Argument over Position

Luke's account of the observance of the Lord's Supper contained a story of the contention and strife among the disciples concerning their position in Jesus' ministry. They argued over who would be the most prominent.

In the account of Jesus' prayers in Gethsemane we find Luke focusing on the human response of Jesus during the time of prayer.

 Read Luke 22:41-44 and check your answer to the following questions.[15]

    1. Did Jesus want to die on the cross for our sins?
        ❏ Yes   ❏ No
    2. Did Jesus sweat blood?
        ❏ Yes   ❏ No
    3. Was Jesus determined to do God's will whether it cost Him or not?
        ❏ Yes   ❏ No

Agony in Gethsemane

Luke suggested that the prospect of imminent pain and death caused such emotional turmoil that Jesus dripped sweat as if He were bleeding (22:44). Jesus wanted to do God's will more than He wanted to escape death. He resolved to drink the cup of suffering and death that led to the cross. Following God's will sometimes leads us to suffering as well. We must desire God's will more than we desire ease or pleasure.

The Trial of Jesus (22:54–23:25)

Before the Jewish Sanhedrin

FRIDAY

Before Pilate

The record of Jesus' trial in Luke involved an appearance before the Jewish Sanhedrin and before Pontius Pilate. Luke did not describe in detail the appearances Jesus made before Annas and Caiaphas, although he mentioned that Jesus was in the house of the high priest (22:54). However, Luke added that in addition to the appearance before Pilate, Jesus also appeared before Herod Antipas (23:6-12).

Before Herod

Herod had come to Jerusalem to observe the Jewish passover in an effort to maintain a good relationship with his Jewish population. Because Pilate did not want to take responsibility for putting Jesus to death, he sent Jesus to Herod when he learned that Jesus came from Galilee. Herod was curious to see Jesus perform a miracle, but Jesus did not answer him a word. Herod eventually returned Jesus to Pilate for the completion of His trial. When Herod returned Jesus to Pilate, Pilate made another unsuccessful effort to release Jesus.

 Read Luke 23:13-25 and answer this question: Why do you think Pilate permitted a man he knew to be innocent to be crucified? Write your answer here.

_____

Pilate followed a custom of the Passover season in offering to release a prisoner as a sign of good will. Pilate asked the crowd whether they preferred Jesus or Barabbas, a rebel against Rome. Pilate felt that the crowd would prefer Jesus, but the coaching of the Pharisees led the crowd to call out for Barabbas. When Pilate realized that he could not persuade the crowd to change their opinion, he went along with them and delivered Jesus to be crucified (23:18-25). Pilate's behavior shows an example of self-serving action. He surrendered his integrity to save his position from possible Jewish protest.

---

15. Answers: 1-No (not if God had some other means of providing salvation); 2-Yes; 3-Yes.

The Crucifixion of Jesus (23:26-49)

Luke recorded the weeping of the women as Jesus proceeded to the place of execution (23:26-31).

🌿 **Read Luke 23:26-34 and answer these questions.**[16]

1. In His last hours and suffering, was Jesus more concerned for Himself or for others?

_____

2. To what fate was Jesus probably referring in his prophecy to the women?

_____

The Repentant Thief

Jesus responded to their weeping by warning them about the coming judgment on Jerusalem. Only Luke mentioned the repentance of one of the two thieves on the cross (23:39-43).

🌿 **Read Luke 23:39-43 and put a check beside the true statements.**[17]

❑ 1. Jesus indicated that both thieves would be with Him in paradise.
❑ 2. As long as there is life, there is spiritual hope.
❑ 3. The two thieves portray how people respond to Jesus today.
❑ 4. People should delay trusting Jesus for salvation until late in life.
❑ 5. The thief probably did not make it to heaven because he was not baptized.

Hope for Everyone

Jesus' promise that the repentant thief would join Him in paradise provides an encouragement for all who have been far away from God. There is hope for them in God's sight. However, people should not be encouraged to wait for a "death-bed" conversion. Many people enter into eternity without making adequate preparation for it, even at the end of life.

The first and last of Jesus' words from the cross appear in Luke. In 23:34 Jesus prayed for the crowd that crucified Him and jeered at Him when He said, "Father, forgive them, for they do not know what they are doing." He also prayed the final cry from the cross in anticipation of the fellowship He would enjoy with God immediately after death. With hope He said, "Father, into your hands I commit my spirit" (Luke 23:46).

The Resurrection and Ascension of Jesus (24:1-53)

SUNDAY

Women Meet Angels

Peter's Rapid Race

Two on Emmaus Road

Luke recorded the time of the resurrection exactly as Matthew and Mark had. Early on Sunday morning the women came bringing spices to complete Jesus' burial. Luke mentioned that as the women were inside the tomb wondering, two angels appeared (24:4). He also mentioned how Peter hurried to the tomb after he had heard the report of the women's meeting with the angels (24:12). Only Luke presented the account of Jesus' appearance to the two disciples on the road to Emmaus (24:13-35).

---

16. Answers: 1-obviously others; 2-the destruction of Jerusalem in A.D. 70.
17. Answers: 2, 3. .

🌿 **Read 24:13-35 and mark the following statements *T* (true) or *F* (false).**[18]

___ 1. The two disciples had concluded after Jesus' crucifixion that He was not the one who was to redeem Israel.
___ 2. Jesus talked with the two disciples the day He was raised from the dead.
___ 3. The two disciples had not heard of the empty tomb.
___ 4. Jesus rebuked the two disciples for not believing the Scriptures.
___ 5. Scriptures from two Old Testament books bear witness to the Lord Jesus Christ.
___ 6. The disciples at Jerusalem were shocked to hear the report of the two disciples that Jesus had walked and talked with them.

Jesus' Surprise Appearance

Jesus made a surprise appearance to the disciples (24:36-49) that also is described in John 20:19-23. He showed the disciples the marks of His wounds. At first they refused to believe. He dispelled their disbelief by eating food to show the reality of His life.

He Finished His Earthly Work

Luke is the only Gospel containing reference to the ascension. In the ascension Jesus disappeared from the view of the disciples. There seemed to be an air of finality about His disappearance. However, in His ascension Jesus closed one chapter and began another. He finished His earthly work. He took up His heavenly res-idence. And He began His heavenly work through His church.

🌿 **SUMMARY REVIEW**

To review this unit, see if you can mentally answer the following questions. You may want to write the answers on a separate sheet of paper. Mark your level of performance on the left: circle *C* if you can answer correctly and circle *R* if you need to review.

C R 1. Who was Luke, and what New Testament books did he write under the inspiration of the Holy Spirit?
C R 2. To what audience did Luke write?
C R 3. List one fact included in Luke's account of the birth of Jesus that is not found in Matthew.
C R 4. How and why are the genealogies in Matthew and Luke different?
C R 5. How does God think we should feel toward our material posses sions; concerning those in need (see Luke 16:19-31)?
C R 6. How does God feel toward sinners? Justify your answer from the story of the Prodigal Son in Luke.
C R 7. List two facts about the crucifixion that Luke alone records.

Review this week's material to find the answers.

"When he had led them out to the vicinity of Bethany, he lifted up his hands and blessed them. While he was blessing them, he left them and was taken up into heaven. Then they worshiped him and returned to Jerusalem with great joy. And they stayed continually at the temple, praising God."

—Luke 24:50-53

RESPONDING TO GOD'S WORD

🌴 **Read Luke 24:50-53. Imagine that you were present for this occasion. Picture Jesus blessing you and ascending to heaven. See the other disciples. Worship with them. Share in the joy. Thank the Lord for His mercy, grace, peace, and joy with which He has blessed your life.**

---

18. Answers: 1-T, 2-T, 3-F, 4-T, 5-F (more than two!), 6-F (they had already heard from Peter)

Unit 6 The Gospel of John

Reading Through the New Testament

☐ John 4–6
☐ John 7–8
☐ John 9–11
☐ John 12–13
☐ John 14–16
☐ John 17–19
☐ John 20–21

UNIT LEARNING GOAL: The study of this unit should help you understand the uniqueness of the Gospel of John. You will be able to:
• Describe the perspective from which John viewed Jesus' ministry.
• Explain the purpose of John's Gospel.
• List at least four of Jesus' "I am" statements.
• Illustrate how Jesus related to people as shown by His interviews.
• Write your explanation of the eternal security of the believer.
• Identify the various ministries of the Holy Spirit.

Author of John: John, the beloved disciple (John 19:25-27)

Date of John: around A.D. 85-95

Theme of John: God's Son Reveals the Father

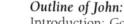

Outline

Outline of John:
Introduction: God's Son Reveals the Father to the World (1:1-18)
  I. Early Ministry of God's Son (1:19–3:36)
  II. Judean and Galilean Ministry of God's Son (4:1–12:50)
  III. God's Son Ministers to His Disciples (13:1–17:26)
  IV. God's Son Submits to Crucifixion (18:1–19:42)
  V. The Resurrection of God's Son (20:1–21:25)

"In the beginning was the Word, and the Word was with God, and the Word was God."

—John 1:1

Key Passage: John 1:1-18 (note especially, vv. 1, 14, 18)

Importance of John
It is the Gospel that is apart from the three (sometimes called the Synoptic Gospels, meaning "to see together"). John recorded much not found in the other Gospels, emphasized the deity of Christ, and dealt more with the *meaning* of events, not just the events themselves.

"We have seen his glory, the glory of the One and Only, who came from the Father, full of grace and truth."

—John 1:14

Special Characteristics of John
1. Written to produce faith in Jesus (20:30-31)
2. Supplements the Synoptics
3. Emphasizes the Judean Ministry
4. No parables; Miracles function as signs to point to God (see 2:11)
5. Dramatizes Jesus' claims of Deity

Fill in Gospels Below

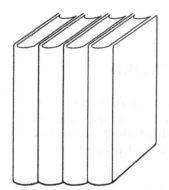

Day 1   The Uniqueness of the Gospel of John

UNIT 6

The Importance of the Gospel

John's Gospel is usually studied apart from the other three Gospels (sometimes called the Synoptic Gospels (from *syn* with or together and *opteo* to see, thus *to see together*). John recorded much that is not found in the other Gospels and dealt more with the *meaning* of events, not just the events themselves.

Emphasizes Person of Christ

John's Gospel also emphasizes the Person of Christ. He wanted to show by various evidences that Jesus is the Son of God. He supported the belief that Jesus is God's Son with seven miraculous signs that appear in the first half of the book.

Awareness of Theology

John also wrote with a deep awareness of theology (right doctrinal belief). In John 1:1-18 he elaborated on the importance of Jesus' incarnation. In 8:58 John included a statement of Jesus' preexistence.

Attractive Simplicity

Despite the doctrinal depth of John's statements about Jesus, his description of Jesus carries an attractive simplicity. John penned his sentences in a simple style and the events he included catch our attention.

To Instruct Christians

John's Gospel was probably the last Gospel to be written. Its action covered the final two or three years of Jesus' life. John wrote these words when the church contained second- and third-generation Christians who needed more instruction about Jesus and new defenses to meet the false teaching threatening the church.

Jesus Is God

Christians who read this Gospel come away fortified in their conviction that Jesus is God's Son. The words and works of Jesus that John selected leave room for no other conclusion. We respond wrongly to Jesus if we merely call Him a great teacher or a moral example. Anyone who claims to be "one" with the Father (John 10:30) and raises the dead to life (John 11:38-44) must be called "God."

🌿 **Check the important aspects of John's Gospel in the following list.[1]**

    ❑ 1. John's Gospel features seven miraculous signs that support the idea that Jesus is God's Son.
    ❑ 2. John's Gospel has much material not found in the other Gospels.
    ❑ 3. John's Gospel was probably the last one written.
    ❑ 4. John's Gospel clearly presents Jesus' incarnation.
    ❑ 5. John's Gospel tells about the last two years of Jesus' public ministry.
    ❑ 6. John's Gospel was timely for second- and third-generation Christians who were confronting false doctrines.

Author and Date of the Gospel

The Disciple Whom Jesus Loved

The disciple whom Jesus loved was the author of John's Gospel (21:24), and he:
• was at the last supper (13:23-24)
• may have helped Peter get into the palace of the high priest (18:15-16)
• was assigned to care for Jesus' mother (19:25-27)
• went with Peter to the empty tomb (20:2-8)
• was among those who saw Jesus at the Sea of Tiberias (21:7)

---

1. Answers: You should have checked all six.

John the Apostle best qualifies to fulfill these conditions.

🌿 **Check the correct ending for each of the following statements.[2]**

1. The following passages of Scripture (John 13:23; 18:15-16; 19:25-27; 20:1-8; 21:7, 20-24) deal with:
   - ❏ a. the fact that Jesus is the Son of God
   - ❏ b. Peter's statements of loyalty and love
   - ❏ c. John, the disciple whom Jesus loved
   - ❏ d. Jesus' coming death
2. John 21:20-24 reveals
   - ❏ a. that Peter loved Jesus
   - ❏ b. that the disciple whom Jesus loved wrote this Gospel
   - ❏ c. that what is written in John is true
   - ❏ d. that the disciple who wrote this Gospel would not die

Early Fathers Said John

The early fathers of the church did not hesitate to say that the apostle John wrote this Gospel. From the time of Irenaeus (middle of the second century A.D.) there was almost unanimous agreement about this.

Author Was Jewish

We can learn by reading John's Gospel that the author was a Jew who wrote in a Jewish style and knew the geography of the Holy Land (5:2; 9:7). His references to the temple in 2:14-15; 8:20; and 10:23 show that he knew the layout of the city before its destruction. He noted small details about Jesus' work, such as the five barley loaves and the two small fish in 6:9 and the fragrance of Mary's ointment in 12:3. He knew the private conversations of Jesus and some of Jesus' own inner thoughts (6:6, 61, 64). Again, John could best insert these descriptions.

One of Inner Circle

Three of Jesus' disciples were in His inner circle. They were with Him at the Garden of Gethsemane (Matt. 26:37). One of these is likely the "beloved" disciple. Peter did not write the Fourth Gospel, for he appeared in it frequently in the third person (13:23-24). James, the son of Zebedee, was martyred by Herod Agrippa too early to have been the author (Acts 12:2). Again, John the apostle best qualifies as the "beloved" disciple.

John's Gospel has little information that allows us to date it precisely. The discovery of a small fragment of a copy of John 18 in Egypt in 1935 revolutionized the dating of the Gospel. Scholars dated the fragment from the early part of the second century. This made it likely that the original writing was earlier, back into the first century. The statement in John 21:23-24 suggests that the disciple whom Jesus loved must have reached an advanced age when he wrote the Gospel.

Around A.D. 85 or 90

Many scholars assume that John wrote after the other three Gospels and added information which they did not contain. Many scholars place the date of writing around A.D. 85 or 90.

Theme and Purpose of the Gospel of John

John's Gospel has the clearest purpose statement of any of the Gospel writings.

🌿 **1. Read John 20:30-31 and write here a summary of John's purpose for writing his Gospel.[3]**

_____

---

2. Answers: 1-c, 2-b,c.

2. Why do you think John chose the material about Jesus he included in his Gospel? _____

3. Is the Gospel of John a good book to recommend to a lost person?

_____

"These are written that you may believe that Jesus is the Christ, the Son of God, and that by believing you may have life in his name."

—John 20:31

John hints that he has selected some incidents out of the many he knew about Jesus. Those he selected aimed at producing faith in Jesus. John's descriptions of events in Jesus' life often showed a dual response of both faith and disbelief in Jesus Christ. Many who heard Jesus responded in faith and received eternal life, while others chose to reject Jesus and fell under condemnation (John 3:18,36).

Special Characteristics of the Gospel of John

John performed the special service of recording additional material the Synoptic writers had not presented about Christ. He emphasized the Judean ministry of Jesus.

🌿 **Read John 2:13; 6:4; and 12:1. In light of these verses, estimate the length of Jesus' public ministry and write your answer here:[4]** _____

John made clear that Jesus' public ministry lasted longer than a single year. A quick reading of the Synoptic Gospels might lead us to select one year as the length of ministry. John showed that there were three Passovers (2:13; 6:4; 12:1) and perhaps four (5:1) during Jesus' public ministry. This fact showed that Jesus' public ministry lasted over two years and perhaps more than three years.

Jesus' Significant Speeches

John also preserved many of Jesus' significant speeches. In John we learn about Jesus' witness to Nicodemus (John 3:1-21), His conversation with the woman at the well (John 3:1-26), and His discussion about the bread of life (John 6:25-71).

John vividly presented the claims of Jesus. Some of the claims are presented dramatically, some accompany miracles, and some are based on nature.

Emphasized Deity of Jesus

John also placed special emphasis on the deity of Jesus. The Synoptic Gospels claimed that Jesus was the Son of God, but John set forth this truth in bolder, clearer language. Jesus claimed to be preexistent (John 17:5). He accepted worship without rebuke to the worshiper (John 20:28). He claimed that His works showed that He came from the Father (John 5:36).

🌿 **Put a check by each special characteristic of the Gospel of John.[5]**
- ❑ 1. Parable of the prodigal son
- ❑ 2. Jesus' conversations with Nicodemus and the woman at the well
- ❑ 3. Jesus' claim to be the true vine and the way, the truth, and the life
- ❑ 4. Sermon on the mount
- ❑ 5. Lord's Prayer
- ❑ 6. Boldest statements of the Deity of Jesus

---

3. Answers: 1-To lead people to believe in Christ and receive eternal life; 2-He included material that would help people believe in Jesus; 3-Yes.
4. Answer: Between two and three years.
5. Answers: 2, 3, 6.

RESPONDING TO GOD'S WORD

Read John 1:1,14; 5:36; 17:5; 20:28. Can anyone doubt that John presented Jesus as Deity? Spend time in worship of your Lord and God.

Day 2 — *Beholding Jesus' Glory*

UNIT 6

John records only seven miracles performed by Jesus. He called them signs, perhaps to stress that Jesus' physical miracles pointed to spiritual truths and to God.

SEVEN SIGNS IN JOHN'S GOSPEL

1. Changing water into wine (2:1-11)
2. Healing an official's son (4:46-54)
3. Healing the paralyzed man (5:1-9
4. Feeding the five thousand (6:1-15)
5. Walking on water (6:16-21)
6. Healing the man who had been born blind (9:1-41)
7. Raising Lazarus from the dead (11:38-44)

John also presented the divine claims of Jesus in an especially vivid fashion. We call them the "I am" passages because Jesus began them by declaring, "I am …" Some of the claims are dramatized claims. Jesus stressed His ability to satisfy the spiritual needs of mankind; and He often performed miracles that showed His ability to meet our deepest needs (John 6:1-14) and to grant spiritual life (John 11:1-44). Jesus claimed to be the light of the world (John 8:12), the true vine (John 15:1), and the way, truth, and life (John 14:6). These statements appear in 6:35; 8:12; 10:7; 10:11; 11:25; 14:6; and 15:1.

Beside each of the "I am" sayings, write a word or phrase that expresses needs in your life that Jesus can meet. I have answered the first one for you.[6]

1. "I am the bread of life": satisfaction of spiritual hunger.

2. "I am the light of the world": _____

3. "I am the gate for the sheep": _____

4. "I am the good shepherd": _____

5. "I am the resurrection and the life": _____

6. "I am the way and the truth and the life": _____

7. "I am the true vine": _____

Seven "I Am" Sayings of Jesus

- "I am the Bread of life" (John 6:35)
- "I am the Light of the world" (John 8:12)
- "I am the Gate for the sheep" (John 10:7)
- "I am the good Shepherd" (John 10:11)
- "I am the Resurrection and the Life" (John 11:25)
- "I am the Way and the Truth and the Life" (John 14:6)
- "I am the true Vine" (John 15:1)

---

6. Possible answers (yours may differ): 2-spiritual enlightenment; 3-salvation/security/fellowship; 4-guide and protector; 5-hope at death; 6-the way to the Father; 7-vitality and productivity.

The Eternal Word (1:1)

John's Gospel reached back into eternity for its beginning, and it presented a picture of Jesus Christ as God's Son.

🌿 **Read John 1:1-14 and check here when you have finished:** ❑

Here John presented the circumstances of the Word prior to the incarnation. We know that John used the term "Word" to refer to Jesus, but John did not clearly make this identification until 1:14. In verse 1 John stated three facts about the Word.

Word Existed Before All Time

First, the Word existed before all time. "Beginning" refers to the creating of the world. The term "Word" reminded the Jews of the method God used to make the heavens. God spoke His word and made the heavens (Ps. 33:6). Just as God's spoken word created the world, God's personal word Jesus revealed who God was. John stated that God's personal word existed before the world was created.

Second, John taught that God's Word was distinct from God Himself. The term "God" in 1:1 is probably a reference to God the Father. "The Word was with God" showed perfect communion and active contact between the Word and God.

Word Is Deity

Third, John proclaimed the deity of the Word. John taught that the Word possessed deity. In a simple but profound manner, John presented the truth that the Word was an eternal being. He laid the foundation for our belief in the Trinity by distinguishing the Word from God the Father. He also prepared us to respond with praise and commitment to Jesus when we recognize that He is God.

🌿 **Read John 1:1 and fill in the blanks.**[7]

1. John affirmed that the Word _____ before all _____.

2. John taught that the Word was distinct from _____ the _____.

3. John proclaimed the _____ of the Word.

The Incarnation (1:14-18)

For the first time John declared in verse 14 that the Word and Jesus were identical. After identifying the two, John stated the *fact* of the incarnation, witnessed to the *glory* of the incarnation, and described the *character* of the incarnation.

The True God-Man

In describing the incarnation, John taught that Jesus became something which He had not been previously. He did not cease to be God, but He became a complete, real man. Jesus was truly the God-man.

He Exhibits God's Glory

In witnessing to the glory of the incarnation, John showed Jesus as the very glory of God. In the Old Testament, God prohibited looking directly upon His glory (Ex. 33:20). Now God's people see the true glory of God in the person of Jesus.

One and Only Son

Through the incarnation Jesus became the "One and Only Son" of the Father. The term "One and Only" indicated the uniqueness of Jesus. Jesus had a special relationship with the Father. He was the one through whom God's promises operated.

_____

7. Answers: 1-existed, time; 2-God, Father; 3-Deity.

🌿 Match the following phrase on the left with the correct phrase on the right. Write the correct letters in the blanks.[8]

_____ 1. The fact of the incarnation   A. Jesus became the unique, "One and Only Son" of the Father

_____ 2. The glory of the incarnation   B. Jesus revealed the true glory of God.

_____ 3. The character of the incarnation   C. Jesus became the complete God-man.

Grace and Truth

As John looked at Jesus, he saw grace and truth. Grace referred to God's steadfast love. Truth referred to God's complete reliability. God has shown His grace in sending His Son to provide for our needs. He is faithful, and we can trust Him to meet those needs. We always will need an abundant supply of God's grace in our lives. Through Jesus we boldly can stake our claim to this grace (Heb. 3:14-16).

Nicodemus's Dramatic Conversion (3:1-15)

🌿 Read John 3:1-15 and put a check here when you have finished: ❑

Israel's Teacher

The miracles of Jesus attracted Nicodemus to Jesus. He approached Jesus with a courteous greeting (3:1-2), but he fell far short of giving to Jesus a recognition of His deity. He simply was calling Jesus a great teacher. Jesus startled Nicodemus by challenging him to be born again (3:3). The term "born again" can mean either that Nicodemus needed to be born from above or that he needed to be born a second time. Nicodemus seems to have understood Jesus' challenge in the second way (3:4).

Factors in Conversion
- Repentance
- Holy Spirit's Work
- Faith

In 3:5-15 Jesus pointed out the factors involved in conversion.
- First, He pointed out that baptism ("born of water") symbolized the repentance from sin that a believer must show (3:5).
- Second, he pointed out that the Holy Spirit would transform Nicodemus' life ("born of the Spirit" 3:6-8).
- Finally, He showed the necessity of faith or personal commitment to Him in order to receive eternal life (3:10-15).

🌿 A. Mark the following statements *T* (true) or *F* (false).[9]

_____ 1. Nicodemus probably talked with Jesus to catch Him in some heresy.
_____ 2. Nicodemus believed Jesus' teachings because he knew of the miraculous signs Jesus had performed.
_____ 3. Nicodemus did not at first understand the meaning of "born again."
_____ 4. John's words about water and Spirit in verse 5 may be understood as pointing to baptism as a symbol of repentance from sin and to the Holy Spirit as the One who could make possible a person's new life.
_____ 5. Nicodemus could not be saved unless he understood all the details of Jesus' teachings.
_____ 6. Any person who believes in Jesus may have eternal life.

B. Read John 7:50-52; 19:39. In light of these verses, do you think Nicodemus became a true believer in Jesus?   ❑ Yes   ❑ No

Two Evidences of Conversion

John did not show us any immediate response by Nicodemus. However, we can find two evidences of his movement toward Jesus. In 7:50-52 Nicodemus earned

---

8. Answers: 1-C, 2-B, 3-A.
9. Answers: A:1-F, 2-T, 3-T, 4-T, 5-F, 6-T. B: Your response; I marked Yes.

the anger of some fellow members of the Sanhedrin when he asked them to give Jesus a hearing before they condemned Him. Risking this opposition took some commitment to Jesus. In 19:39 Nicodemus assisted Joseph of Arimathea in burying Jesus. Someone who buried an accused criminal such as Jesus could risk further contempt and hatred from the Jews. Nicodemus' action gave evidence that he had made a faith commitment to Jesus.

RESPONDING TO GOD'S WORD

Spend a few minutes meditating on your own conversion to Christ. List below similarities or differences to Nicodemus's conversion.

1. _____

2. _____

3. _____

Day 3   *Unique Episodes in John*

UNIT 6

Spirit Comes After Jesus Was Glorified

An Invitation to Full Living (7:37-39)

Read John 7:37-39 and put a check when you have done so: ❏

Jesus' words here represent one of the richest promises in Scripture. Jesus was prophesying concerning the coming of the Holy Spirit. He presented an invitation and a promise. John added an explanation. In 7:37 Jesus presented an invitation to come to Him and believe with a faith that led to commitment. In 7:38 John presented a promise that the one who believed on Jesus would experience the overflowing presence of the Holy Spirit. In 7:39 we learn the nature of His promise. The Holy Spirit would come when Jesus was glorified following the completion of His earthly ministry. To experience "the streams of living water" Christ promised, we come to Jesus in believing commitment.

Read John 7:37-39, and write brief answers to the following questions.

1. In 7:37 what was the invitation: _____

2. In 7:38 what was the promise:_____

3. In 7:39 what was the explanation:_____

See the above paragraph for answers.

Jesus' View Toward Sin (7:53–8:11)

Most modern versions of the New Testament contain a note warning that verses 7:53–8:11 do not appear in this place in the best New Testament manuscripts. Some versions omit the incident from the text altogether and put it in a footnote.

Some ancient manuscripts actually locate the incident in other sections of John's Gospel. Even if this incident may not have originally appeared in this place or even in what John wrote, we still accept that it happened in Jesus' ministry. It is in agreement with what we know about Jesus' character. We can state that it is a historical truth, but some may feel that it was not originally in what John wrote.

🌿 **Read John 7:52–8:11 and check the correct ending for each of the following statements.**[10]

    1. Jesus was teaching people in:
       ❏ a. the local synagogue   ❏ b. the temple courts   ❏ c. the city square

    2. The Pharisees and teachers of the law brought to Jesus a woman:
       ❏ a. who had been bribed to play the role of one taken in adultery
       ❏ b. who was falsely accused of adultery.
       ❏ c. who was guilty of adultery

    3. The Pharisees and teachers of the law thought that Jesus' answer:
       ❏ a. would put Him in disfavor with the people
       ❏ b. would enlighten them
       ❏ c. neither of the above

    4. Jesus wrote on the ground:
       ❏ a. a record of the accusers' sins
       ❏ b. the names of people with whom the accusers had committed adultery
       ❏ c. we know not what

    5. Jesus' answer _____ the accusers.
       ❏ a. confused   ❏ b. shamed   ❏ c. disgusted

    6. Jesus told the woman that He did not condemn her and that she should:
       ❏ a. not condemn others ❏ b. not condemn herself ❏ c. leave her life of sin

Adulterous Woman

The enemies of Jesus tried to catch Him in a trap. The woman was guilty. Jesus did not dispute this. The Old Testament directed that an adulterer and an adulteress be stoned to death (Deut. 22:22-24). If Jesus did not confirm the death penalty, His enemies could charge Him with denying God's law. If He affirmed the verdict of the Pharisees, He could be seen as lacking compassion.

Jesus' reply put His accusers on the defensive. The accusers likely had seen the act of adultery in progress and had not stopped it. They would have condoned the offense contrary to the Old Testament (Deut. 22:22-27). Jesus indicated that only the guiltless could carry out the sentence. These enemies of Jesus were not guiltless.

Jesus Did Not Condemn

The enemies of Jesus left one by one, probably stricken in conscience. Jesus' reply to the woman was respectful. He did not condemn her, but He did not accept or gloss over her sin. He called her to make a clean break with sin. He did not pronounce a word of forgiveness because the woman had not confessed.

Love Sinner; Hate Sin

Christians should not condone sin or evil. However, we must not refuse to help the sinner while we oppose sin. Jesus clearly called us to do both. Beware of being more eager to accuse the guilty than to help the needy. Being nonjudgmental toward others (Jas. 4:11-12), while holding firmly to our Christian convictions, is difficult. However, we must apply both emphases as we live in an immoral society.

---

10. Answers: 1-b, 2-c, 3-a, 4-c, 5-b, 6-c.

🌿 **Check the correct ending or endings.**[11]

When we see people involved in obvious or gross sin, we should:
- ❏ a. Remind ourselves of what is wrong in the sinful activity
- ❏ b. Point out the sin to others as a warning
- ❏ c. Resolve not to associate with those people any more
- ❏ d. Realize that we also sin, even though our sins may not be obvious
- ❏ e. Think of ways we can offer help and hope

The Eternity of Jesus (John 8:51-58)

Jesus' words here sound puzzling to most of us, but they are a clear claim to eternal existence and to Deity. Jesus described Abraham as one who "was," or who became. This meant that Abraham's existence started at birth. There was a time for the beginning of Abraham. By contrast Jesus had existed continuously. Jesus could say, "I am."

Claim to Deity

The clause "I am" represents one way of expressing Deity. A similar phrase appeared in Exodus 3:14 to refer to the divine name of God. Jesus' use of the words was clear claim to Deity. Jesus' hearers viewed His words as a claim to Deity. They took up stones to throw at Him for blasphemy. At this point the protective hand of God shielded His Son from harm.

Does Sin Cause Suffering? (John 9:3-4)

🌿 **Read John 9:1-12 and check the statements with which you agree.**[12]

- ❏ 1. All suffering is caused directly by sin.
- ❏ 2. Some suffering is caused directly by sin.
- ❏ 3. God caused the man to be born blind so that Jesus could heal Him.
- ❏ 4. Bad things don't happen to good people.
- ❏ 5. Most judgment of God on sin happens in this life.
- ❏ 6. We cannot determine the ultimate cause of some suffering.
- ❏ 7. We are not to judge suffering people but to help them.

Relation Between Sin and Suffering

This is a crucial passage because it talks about a possible relation between sin and suffering. Jesus' disciples had seen a man blind from birth. They wondered aloud about the cause of his blindness. They were convinced that the blindness was due to sin. They asked the question, "Who sinned, this man or his parents, that he was born blind?" Had the parents sinned? Some rabbis followed the idea that an infant could sin in the womb. Was that the explanation of the man's blindness?

Jesus did not make a statement about all human suffering. What He said spoke only of this particular blind man and his needs. Jesus first stated that the blindness was not due to sin. He then added that the purpose of the man's blindness was that a divine work might take place in him and reveal the glory of God. This does not mean that God made the man blind so that years later God might get the glory for healing him. Rather, in this case Jesus overruled the disaster of a man born blind, gave him his sight, and gave him the opportunity to turn to Him in faith.

The question of the cause of sin, the mystery of suffering, and God's sovereignty has occupied our thinking for centuries. Jesus did not give a full answer in this passage, nor do most of us fully understand these matters. However, we know that

---

11. Answers: a, d, e.
12. Answers: Hopefully you checked 2, 6, and 7.

His Grace Is Abundant

God does not deliberately and maliciously cause pain and hardship just so He might receive glory when the sick recover. And He at times shows His mercy to certain ones by removing the burdens of sickness and weakness after times of hardship. He may sometimes leave the hardship with us. In either case we can claim an abundant supply of His grace (2 Cor. 12:9-10).

RESPONDING TO GOD'S WORD

Spend a few moments thinking of episodes of suffering in your life or that of someone you know. Check the boxes below that you think apply to your suffering.

❑ 1. My suffering was not caused directly by sin.
❑ 2. God did not cause my suffering just so Jesus could heal me.
❑ 3. I may never know the ultimate cause of my suffering.
❑ 4. Bad things do happen to good people.
❑ 5. God was with me and helped me in my suffering.
❑ 6. My suffering better qualifies me to help others who suffer.

Day 4   *Jesus Cares for His Own*

UNIT 6

Our Eternal Security (John 10:27-28)

🌿 **Read John 10:27-30 and answer the following questions.**[13]

A. Two characteristics of those who have placed their faith in Jesus are that

they _____ to Him and they _____ Him.

B. Jesus gives them _____ _____, and they shall _____.

C. How secure are those who belong to Christ (vv. 28-29)? _____.

Eternal Security

This passage contributes directly to the discussion of the doctrine of eternal security. The passage here emphasizes that eternal life is a gift we keep because Jesus holds us firmly in His grip. Nothing can snatch us from His firm hold. The verse is not a promise that believers will never have earthly disasters. It is not a statement that we will always serve God faithfully. It does suggest that we are saved no matter what earthly hardship falls on us.

Salvation Makes Us Responsible

Scripture teaches that believers "through faith are shielded by God's power" (1 Pet. 1:5) and that they also must avoid the practice of sin (1 John 3:6). Those who continually practice sin show that they are not God's children. Those who are God's children do not practice sin because God keeps them by faith.

Jesus' words in John 10:27-28 must never be used to excuse sin in our lives. They are not meant to encourage sin or careless living. They are a source of rich

---

13. Answers: A-listen, follow; B-eternal life, never perish; C-absolutely secure.

encouragement and hope for all fearful, wavering Christians who doubt, question and wonder about their relationship to God. We can rest assured that God keeps His people tightly bound to Him.

God Keeps His People

🌿 **Mark the following statements *T* (true) or *F* (false).**[14]

_____ 1. Jesus' promise that His own cannot be snatched from the Father's hand means in part that believers are secure from earthly disasters.
_____ 2. Jesus' words about His sheep hearing and following Him mean that genuine Christians do not make a practice of a life of sin.
_____ 3. If a person is saved, how that person lives does not matter.
_____ 4. Seeking to obey Christ is an indication of genuine faith.
_____ 5. A person's salvation depends on that person's living a righteous life.

Love Is Evidence of Our Christian Faith (John 13:34-35)

🌿 **A. Read John 13:34-35 and check the following examples for which those verses could be a solution.**[15]

❏ 1. I stay home because they're always getting mad in business meetings.
❏ 2. I guess they made her the teacher of our class because she's been to college; she thinks she is better than we are.
❏ 3. Yeah, he got his feelings hurt; let him stew in his own juice.
❏ 4. Sure they need money; they will always need money because they do not know how to manage.

B. Circle the following action that would most likely convince a non-Christian that Christianity is real.

Visiting lost people   Working in a church organization
Giving more than a tithe   Loving one another as Christ loved
Regular church attendance   Visiting people who are sick

Love One Another

Jesus' words here contain a command, a pattern, and a result. The command is to love one another. The love He called for is a sacrificial and uncalculating. Although our love also should include all peoples of the world, Jesus here focused on the love we as believers have within our own fellowship. When a Christian fellowship shows a sacrificial, unselfish love within itself, it demonstrates to outsiders that the believers have been genuinely changed by the love of Jesus.

Love as Jesus Loved

The pattern is that we love as Jesus loved. Jesus provided an example of unselfishness, commitment, and depth which left His disciples a visible example to imitate. The result was evidence others could recognize. The practice which convinces a suspicious world of the truth of our commitment to Jesus is the evidence of love in the Christian brotherhood. Our church attendance, our right theology, or our religious activity will not convince outsiders that we know Jesus. When they behold our love for one another, they see evidence they cannot ignore.

Love also can be extended to unbelieving friends. You will convince some non-Christian friends of your genuine love for Jesus by baking a cake, mowing a yard, or expressing forgiveness to them or to some Christian friend. The result might draw an outsider into Christ's kingdom.

---

14. Answers: 1-F, 2-T, 3-F, 4-T, 5-F. If you missed more than one of these, read the section on "Eternal Security" again, carefully reading all the related Scriptures.
15. Answers: A-I know you checked them all; I could not think of a situation to which love in action would not be an answer! B-loving one another as Christ loved.

Our Source of Spiritual Strength (15:1-10)

🌿 Mark the following statements *T* (true) or *F* (false).[16]

___ 1. God is concerned that Christians live spiritually productive lives.
___ 2. God will work in the lives of His people to help them become more spiritually productive.
___ 3. Spiritual cleansing comes from responding positively to the gospel.
___ 4. Spiritual productivity cannot occur in one who is not remaining in close fellowship with the Lord.
___ 5. Those who remain in close fellowship with the Lord will experience answers to their prayers.
___ 6. Christians who are spiritually productive bring glory to God.
___ 7. Obeying Jesus' commands is necessary for staying in close fellowship with Him.

Jesus the True Vine

Jesus used the picture of a vine to teach that fruitfulness in the Christian life depended on a right relationship to Him. In verse 1 He identified Himself as the true vine. He called the Father the cultivator of the vine. In verse 2 Jesus assured His listeners that God would do all that was necessary to lead the vine to produce fruit. Men's gathering of dead branches to build a fire does not teach that a believer can lose his salvation. Rather, the only useful purpose dead vines can serve is to bring warmth for others.

Cleansing for Disciples

In verse 3 Jesus showed that responding to the message of His word brought cleansing for His disciples. In verses 4-5 Jesus showed the urgency of remaining in vital union with Him. He promised spiritual fruit for those who remained in Him. In verse 6 He warned that rejection and uselessness lay ahead for those who did not keep a vital link with Him.

Abiding Demands Obedience

Abiding in Jesus demands obeying Him. If we abide in Jesus, we will experience fruit. We will produce service and work that will glorify God (v. 5). We also will have privileges in prayer (v. 7) and experience an abiding in God's love. When we practice complete obedience to God, our lives will experience the richest blessings God can give.

The Holy Spirit and the World (16:5-11)

🌿 Read John 16:5-11 and put a check here: ❏

Holy Spirit and Unbelievers

In these verses Jesus explained the work of the Holy Spirit in the lives of unbelievers. In verse 8 He explained that the Holy Spirit had come to convict the world. Conviction involved making the truth so clear that no one could deny it.

John mentioned that the Holy Spirit exposed three things.
- First, He showed sin (v. 9). The Holy Spirit made the world aware of its guilt before God.
- Second, the Holy Spirit convicted the world of Christ's righteousness. This meant that the Holy Spirit showed that Christ's death and resurrection made it possible for us to become righteous before God.
- Finally, the Holy Spirit showed that Satan had been judged and defeated.

---

16. Answers: All are true.

🌿 Match the following scriptural phrase on the left with the correct explanation of that phrase on the right. Write the correct letters in the blanks.[17]

___ 1. Convict in regard to sin
___ 2. Convict in regard to righteousness
___ 3. Convict in regard to judgment

A. Show the person that he or she is righteous before God
B. Show the person that he or she is sinful before God
C. Show the person that Satan has been condemned and defeated
D. Show the person that Jesus is righteous and can make him or her righteous

Spirit Helps Unbelievers Understand

When we tell others about Jesus, the success of our effort does not depend on our cleverness or persuasiveness. The Spirit of God helps outsiders understand the consequences of Jesus' death and draws these people to faith in Christ.

🌿 Which of the following is the most crucial factor in witnessing to a lost person about the salvation available in Jesus Christ? Check your answer.[18]

❑ 1. A clear presentation of the gospel
❑ 2. Using Scriptures
❑ 3. The work of the Holy Spirit
❑ 4. Knowing the person to whom you witness
❑ 5. Good timing
❑ 6. Privacy

RESPONDING TO GOD'S WORD

🌴 Review the Scriptures you have read in today's study of the Gospel of John and jot down your responses to the following.

1. Which passage seemed to speak to your life today?_____

2. What action should you take in light of this passage? _____

Pray and commit this matter to the Lord right now.

Day 5   *Jesus Final Acts*

UNIT 6

It Is Finished (19:30)

🌿 Read John 19:28-30 and check the correct answer or answers for each of the following questions.[19]

1. How would you characterize the words "It is finished" in normal, everyday conversation?
❑ a. factual   ❑ b. discouraging   ❑ c. encouraging   ❑ d. hopeful

---

17. Answers: 1-B, 2-D, 3-C.
18. Answers: Of course all of these could be important, but the crucial factor is 3.

2. In what sense do you think Jesus used the phrase "It is finished"?
  ❏ a. His life was finished.
  ❏ b. His mission was finished.
  ❏ c. His movement was finished.
3. What do Jesus' words "It is finished" have to do with us today?
  ❏ a. The salvation He purchased is available to us.
  ❏ b. We have no work to do.
  ❏ c. We do not have to go to church.

When we say, "It is finished," we generally mean that it is all over. It is often a discouraging word. That was not what Jesus meant. When Jesus spoke these words, it was a shout of victory. He had done everything He came to do, and it was completed.

He Paid for Our Salvation

Jesus' words are true both chronologically and theologically. Jesus' life was at an end. He was dying. His words stated that. He also had finished all that the Father had sent Him to do. He had paid for the salvation of all of those who would believe.

"All to Him We Owe"

The verb translated "It is finished" was used in the sense of paying a debt. Jesus was effectively saying, "The debt of sin has been paid." We say the same thing when we sing the hymn, "Jesus Paid It All." Because Jesus has paid for our sins, we can come to Him and find salvation and forgiveness.

A Pilgrimage of Faith (John 20:24-29)

We can read about "Doubting Thomas" four times in John's Gospel.

🌿 **Read John 11:7-8, 16 and 14:5. Check the following traits that these verses reveal about Thomas.[20]**

❏ 1. Industrious	❏ 2. Faithful	❏ 3. Optimistic
❏ 4. Grudging	❏ 5. Pessimistic	❏ 6. Hot tempered
❏ 7. Loyal	❏ 8. Outspoken	❏ 9. Questioning

Thomas: Loyal but Pessimistic

In 11:16 and 14:5 we see Thomas as a loyal but pessimistic follower of Jesus. In 21:2 we see him fishing on the Sea of Galilee with Peter and others. In 20:24-29 we see him move into the spotlight of full faith.

"Unless I See, I Will Not Believe"

Thomas had not been present when Jesus appeared to the other ten disciples on resurrection evening (20:19-23). When he learned of their experience he said, "Unless I see the nail marks in his hands and put my finger where the nails were, and put my hand into his side, I will not believe it." Thomas was only demanding the same evidence the other disciples had received in the earlier appearance. If Thomas had been present when Jesus first appeared, he might have believed then.

Thomas prescribed the evidence on which he would believe (v. 25). When Jesus made a personal appearance to him, he showed a responsible faith (vv. 26-28). Jesus commended Thomas' faith in verse 29, but He reserved higher praise for those who can trust without demanding such physical evidence.

Jesus' approach to Thomas was gentle and gracious. Thomas's initial response to the evidence for the resurrection was slow. When he did respond, his faith outstripped the other disciples. He worshiped Jesus and called Him God.

---

19. Answers: 1-a and b; 2-a and b; 3-a.
20. Answers: Your response; I checked 2, 5,7, 8, 9.

Restoring a Fallen Leader (21:15-19)

✎ Read John 21:15-19 and put a check here when you finish: ❑

Agapao
Deep, Unselfish Love

Phileo
Love of Friendship

Peter's Love Limited

Jesus' Love Unlimited!

In John 21:15-19 Jesus asked Peter about his love. In His first two questions He used the Greek verb *agapao* (which refers to a deep, rich, sacrificial love such as God has for sinners). In His final question in verse 17 He used the verb *phileo* (which often describes the love of friendship). Peter responded to Him each time with the verb *phileo*. The change in words may indicate a change in meaning.

Even though Peter now recognized how limited his love for Jesus was, Peter still affirmed his love for the Lord three times. Jesus then gave Peter a commission three times. The giving of this commission completed the process of bringing Peter back to a place of leadership among the apostles. Peter later demonstrated his love by his bold, daring service in Acts.

✎ Check the correct ending for each of the following statements.[21]

1. After Peter had denied Christ the night He was arrested, he probably felt
   - ❑ a. that he would no more be of any use in God's kingdom
   - ❑ b. that the Lord would understand the circumstances and overlook what he had said
   - ❑ c. that he was justified in what he had done
2. The two Greek words for love used in verses 15-17
   - ❑ a. refer to sacrificial love and love of friendship
   - ❑ b. may indicate a change in meaning
   - ❑ c. both of the above
3. Perhaps the reason Jesus asked Peter three times if Peter loved Him was
   - ❑ a. for emphasis
   - ❑ b. to make Peter feel bad
   - ❑ c. to remind Peter of his repeated denials
4. Jesus' fresh new assignment to Peter
   - ❑ a. overwhelmed him
   - ❑ b. made him wonder whether Jesus had made a mistake in relying on him who had proved to be so unreliable
   - ❑ c. assured him that he was forgiven and that Christ valued his service
5. That Jesus' assignment to Peter was wise is shown in
   - ❑ a. the Gospel of Matthew
   - ❑ b. the Book of Acts
   - ❑ c. the Book of Romans

SUMMARY REVIEW

To review this unit, see if you can mentally answer the following questions. You may want to write the answers on a separate sheet of paper. Mark your level of performance on the left: circle C if you can answer correctly and circle R if you need to review.

C R 1. List two ways the Gospel of John is different from the other three Gospels.

C R 2. Why did John say he wrote his Gospel?

C R 3. List four of Jesus' "I am" statements.

C R 4. How did Jesus relate to Nicodemus? the adulterous woman? Thomas? Peter?

---

21. Answers: 1-a, 2-c, 3-a, 4-c, 5-b.

C R   5. Explain the doctrine of the eternal security of the believer in one sentence.

C R   6. List two ministries of the Holy Spirit.

Review this week's material to find the answers.

To review our study of all four Gospels during the last four weeks, check the correct answer for each of the following questions.[22]

1. Which Gospel was probably written first?
   ❏ a. Matthew   ❏ b. Mark   ❏ c. Luke   ❏ d. John
2. Which Gospel was probably written last?
   ❏ a. Matthew   ❏ b. Mark   ❏ c. Luke   ❏ d. John
3. Which Gospel probably was directed toward Gentiles?
   ❏ a. Matthew   ❏ b. Mark   ❏ c. Luke   ❏ d. John
4. Which Gospel probably was directed toward Jews?
   ❏ a. Matthew   ❏ b. Mark   ❏ c. Luke   ❏ d. John
5. Which Gospel may have been directed toward Romans?
   ❏ a. Matthew   ❏ b. Mark   ❏ c. Luke   ❏ d. John
6. Which Gospel provides the most information on Mary, the mother of Jesus?
   ❏ a. Matthew   ❏ b. Mark   ❏ c. Luke   ❏ d. John
7. Which Gospel emphasizes Jesus' claims to deity?
   ❏ a. Matthew   ❏ b. Mark   ❏ c. Luke   ❏ d. John
8. Which Gospel emphasizes prayer?
   ❏ a. Matthew   ❏ b. Mark   ❏ c. Luke   ❏ d. John
9. Which Gospel includes the parable of the prodigal son?
   ❏ a. Matthew   ❏ b. Mark   ❏ c. Luke   ❏ d. John

RESPONDING TO GOD'S WORD

Meditate on the conversation of Jesus and Peter. In what ways have you failed Jesus? through this Scripture do you hear His voice calling you to renewed commitment and service? In prayer thank Him for His grace and renew your vows to Him as your Lord.

---

22. Answers: 1-b, 2-d, 3-c, 4-a, 5-b, 6-c, 7-d, 8-c, 9-c.

Unit 7 — The Book of Acts, Part 1 (Acts 1–12)

Reading Through the New Testament

- ☐ Acts 1–2
- ☐ Acts 3–4
- ☐ Acts 5–6
- ☐ Acts 7–8
- ☐ Acts 9–10
- ☐ Acts 11
- ☐ Acts 12

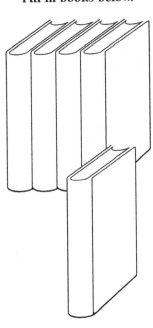

Outline

Fill in books below.

UNIT LEARNING GOAL: The study of this unit should help you understand the history of New Testament churches as recorded in Acts. You will be able to:
- Write the theme and the two-point outline of Acts.
- Describe the events which occurred on Pentecost after Jesus' ascension.
- Relate how and why Christians receive the Holy Spirit.
- Illustrate Peter's key role in leading the early Christians.
- Explain the various ways God used early Christians to witness.

Author of Acts: Luke, the author of the third Gospel

Date of Acts: Mid-60s

Theme of Acts: God's Holy Spirit Spreads the Gospel

Outline of Acts:
 I. Progress of the Gospel Among Jews (1:1–12:25)
 II. Progress of the Gospel Among Gentiles (13:1–28:31)

Importance of Acts: It is the only historical book in the New Testament.

Special Characteristics of Acts:
1. Indicates the spread of the gospel from Jerusalem to Rome
2. Shows the beginning and progress of a Spirit-guided church
3. Spotlights the work of Paul
4. Defends Christians against false accusations

ASIA MINOR

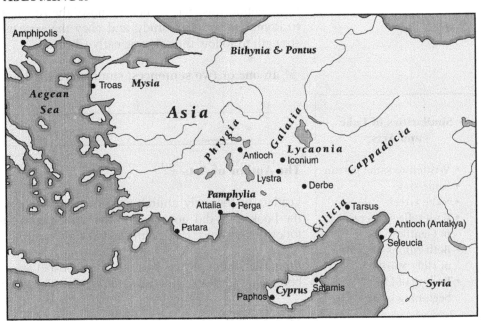

Day 1　Introduction to Acts

UNIT 7

The Importance of Acts

🌿 Read Luke 1:1-4; 24:45-52; Acts 1:1-9. Mark the following statements *T* (true) or *F* (false).[1]

___ 1. Both books are addressed to Theophilus.
___ 2. Both books describe the birth of Jesus.
___ 3. Both books have Jesus' instruction to be witnesses of Him.
___ 4. Both books have the account of the crucifixion.
___ 5. Both books have Jesus' instruction to wait in Jerusalem.
___ 6. Both books have Jesus' ascension.
___ 7. The first verses of Acts are essentially a review of the last verses of the Gospel of Luke.

Begins Where Luke Ended

Acts begins where the Gospel of Luke ended, with the fulfillment of Jesus' command for the disciples to bear witness (Luke 24:48; Acts 1:7-8). Jesus' ascension was the final event in Luke's Gospel and is also recorded at the beginning of Acts.

Christ Empowers Church to Witness

Growth of Church

Acts shows the strength of the ascended Christ in empowering the church for witness. It records the growth of the church by proclaiming the gospel. When Acts begins, the church is confined to Jerusalem, and the disciples are timid and fearful. Acts records their being filled with the Holy Spirit, their bold proclamation of the gospel, and the widespread results of their preaching and teaching. In three decades God's power brought the gospel from the remote area of the Roman Empire called Jerusalem to a central place in the capital city of Rome.

Progress from Jerusalem to Rome

Acts presents a church sensitive to the leadership of the Holy Spirit. It does not present all the locations into which Christianity spread. Although the gospel spread rapidly into Mesopotamia, throughout Africa, and around the Black Sea, Acts does not mention this fact. Rather, it shows the progress of the gospel from Jerusalem to Rome. As we read, study, and obey the appeals of Acts, we can find spiritual strength to follow these heroic early Christians.

🌿 **In one or two sentences, summarize the importance of the Book of Acts.[2]**

_____

_____

Similarities of Luke and Acts

• Written to same person
• Same style
• Same Greek
• Both reflect interest in Gentiles
• Both emphasize work of Holy Spirit
• Ending of Luke fits beginning of Acts

The Author of Acts

Leaders in the early church agreed that Luke was the author of Acts, although the book itself did not mention the author by name. However, Acts contains the following evidence that points to Luke as its author.

First. The author of Acts and the Third Gospel appear to be the same person. Both books are addressed to the same person, Theophilus, a name that means *friend*

---

1. Answers: 1-T, 2-F, 3-T, 4-F, 5-T, 6-T, 7-T.
2. Compare your answer to mine: Acts shows the strength of the ascended Christ in empowering the church for witness. It shows the growth of the church from Jerusalem throughout the Roman Empire.

of God. The opening words of Acts refer to a "former book" that suggests the Gospel of Luke. Both Luke and Acts are written in a similar style with the use of a cultured type of Greek. Both books have a similar interest in Gentiles and the work of the Holy Spirit. The ending of the Third Gospel also leads naturally into the beginning of Acts.

🖉 Fill in the blanks.[3]

1. The Books of Acts and Luke do not tell us who the _____ is.

2. Both Books are addressed to _____, which means _____ of ____.

3. Acts 1:1 mentions a _____ _____, which suggests the Gospel of Luke.

4. Both Books are written in a similar _____.

5. Both Books indicate an interest in _____ and in the Holy Spirit.

6. Facts in items 2—5 suggest that the Books of Acts and Luke were written by the _____ _____.

Companion of Paul

Second. The author of Acts was a companion of Paul. Three sections of Acts use the first person pronoun *we* (Acts 16:10-17; 20:5–21:18; 27:1–28:16). The best explanation of these sections is that they represent the personal observations of a companion of Paul. The writer of these "we" sections accompanied Paul to Philippi, joined him at Philippi on the third missionary journey, and accompanied Paul to Rome.

Luke with Paul During Imprisonment

Luke best fits as the author of these "we" sections. We know that Luke was with Paul on the occasion of Paul's Roman imprisonment (Col. 4:14). Several other potential authors of Acts (including Timothy) are excluded because the author of these sections mentioned them as separate from him in Acts 20:4-5.

A Gentile and a Physician Highly Educated

Third. Luke is not a prominent New Testament character, and there is no reason to explain why ancient writers viewed him as the author of Acts unless he wrote it. Tradition presents Luke as a native of Antioch in Syria and places his death in Boeatia, a province of ancient Greece, at the age of 84. Paul referred to Luke as a Gentile and a physician (Col. 4:10-14). His use of cultured Greek suggests that he was a highly educated man. Luke's life shows that God can channel the abilities of an educated mind into effective opportunities for service.

🖉 Mark the following statements *T* (true) or *F* (false).[4]

Luke's life teaches us that:
____ 1. Educated people aren't as spiritual as less educated.
____ 2. God can use an educated mind for effective service.
____ 3. Our present training can prepare us for future service.

The Date of Acts

No Mention of Jerusalem's Fall in A.D. 70

The final verses of Acts indicate that Paul spent at least two years prison in Rome (Acts 28:30-31). The book ends abruptly, and the ending suggests that Paul still awaited trial when the words were written. Luke included no information about

---

3. Answers: 1-author, 2-Theophilus, friend of God; 3-former book, 4-style, 5-Gentiles, 6-same person.
4. Answers: 1-F, 2-T, 3-T.

the outcome of Paul's trial. If Paul had died, Luke likely would have mentioned it. Acts also shows no evidence of the Jewish Wars and the fall of Jerusalem in A.D. 70.

Book Written in Mid-60s

Acts shows the early church discussing the terms for Gentile admission (Acts 15:6-35). This suggests that Acts was written when these issues were important. A common date for Paul's Roman imprisonment is A.D. 61-63. Luke may have gathered his material for writing Acts during Paul's two-year imprisonment (Acts 28:30). He probably wrote the book in the mid sixties.

The Trustworthiness of Acts

Remarkable Accuracy of Material

Luke presents with remarkable accuracy many facts, figures, and personalities in Acts. Luke is the only Gospel writer to present chronological information which allows us to date the period of the ministry of John the Baptist and also of Jesus (Luke 3:1-2). Luke also presented much chronological information in Acts (see 17:2; 18:11; 19:8,10; 20:31). Luke was accurate in titles for officials. He correctly identified Gallio in Acts 18:12 as a proconsul (KJV uses "deputy"), and he used the correct names of other officials in Acts 16:38; 17:8; and 19:31. An error at this point would be like calling the president of the United States the "governor of the United States." Luke always had his facts straight.

Unusual Knowledge of Nautical Information

Luke also showed nautical information in his description of Paul's voyage to Rome and shipwreck in Acts 27. Sailing on the Mediterranean was virtually impossible from October through February due to stormy conditions, especially blasts of wind from the northeast. Luke mentioned such a storm in Acts 27:14 and accurately described the actions of the sailors in attempting to save the ship and their lives.

RESPONDING TO GOD'S WORD

Write here an example that illustrates that even today Christians are sometimes misunderstood or falsely accused by unbelievers.

_____

What can Christians do to counter such misunderstandings or false accusations? Write your ideas here.

_____

Ask God to help you respond helpfully to unjust criticism or condemnation that comes to you because of your commitment to Christ.

Day 2 *Beginning of Acts*

UNIT 7

The Purpose of Acts

What Jesus Continued

In Acts 1:1 Luke indicated that his purpose in writing his Gospel had been to set out what Jesus began to do and to teach. This statement implies his purpose in writing Acts was to indicate what Jesus *continued* to do and teach through the church after the ascension. In addition to this purpose Acts also accomplishes further goals.

🖊 Write here a one-sentence statement of Luke's purpose in writing Acts.

_____

"Acts of the Holy Spirit"

Luke showed that the progress of the church was guided by the Holy Spirit. Statements appearing in Acts 1:2; 13:4; and 16:6-7 highlight the sovereign role of the Holy Spirit in the spread of the gospel. In fact, we could refer to Acts as "The Acts of the Holy Spirit."

Progress of the Gospel

Acts presents a selective account of the progress of the gospel from its birth in Jerusalem to its penetration throughout the Roman Empire. It presents such important events as:
- the ascension of Christ
- the outpouring of the Holy Spirit at Pentecost
- Peter's preaching to the Gentiles
- Paul's missionary journeys
- the spread of the gospel to Rome

The Book of Acts records the fulfillment of Christ's promise of power for the church in 1:8. The experience of the church in following the leadership of the Holy Spirit and in preaching with power and boldness provides a pattern to inspire and challenge Christians today.

Rome the Goal

Luke did not show the spread of the gospel throughout Africa and Asia but on a road from Jerusalem to Rome. The gospel began in the cradle of Judaism and moved steadfastly to the dominant city of the Roman Empire. Rome was the goal of Paul's missionary journeys.

🖊 Put a check by the name of the most prominent Christian leader in the Book of Acts.[5]

    ❑ 1. Peter
    ❑ 2. James
    ❑ 3. Barnabas
    ❑ 4. Paul
    ❑ 5. Timothy
    ❑ 6. Titus

Paul's Achievements

Luke highlighted the heroic achievements of the apostle Paul. Personalities such as Peter, Barnabas, Timothy, and James have prominent mention, but Luke focused primarily on the role of Paul. Luke showed Paul's involvement in miracles of healing (Acts 14:8-10), exorcism (Acts 16:18), and powerful preaching (Acts 19:8-10). He showed Paul's great courage under trial and pressure (Acts 27:21-26). Luke also presented the conversion testimony of Paul on three separate occasions (Acts 9; 22; 26).

Christians Falsely Accused

Luke showed the innocence of Christians as they faced various false accusations. In Ephesus Paul was on friendly terms with local leaders, and the town clerk pronounced him guiltless of any illegal activity (19:35-41). In Philippi the officials apologized for imprisoning him (16:35-40). In Corinth Gallio refused to hear accusations against Paul (18:12-17). The Roman governor Festus and the Jewish king Agrippa agreed on Paul's innocence (26:30-32).

_____

5. Answer: 4.

🌿 Read Acts 16:19-20; 35-40; 18:12-17; 19:31,35-41; 26:30-32. Circle the following crimes of which Paul was guilty.[6]

robbery   blasphemy   advocating unlawful customs
inciting rebellion   inciting riot   promoting illegal worship

Theme of Acts: God's Holy Spirit Spreads the Gospel

1. Progress of the Gospel Among Jews (1:1–12:25)
2. Progress of the Gospel Among Gentiles (13:1–28:31)

The material of Acts falls into two natural divisions. From 1:1 to 12:25 Luke showed the witness of the church in a primarily Jewish culture. From 13:1 to 28:31 Luke presented the witness of the church in a primarily Gentile culture.

The Ascension of Jesus (1:9-11)

The ascension of Jesus signaled the end of the postresurrection appearances of Jesus and represented His entrance into the ministry of His heavenly priesthood (Heb. 1:3; 7:25). After the ascension Christians experienced their relationship with Jesus in the realm of the spiritual rather than in the realm of the physical.

On the Mount of Olives

The ascension occurred while the disciples were gathered on the Mount of Olives (1:12). The cloud into which Jesus arose symbolized the presence of God's glory and His approval of Jesus' work. The two young men were angels.

🌿 A. Read Acts 1:9-12 and complete the following sentences.[7]

1. The place from which Jesus ascended was the _____ of _____.

2. The cloud symbolized God's _____ and _____.

3. The two men were _____.

B. Read Acts 1:11 and check the following statements with which you agree.
❑ 1. The angels said that Jesus no longer would have anything to do with the disciples.
❑ 2. The angels said that Jesus is now in heaven.
❑ 3. The angels said that Jesus' ministry in relation to earth was over for good.
❑ 4. The angels said that Jesus would return in a secret way.
❑ 5. The angels said that Jesus would return as He departed.

Return in Same Manner

The angels first promised that Jesus would return in the same way that the disciples had seen Him go. This indicated that Jesus' return would be accompanied with a visible evidence of the divine glory.

Jesus Assumed His Throne

In his sermon on the Day of Pentecost, Peter viewed the ascension as the event in which Jesus assumed His throne. The throne was not on earth but in heaven (Acts 2:33-35). God displayed His mighty power in the resurrection and ascension of Christ (Eph. 1:19-23). He makes this power available today to individuals and churches.

---

6. Answers: Luke made plain that Paul was not guilty of any crimes.
7. Answers: A-1. Mount of Olives; 2. glory and approval; 3. angels. B-Hopefully you checked 2 and 5.

RESPONDING TO GOD'S WORD

What can you do to help the gospel make progress in your church and community? Write your response here.

_____

In prayer make yourself available to God in His work of advancing the gospel in your world.

Day 3   *Empowering of the Church*

U N I T   7

The Day of Pentecost (2:1-13)

The Jewish Feast of Pentecost occurred 50 days after the Passover. Jews also called it the Feast of Weeks because it came after seven weeks of harvesting grain.

 What world-changing event had happened during the preceding Passover season? Write your answer here.[8]

_____

For Christians the significance of Pentecost is that the relationship of the Holy Spirit to each believer became more intimate after Pentecost. That day was the fulfillment of Jesus' promise that the Spirit would be with them and would dwell in them (John 14:17). The coming of the Holy Spirit gave the church the power necessary for its mission.

Sounds and Sights

On the Day of Pentecost God sent both sounds and sights. The sound resembled that of wind (2:2). The sight resembled that of fire. The Greek word for *spirit, pneuma,* can refer either to wind or to the spirit, depending on the context. This fact shows a close association of the two ideas of wind and spirit. Fire as a symbol of the divine presence was common among the Jews (see Ex. 3:2-5; 1 Kings 18:16-46).

Filling of the Spirit

The "filling" of the Holy Spirit suggested that believers had received as much of the Spirit as they could hold. He had permeated their beings and filled them with power. The words spoken in "tongues" was recognized by the listeners in their own languages (2:8). The hearers did not need an interpreter to explain the words to them. This suggests that the act of speaking in tongues was a speaking in known languages of the people groups mentioned in 2:9-11.

Crowd Came Together

The crowd may have come together because of a combination of the sound of the wind and the speaking of the disciples. The miracle of speaking in the known languages must have been impressive to the hearers. It did not, however, convince all doubters that something divine in origin was happening. Some with greater spiritual interest asked, "What does this mean?" Others mocked with insensitivity and accused the speakers of drunkenness. Peter's sermon which follows rebuts this senseless charge.

---

8. Answer: The crucifixion and resurrection of Jesus!

🌿 **Read Acts 2:1-13 and check the correct answer for each of the following questions.**[9]

    1. On Pentecost the believers heard:
        ❑ a. a breeze blowing
        ❑ b. a tornado
        ❑ c. a sound like a violent wind
    2. On Pentecost the believers saw:
        ❑ a. tongues of fire on each person's head
        ❑ b. a huge flame
        ❑ c. what seemed to be tongues of flame that separated and came to rest on each of them
    3. The believers began to:
        ❑ a. speak in unknown tongues
        ❑ b. speak in other human languages
        ❑ c. shout and roll on the ground in ecstasy
    4. The believers' excited speaking was:
        ❑ a. a permanent gift
        ❑ b. enabled by the Holy Spirit
        ❑ c. made no sense to the hearers
    5. The hearers from other countries were bewildered:
        ❑ a. to hear Galileans speaking in their native languages
        ❑ b. by such excitement so early in the morning
        ❑ c. by the tongues of flame
    6. The hearers immediately:
        ❑ a. became seekers of truth
        ❑ b. began to mock
        ❑ c. both of the above

Spirit's Presence in All Christians

The event of Pentecost brought the Spirit's presence into the life of all Christians. The Holy Spirit now teaches, leads, and produces Christian character in all believers.

Peter's Sermon (2:14-40)

Peter's Pentecostal sermon contained four elements. First, he responded with a rebuttal to the charge of drunkenness among the disciples (2:14-15). His response was that common sense would instruct his listeners that no one would practice such excessive drinking so early in the morning.

Second, he explained what the noise, sight, and speaking in tongues indicated (2:16-21). He explained the experience as the fulfillment of promises made in Joel 2:28-32. Peter felt that the days of the fulfillment of God's purpose had arrived. The powerful outpouring of the Spirit on men and women was one sign.

Jesus, God's Messiah, Accomplished Salvation

Third, he presented Jesus' life, death, and resurrection as the apex of divine action for our salvation (2:22-36). He presented facts about Jesus' life which included His performance of miracles. He describes Jesus' crucifixion as ordained by God (2:23). He referred to David's words in Psalm 110:1 and stated that the words were fulfilled in the resurrection of Christ. He proclaimed the ascension and exaltation of Christ (2:33-35).

Appeal for Repentance, Faith, and Baptism

Peter concluded with an appeal to the people (2:37-39). His appeal in 2:38 promised the gift of the Holy Spirit to those who expressed repentance and faith as symbolized by baptism. Peter did not link the gift of the Holy Spirit merely with

---

9. Answers: 1-c, 2-c, 3-b, 4-b, 5-a, 6-c.

the act of baptism but with baptism as a visible sign of repentance and faith. Christians receive the Holy Spirit by repentance and faith in Jesus Christ, and baptism is the outward sign of this conversion.

Answer the following questions.[10]

1. From which two Old Testament Books did Peter quote?

   a. _____   b. _____

2. What three things did Joel prophesy? Check your answers:
   ❏ a. The coming of the Holy Spirit on people
   ❏ b. Signs and wonders
   ❏ c. Satanic activity
   ❏ d. The end of the world
   ❏ e. The Lord will save those who call on Him

3. Does Peter's sermon teach that Jesus' death was included in God's plan to provide redemption?
   ❏ Yes   ❏ No

4. How would you answer one who says, "Acts 2:38 seems to teach that baptism is essential to receive the Holy Spirit"? Check your answer.
   ❏ a. Peter meant that baptism is essential to receive the Holy Spirit.
   ❏ b. Peter was communicating that those who express repentance and faith as symbolized by baptism would receive the Holy Spirit.
   ❏ c. Peter should not have said "and be baptized."

RESPONDING TO GOD'S WORD

How has the Holy Spirit worked in your life since you have believed? Write a brief response here.

_____

Ask God to fill you with His Spirit and enable you this week to be the ministering Christian He wants you to be.

Day 4   *Life in the Early Church*

UNIT 7

Doctrine, Fellowship, Prayer

Characteristics of a Spiritual Church (2:42-47)

To these early Christians doctrine was important because it provided information about Christ. The sense of fellowship quickly united the three thousand people who had been converted on the Day of Pentecost (2:41). In breaking bread the early Christians were commemorating the death of Christ and expressing a hope for His return (see 1 Cor. 11:26). The prayers of the early church included both praise and fervent intercession (see example in 4:23-31).

---

10. Answers: 1a-Joel, 1-b-Psalms; 2-a, b, e; 3-Yes; 4- Your response, I checked b.

Awe, Unity, Joy

Christians lived among one another with a sense of awe, and they expected God to show Himself in miraculous, supernatural ways. The church had a unity and compassion which led individual members to share their own goods with the needy among them. Christians had a sense of joy, and they abounded in praise to God.

A. Read Acts 2:42-47. Mark the statements *T* (true) or *F* (false).[11]
____ 1. Acts 2:44-45 teaches that Christians should pool their resources so that all believers will have equal shares of everything.
____ 2. "Breaking of bread" probably includes participating in the Lord's Supper.
____ 3. The church had many after-church fellowships.
____ 4. The love of Christians for one another was expressed in their material generosity.

B. Check the following items that characterized the church in Acts 2:42-47.
❏ 1. compassion   ❏ 2. fellowship   ❏ 3. praise
❏ 4. prayer   ❏ 5. proclamation ❏ 6. sense of the miraculous
❏ 7. singing   ❏ 8. unity   ❏ 9. visiting the sick

The Church at Prayer (4:23-31)

In this passage the Jerusalem Christians faced a difficult dilemma, for the Jewish Sanhedrin had just reprimanded Peter and John for an act of healing and a bold proclamation of Jesus' saving power (4:13-22). Peter and John responded that they would continue to preach what they had seen and heard. A timid Christian would have withdrawn to the safety of his own private world. However, that was not the response of Peter, John, and the other Jerusalem Christians.

Read Acts 4:23-31 and answer the following questions.[12]
A. Of the verses that contain the believers' prayer (vv. 24-30), how many verses are devoted to praising God for what He has done? _____

B. How many verses are devoted to petition? _____

C. What is one implication of A and B?_____

D. What did they ask for themselves? _____

E. What did God give them? _____

Luke mentioned three marvelous results of the prayer in 4:31.
• First, the room shook.
• Second, the disciples were filled or dominated by the Holy Spirit.
• Third, the power of the Spirit led them to speak with boldness.

When we face difficulty and opposition, we must not surrender to self-pity or resentment. We must ask God for boldness to continue living and witnessing for Him in all circumstances.

First-Century Problems (Acts 5–6)

Sometimes it is easy to think that early Christians did not have problems in their churches because their spiritual depth prevented it. When we read such passages

---

11. Answers: A: 1-F, 2-T, 3-F ("fellowship" does not necessarily mean a social gathering), 4-T. B:All except 7 and 9.
12. Answers: A-5;B-2; C-You may have written that we should spend more prayer time in praise; D-Boldness to speak God's Word; E-Boldness to speak God's Word

as Acts 5 and 6, we realize that even the first-century Christians faced many of the same problems we face today. Their response to these problems gives us a pattern to follow in the many problems churches face today.

Problem of Sin in the Church (Acts 5)

When Satan attacks the church, he often uses a dual approach, persecution from *without*, and deception and division from *within*. The account of Ananias and Sapphira (Acts 5:1-11) does not just give us the first recorded instance of church discipline nor is it primarily a story of selfishness and greed. More importantly, the account of Ananias and Sapphira teaches us the seriousness with which God views hypocrisy among believers, and reflects the potential damage hypocrisy can inflict on a congregation of believers.

Lied to God

Peter made it clear that Ananias and Sapphira's sin was in lying to the church about giving the full purchase price of the property, yet actually withholding part of it (v. 8). And therefore, they had lied to the Holy Spirit (v. 3), who is God (v. 4), in testing His ability to know about the matter (v. 9).

Drastic Punishment

Their sin was both corporate and individual (note v. 2). God dealt with their sin directly and swiftly. His method (involving their individual deaths) seems drastic by modern standards, but gives some indication of how seriously God views sin within the church.

🌿 **Mark the following statements *T* (true) or *F* (false).**[13]
Ananias and Sapphira's sin:
___ 1. Was against God
___ 2. Was not corporate (together) but individual
___ 3. Was punished in a way that made clear how God viewed their sin

Caring for Needs Important (Acts 6)

The early church felt that caring for the physical needs of widows in the congregation was an important task. Among the congregation were two types of widows. Some widows were Jews who had lived in Jerusalem and were fully Jewish in their background. They followed Jewish customs and spoke Aramaic or Hebrew. Luke called them "Hebrews." Other widows were Jews who had been living outside Jerusalem. They had returned to Jerusalem as their homeland. They were more Greek in their language and customs, but they were Jewish in their ethnic background. Luke called them "Grecians." The "Grecian" widows were smaller in number than the "Hebrews" and it was easy to overlook them and allow them to live in need.

Appointment of the Seven

The Jewish Christians who spoke Greek complained that their widows were not being treated fairly. The busy apostles could not minister effectively and also worry about details. They were overworked administrators, who became inefficient because of the volume of work (and perhaps because of their calling). The apostles called the church together to settle the problem. They refused to leave the preaching of the gospel and make the ministry to the widows a full-time task. They felt that the task was important enough to suggest that the church choose seven spiritual, capable men to perform the job. If these seven men ministered to the widows, the apostles could focus on prayer, preaching, and teaching (6:4).

God's Word Increased

The church responded by selecting seven men with Greek names. They chose seven Greek-speaking Hebrew Christians, an evidence of going the second mile in seeking reconciliation between the "Grecians" and the "Hebrews." Luke listed the result of this unified decision in 6:7. When the apostles were able to focus on the ministry of prayer and proclamation, God's word increased, and the number of believers grew rapidly. Even Jewish priests were converted to Christ.

---

13. Answers: 1-T, 2-F, 3-T.

Check the following principles that can be derived from Acts 6:1-7.[14]

> **Principles for Dealing with Problems**
>
> - Spiritual worship must not exclude ministry
> - We must seek solutions, not blame
> - We must be flexible, willing to try new ways
> - We must remain united to remain powerful

❑ 1. Families should care for their members.
❑ 2. Seek solutions rather than persons to blame.
❑ 3. Be flexible enough to organize to meet needs.
❑ 4. Give priority to giving.
❑ 5. Work together to maintain unity.
❑ 6. Both proclamation and ministry are important church tasks.

RESPONDING TO GOD'S WORD

Reflect on the content of your prayers. Is praise a regular element? In your regular petitions, do your prayers reflect the purpose of accomplishing God's will in the world? Write here one improvement in your prayer life that you will try to make this week.

_____

_____

Day 5   *Witnessing for Jesus*

UNIT 7

Witnessing by Martyrdom (6:8–7:60)

Read Acts 6:8–7:60 and check here when you have finished: ❑

Stephen's ministry for Christ was very powerful (v. 8), even though short-lived. His character was impeccable and his witness for Christ radiant (6:15; 7:55-60). Although his preaching was powerful (7:51-54), and his recorded sermon much longer than Peter's at Pentecost, Scripture records few results of his ministry.

Saul Impressed by Stephen's Witness

However, Acts 8:1 records that Saul witnessed and assented to his martyrdom. Years later, Paul alludes to the impact Stephen's witness had on him when he stated before a crowd in Jerusalem. "When the blood of your martyr Stephen was shed, I stood there giving my approval and guarding the clothes of those who were killing him" (Acts 22:20).

Read Acts 8:5-24 and check the correct answer for each question.[15]

1. Simon the sorcerer was truly converted.
   ❑ a. yes   ❑ b. no   ❑ c. probably   ❑ d. probably not
2. Simon solved most of his problems by believing in Jesus.
   ❑ a. yes   ❑ b. no   ❑ c. probably   ❑ d. probably not
3. Simon made a public profession, was baptized, and publicly joined the apostles.
   ❑ a. yes   ❑ b. no   ❑ c. probably   ❑ d. probably not
4. Simon stands as a typical example of a worldly Christian.
   ❑ a. yes   ❑ b. no   ❑ c. probably   ❑ d. probably not

---

14. Answers: 2, 3, 5, 6.
15. Answers: Your answer. I put 1-c, 2-b, 3-a, 4-a.

Witnessing and Worldliness (8:5-24)

Does Walk Match Talk?

Sometimes we witness to an interested person, or have a part in someone's conversion, only to find that their subsequent life does not seem to measure up to their conversion testimony. Such was the case with one of Philip's converts in Samaria.

Philip's Powerful Ministry

Philip was blessed with God-honoring miracles and many conversions in Samaria, and "there was great joy in that city" (Acts 8:8). Simon the sorcerer, called "The Great Power" (v. 10) by the people, also believed and was baptized (v. 13). He became a constant companion of Philip, and later of Peter and John when they arrived.

Simon's Spiritual Problems

Simon marveled at Philip's "signs and miracles" (v. 13), and at the way believers received the Holy Spirit when Peter and John placed their hands on them (v. 17). He offered money to the apostles if they would pass this ability on to him, but was immediately rebuked by Peter. Peter indicated that Simon—
- did not understand spiritual matters (v. 20);
- could not share in a spiritual ministry (v. 21);
- had a heart not right before God (v. 21);
- had committed wickedness (v. 22);
- was full of bitterness (v. 23);
- was a captive to sin (v 23).

Some have suggested that Simon was not really saved, while others have pointed out that Simon may have been genuinely converted, but still remained very much a slave to his background. If Simon were truly a Christian, we may be sure that he was a worldly one. If Simon were unconverted, we may assume that his belief in 8:13 was, not a trust in Christ, only an admission of the reality that a powerful God lay behind Philip's preaching. It is difficult to determine whether Peter's words of rebuke in 8:20-23 sound like words spoken to a Christian or to a lost person.

Witnessing One-on-One (8:26-40)

Read Acts 8:26-40 and check here when you have finished: ❏

Philip had been preaching in a city of Samaria (vv. 4-8) when God directed him to a road leading to Gaza. Though Luke calls it "a desert road," we must not suppose that it was deserted. Rather, it was the main road south to Egypt and was one of the most heavily traveled roads.

Philip met a high-ranking official of the Ethiopian government, who had been to Jerusalem to worship God. Probably he was a proselyte to Judaism, for he was studying the Scripture.

Philip knew the Old Testament well enough that, when he heard the man reading, he knew it was from Isaiah. He asked a courteous yet direct question, "Do you understand what you are reading?" (Acts 8:30). When the man replied that he needed help in understanding, Philip began where he had been reading (Isa. 53), and "told him the good news about Jesus" (v. 35).

We are not told in so many words that the Ethiopian accepted Christ. "I believe that Jesus Christ is the Son of God" is not found in any of the best and oldest manuscripts. However, we are sure of his decision because of his demonstration of faith when he requested baptism. Philip was convinced, or he would not have baptized him.

🌿 **Mark the following statements true (T) or false (F).**[16]

_____ 1. The road to Gaza was a deserted road.

_____ 2. Philip decided that it was better to leave his preaching ministry and go to Gaza.

_____ 3. We are not told specifically that the Ethiopian man said he would accept Christ.

_____ 4. Baptism is a public demonstration of our faith.

🌿 **SUMMARY REVIEW**

To review this unit, see if you can mentally answer the following questions. You may want to write the answers on a separate sheet of paper. Mark your level of performance on the left: circle *C* if you can answer correctly and circle *R* if you need to review.

C R   1. Write the theme of Acts.

C R   2. What is a two-point outline of Acts?

C R   3. Who is the most prominent Christian leader in the Book of Acts?

C R   4. What happened on the first Feast of Pentecost, after Jesus' ascension?

C R   5. What did Peter do that showed his leadership of the early Christians?

C R   6. List the characteristics of the early church.

C R   7. Describe two occasions when God used early Christians to witness.

Review this week's material to find the answers.

RESPONDING TO GOD'S WORD

Make a short note here of any unity-threatening matters that your church is presently experiencing (or perhaps could experience).

_____

Write here principles of problem solving in Acts 6:1-7 that can apply to the situation.

_____

Write here ways you can encourage the practice of these principles.

_____

---

16. Answers: 1-F, 2-F, 3-T, 4-T.

Reading Through the New Testament

- ❏ Acts 13–14
- ❏ Acts 15–17
- ❏ Acts 18–19
- ❏ Acts 20–21
- ❏ Acts 22–23
- ❏ Acts 24–26
- ❏ Acts 27–28

UNIT LEARNING GOAL: The study of this unit should help you understand the conversion and ministry of Paul and his influence on New Testament churches. You will be able to:

- Describe Paul's conversion and early years as a Christian.
- Relate how the gospel began to be preached to the Gentiles and identify the first Gentile convert.
- Summarize Paul's three missionary journeys, and identify those who accompanied Paul on these journeys.
- Explain Paul's strategy in proclaiming Christ in the cities he visited.
- Explain the importance of the Jerusalem Council.
- Describe how Paul ended his public ministry and how he got to Rome.

Outline

PAUL'S MISSIONARY JOURNEYS

First Journey (13:1–14:28)
Second Journey (15:36–18:22)
Third Journey (18:23–20:30)

ROMAN EMPIRE IN PAUL'S TIME

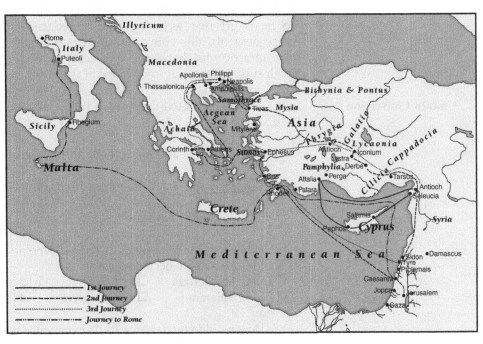

Day 1   *The Conversion of Paul (Acts 9:1-30)*

UNIT 8

🌿 **What are the opening (Acts 1:6-11) and closing (28:30-31) events in the Book of Acts?**

1. Opening: _____

2. Closing: _____

Read the following paragraph to check your answer.

A.D. 29–63

From Jerusalem to Rome

Acts covers events ranging from the time of Jesus' ascension to the first Roman imprisonment of Paul (approximately A.D. 29-63). It moves in geographical order from Jerusalem to the regions of Judea, Samaria, Galilee, Asia Minor, Macedonia, Greece, to the islands of the Mediterranean, and finally to the city of Rome.

🌿 **Without looking back, write here the outline of Acts. Include the references if you can.**[1]

1. _____

2. _____

Saul the Pharisee

Born Saul

Born a Roman Citizen

Paul was given the Jewish name of Saul after his father (or perhaps after King Saul, who was also from the tribe of Benjamin). He was born in Tarsus, a self-governing city loyal to the Roman Empire, making him a Roman citizen. Paul learned several languages and became by his own admission a religious fanatic, "a Hebrew of Hebrews" (Phil. 3:5) with total confidence in his own righteousness. In Philippians 3:6, he records that "as for legalistic righteousness, [I was] faultless." Luke recorded the account of Paul's conversion in Acts 9:22 and 26. The accounts agree in the main idea of what happened, but each account includes additional information which supplements our knowledge of the event.

Saul's Conversion

In 9:1-9 Luke presented the story of Paul's encounter with Christ on the Damascus Road.

🌿 **Read Acts 9:1-9 and answer the following questions.**[2]

1. Complete the "I am" statement from John 14:6. Jesus reflected in dealing

with Saul [Paul], "I am the _____, the _____, and the _____."

2. What was Paul's attitude toward believers in Christ as he traveled to Damascus? Check your answers:
   - ❑ a. Murderous   ❑ c. Angry   ❑ e. Hateful
   - ❑ b. Tolerant   ❑ d. Indifferent   ❑ f. Vicious

3. How would you describe Paul's experience with Christ on the way to Damascus as compared with the way most people experience Him? Check your answer: ❑ a. Typical   ❑ b. Most unusual

---

1. Answers: 1-Progress of the Gospel Among Jews (1:1–12:25); 2-Progress of the Gospel Among Gentiles (13:1–28:31).

4. After Jesus answered Paul's question, by what means did He indicate that

Paul could receive further information? _____

5. For how long was Paul blind? _____

To Damascus to Persecute Christians

Paul went to Damascus armed with letters from the high priest, which gave him the right to extradite Jewish Christians to Jerusalem. On the road to Damascus at noon Christ spoke to Paul in a blinding flash of light. Paul heard a definite voice from the Lord. His traveling companions heard only a sound. Paul addressed Jesus as Lord (9:5) and was blinded after the experience. Paul's friends led him by the hand into Damascus. He remained for three days in Damascus without food or water as he awaited instructions. Paul received help from Ananias in 9:10-19.

Saul Becomes Paul the Apostle

A. **Read Acts 9:10-19 and answer the following questions.**[3]
   1. How would you describe God's means of showing Ananias what He wanted him to do? Check your answer:
   ❑ a. Typical   ❑ b. Unusual

   2. What was Ananias's first response to the Lord's instruction? Check your answers:
   ❑ 1. Eager to obey   ❑ 2. Reluctant
   ❑ 3. Fearful   ❑ 4. Bold

B. **Without looking at the Scripture, try to fill in the blanks.**

"This man is my _____ _____ to carry my name before the

_____, and their _____ and before the people of _____."

C. **Mark the following statements *T* (true) or *F* (false).**

___ 1. Paul probably knew that Ananias could not have known of Jesus' appearing to Paul unless the Lord Jesus had told him.
___ 2. Because of his background in Judaism and his opposition to Christianity, Paul was reluctant to be baptized.

Ananias was a Jewish Christian in Damascus with a readiness to obey God's call. After an initial hesitancy when he learned that God's call included a visit to the persecutor Paul, he went to Paul's residence. When he put his hands on Paul and prayed, sight came again to the future apostle. Paul was baptized, received food, and regained his strength.

Preaching Christ in Synagogues

In Acts 9:20-25 we find the evidence for Paul's conversion. He began immediately to preach Christ in Damascus synagogues. During this time Paul spent an extended period in Arabia and Damascus learning from God the nature of his ministry (Gal. 1:15-19). Paul's growth in ability to witness with convicting power led some of the unbelieving Jews to plot his death. He escaped with the assistance of fellow Christians who lowered him over the wall in a large rope basket. Luke presented the Jerusalem believers' response to Paul in 9:26-30.

_____

2. Answers: 1-Way, Truth, Life; 2-you could have checked a, c, e, f; 3-hopefully you checked b; 4-from another human being; 5-three days.
3. Answers: A1-b; A2-2, 3; B-chosen instrument, Gentiles, kings, Israel; C1-T, C2-F.

🌿 Read Acts 9:26-30 and check the correct answer for each of the following questions.[4]

1. Why would the believers in Jerusalem suspect Paul of lying about becoming a believer in Christ?
   - ❏ a. They thought he was setting a trap for them.
   - ❏ b. They knew he was an immoral man.
   - ❏ c. Both of the above.

2. Who encouraged the believers in Jerusalem to accept Paul as a fellow believer?
   - ❏ a. Peter
   - ❏ b. James
   - ❏ c. Barnabas

3. How could Barnabas have learned what he told the disciples in Jerusalem about Paul?
   - ❏ a. He talked with other believers from Damascus.
   - ❏ b. He evidently risked a visit with Paul.
   - ❏ c. He probably was guessing in order to give Paul the benefit of the doubt.

4. One measure of Paul's effectiveness in leading others to faith in Christ was:
   - ❏ a. the huge numbers who were saved
   - ❏ b. his popularity with the people
   - ❏ c. the opposition against him by the Jews

Barnabas's Recommendation

Understandably Christians in Jerusalem viewed Paul as a potential spy who would fake his conversion in order to gain acceptance to a Christian group and ferret them out. Barnabas stepped forward to risk his reputation by speaking a recommendation for Paul. The Christians accepted Paul, and he preached boldly to the Greek-speaking Jews in Jerusalem. These unbelieving Jews also plotted to kill him.

Paul the Leader

The conversion of Paul provided Christianity an unswerving leader who led the efforts to plant Christianity throughout the Roman world. Paul's background of living as a Jew among Gentiles uniquely prepared him to be an apostle of God's message to the Gentiles. Just as God used Paul's background to prepare him for ministry, God will use our backgrounds in preparing us to carry out unique tasks for His glory.

🌴 RESPONDING TO GOD'S WORD

What evidence can you present that would indicate that you truly are a Christian? Write your answer here.

_____

Pray for God to use you to help others come to know Christ as their Lord.

---

4. Answers: 1-a, 2-c, 3-b, 4-c.

Day 2

The Gospel Goes to the Gentiles
(Acts 10:1-48)

UNIT 8

"Gentile Pentecost"

God Prepares a Gentile Heart

The believers who had received the Holy Spirit at Pentecost in Acts 2 were Jewish Christians. Now we find Gentile believers receiving the Holy Spirit. It is fitting to name this chapter the "Gentile Pentecost." The conversion of Cornelius shows the timing of God in directing Jewish Christians to evangelize Gentiles. Cornelius was a Gentile who had a relationship to Judaism. Later Paul carried the gospel to some Gentiles who had no relationship to Judaism. Crossing these barriers of reaching the Gentiles required direction and guidance only God could give.

A. Read Acts 10:1-8. Check the characteristics of Cornelius that appear in the following list.[5]
- ❏ 1. Baptized
- ❏ 2. Feared God
- ❏ 3. Prayed regularly
- ❏ 4. A Roman (Gentile)
- ❏ 5. Tanner
- ❏ 6. Jew
- ❏ 7. Centurion
- ❏ 8. Gave generously to help others

B. If you knew a person like Cornelius today, what would you assume about that person? Check your answers.
- ❏ 1. That person needs the Lord Jesus Christ as his/her Savior.
- ❏ 2. That person lives a good life and knows Jesus as his/her Savior.
- ❏ 3. That person is going to heaven.
- ❏ 4. That person is going to hell.

C. Had Cornelius died the day before he had a vision, what would have been his eternal destiny? Check your answer.
- ❏ 1. Heaven   ❏ 2. Hell

D. Why did the angel tell Cornelius to send for Peter rather than directly telling him how to be saved? Check your answer.
- ❏ 1. The angel did not know how to tell a human how to be saved.
- ❏ 2. God wanted Peter to have the joy of leading Cornelius to Christ.
- ❏ 3. God has ordained that the gospel be spread through human believers.

Vision of Cornelius

In 10:1-8 Luke narrated the vision of Cornelius. Cornelius was a godly centurion who was a near-proselyte to Judaism and participated in Jewish worship practices. God directed Cornelius to send men to seek Peter, who was then in Joppa (9:43). The three persons Cornelius sent were so eager that they apparently walked most of the night to cover the 35 miles between Caesarea and Joppa.

God Prepares a Prejudiced Preacher

As the men were arriving in Joppa, God was giving Peter a vision to prepare him to receive Gentile guests (10:9-16). Peter was not an overly scrupulous Jew, but he was not prepared to minister directly to Gentiles. God sent him a vision to overcome his reluctance.

Read Acts 10:9-16 and put a check here when you have finished: ❏

---

5. Answers: A-2, 3, 4, 7, 8; B-Your response; probably many of us would assume 2 and 3; C-2; D-3.

Overcoming Prejudice

At noon on the day following Cornelius' vision, Peter was on the flat roof of the house of Simon the tanner. While in prayer, Peter fell into a trance and saw a vision. In the vision Peter saw a large sheet-like object containing four-footed animals, reptiles, and birds. The animals represented a mixture of both clean and unclean animals. Peter was not prepared to follow God's command to "kill and eat." Inwardly Peter recoiled from the command, but God repeated the vision three times in order to impress it on him.

One of the chief reasons Jews avoided table fellowship with Gentiles was that Gentiles ate food considered unclean by the Jews. In the vision God was telling Peter that he had cleansed all types of foods. Responding to that truth would remove a hindrance Peter must have felt in his relationship to the Gentiles.

🌿 **Read Acts 10:17-23. Circle the following words or phrases that describe Peter at this point.[6]**

hard-headed	open to learn	ruled by prejudice	ready to risk
perceptive	closed mind	impulsive	thoughtful
dull	spiritual	worldly	skeptical

In 10:17-23 Peter greeted the messengers Cornelius had sent. The messengers from Cornelius were at the entrance of Simon's house even as Peter was concluding his vision. When Peter met and talked with them, he came to realize that the vision had prepared him to travel with the Gentiles to meet Cornelius. Peter was learning that questions over eating foods should not prevent his making an effort to reach Gentiles with the gospel. After the messengers had spent the night in Simon's home, Peter left with them the next day for Caesarea and Cornelius's home.

In anticipation of meeting Peter, Cornelius had gathered both friends and relatives. Peter related to Cornelius that God had taught him not to regard the Gentiles as unclean or common. Cornelius explained his vision to Peter and then introduced Peter to the group of people he had assembled together.

🌿 **Read Acts 10:34-43 and match the following teachings on the left with the correct verses on the right. Write the correct letters in the blanks.[7]**

___ 1. God anointed and worked through Jesus.	A. verse 34
___ 2. Jesus Christ is Lord of all.	B. verse 35
___ 3. God chose certain people to see Jesus alive again.	C. verse 36
___ 4. Any person can be saved.	D. verse 37
___ 5. God shows no favoritism.	E. verse 38
___ 6. Jesus was killed.	F. verse 39
___ 7. People who believe in Jesus are forgiven.	G. verse 40
___ 8. Peace comes through Christ.	H. verse 41
___ 9. Jesus is the Judge of the living and the dead.	I. verse 42
___ 10. God raised Jesus from the dead.	J. verse 43

The Gospel Preached to Gentiles

Peter presented his sermon in 10:34-43. In a brief introduction (10:34-35) he announced that God accepted persons from all nations who followed the righteousness of repentance and faith in Jesus. In 10:36-43 Peter focused on the life,

---

6. Answers: I circled open to learn, ready to risk, perceptive, thoughtful, spiritual.
7. Answers: 1-E, 2-C, 3-H, 4-B, 5-A, 6-F, 7-J, 8-C, 9-I, 10-G.

death, and resurrection of Jesus. He promised forgiveness through Jesus to anyone who believed on Him. The results of Peter's preaching appear in 10:44-48.

Before Peter concluded his message, the Holy Spirit fell upon the crowd, and they spoke in tongues, and praised God (10:44-46). Peter responded to God's initiative by calling for baptism for these who were obviously converted.

Jerusalem Jews who criticized Peter's effort to reach gentiles heard not only Peter's testimony of what had happened, but also the story of the six believers who accompanied him (11:12). When they heard these combined testimonies, they began to understand that God had a plan to save the Gentiles.

RESPONDING TO GOD'S WORD

Check the following boxes after you have completed the exercise.

❑ Examine your heart for prejudice against some person(s).
❑ If you find prejudice, confess it now to God as sin and ask Him to help you overcome it.
❑ Ask God to show you how to build bridges between you and that person (or persons) over which the gospel of Christ can be carried.
❑ Dedicate yourself in prayer to loving and reaching all people for Christ.

Day 3 *Increasing Gentile Response*

UNIT 8

Paul's First Missionary Journey (13–14)

Read Acts 13:1-5 and answer the following questions.[8]

1. Who set Paul and Barnabas apart for a special work? _____

2. Who sent Paul and Barnabas on their first missionary journey? _____

3. Where did they first proclaim the Word of God? _____

4. To whom did they first proclaim the Word of God? _____

PAUL AND BARNABAS'S ITINERARY		
Antioch of Syria	Island of Cyprus	Perga
Antioch of Pisidia	Iconium	Lystra
Derbe	Return Through Cities to Antioch	

---

8. Answer: 1-The Holy Spirit; 2-The Holy Spirit; 3-Salamis on Cyprus; 4-Jews.

God Himself indicated that Paul and Barnabas should begin their first missionary journey, calling them while they were busily at work in ministry in the city of Syrian Antioch. Paul and Barnabas went to the island of Cyprus and then to the coast and inland district of Asia Minor, where they preached in such cities as Perga, Antioch of Pisidia, Iconium, Lystra, and Derbe.

At Derbe Paul turned around and passed back through the cities he had visited. He prepared his converts for difficulty by urging them to expect persecution and trial (14:22). He completed the journey by returning to Antioch. Several prominent events took place on this journey.

Region of Pamphlia
City of Attalia
City of Perga

At Perga John Mark, who had worked as a helper with Paul and Barnabas, left and returned to Jerusalem. Luke never explained his reason for leaving, but Paul regarded the departure as a serious problem, and refused to take Mark on the second missionary journey (15:36-41).

At Antioch in Pisidia Paul made a deliberate effort to turn to the Gentiles. He began to preach the gospel even to Gentiles who had no contact with the synagogue.

🌿 **Read Acts 13:42-52. Check the correct ending for each statement.[9]**

1. On a scale of 1 to 10, was Paul's preaching in the synagogue at Pisidian Antioch effective?
   ❑ a. 2   ❑ b. 4   ❑ c. 6
   ❑ d. 8   ❑ e. 10

2. When the Jews saw the popularity of Paul and his message, they:
   ❑ a. rejoiced in what God was doing
   ❑ b. plotted Paul's death
   ❑ c. were jealous and talked against his teaching

3. When the Jews strongly opposed Paul and Barnabas, the missionaries:
   ❑ a. announced that they would direct their ministry to the Gentiles.
   ❑ b. left town
   ❑ c. sought to be reconciled with them

Region of Phrygia
Antioch of Pisidia
City of Iconium
City of Laodicea

4. The Gentiles, on hearing that Paul and Barnabas would turn their missionary efforts to them, expressed their:
   ❑ a. scorn   ❑ b. joy   ❑ c. fear

5. The word of the Lord was:
   ❑ a. limited by Jewish opposition
   ❑ b. spread throughout the city
   ❑ c. spread throughout the region

Region of Lycaonia
City of Derbe
City of Lystra

6. When Paul and Barnabas were expelled from Antioch in Pisidia, they:
   ❑ a. gave up their missionary work
   ❑ b. were acutely embarrassed
   ❑ c. went elsewhere to preach the gospel

In Iconium Paul followed the principle of first visiting a synagogue to reach Jews who had a background for understanding the gospel. When the Jews opposed his message, he went to the Gentiles. Stubborn Jews from Antioch of Pisidia hounded Paul's preaching throughout much of the first journey (14:19). However, Paul

---

9. Answers: 1-your response could have been from 6 to 10; 2-c, 3-a, 4-b, 5-c, 6-c.

showed the dogged determination that led him to make such a magnificent contribution in spreading the gospel. The day after a near-fatal stoning in Lystra he left with Barnabas to preach further in Derbe (14:20).

🌿 **Read Acts 14:21-28. Check the statements with which you agree.**[10]

❑ 1. After people are saved, Christians have no further responsibility toward them.
❑ 2. After people are saved, they need no guidance in spiritual matters.
❑ 3. After people are saved, follow-up by more mature Christians is most important.
❑ 4. After people are saved, most of their problems are over.

🌿 **Trace on the map in the margin Paul's first missionary journey. Put a check here when you have done so:** ❑ **Consult the map at the beginning of this unit if needed.**

PAUL'S FIRST MISSIONARY JOURNEY

The Jerusalem Council (15:1-29)

Paul's policy of preaching directly to the Gentiles stirred much opposition in Jerusalem among Christian Pharisees.

Jewish Christians came to Antioch in Syria and taught the necessity of circumcision and a Jewish lifestyle for the Gentiles to be saved. The debate over this issue led to a conference (called the Jerusalem Council) to settle the matter in Jerusalem. The conference involved much discussion and the presentation of various experiences and viewpoints (15:5-12).

Must Gentiles Adopt Jewish Lifestyle?

Some Christian Pharisees insisted that Gentiles needed to submit to circumcision and obey Mosaic law. Peter shared his experience with Cornelius and urged the group not to put the yoke of the Mosaic law on the Gentiles. Both Paul and Barnabas described the outreach among the Gentiles which they had found. The crowd expectantly looked to James, the brother of Jesus, for leadership in a decision on the matter (15:13-21).

🌿 **Read Acts 15:13-21 and check your answer to the following questions.**[11]

1. On what did James base his conclusions?
❑ a. conversion experiences and Scripture
❑ b. his longstanding relationship with Peter
❑ c. the persuasive oratory of Paul

2. On what side did James declare himself?
❑ a. The Jewish Christians
❑ b. Paul and Barnabas
❑ c. Neither of the above

3. What was the significance of James's choice of things from which Gentile believers should abstain?
❑ a. These Jewish religious laws would help save them.
❑ b. These practices would help them grow spiritually.
❑ c. These guidelines would help Jewish and Gentile believers get along.

---

10. Answers: You checked the third statement, right? Right!
11. Answers: 1-a, 2-b, 3-c. (Note: adultery was probably included because sexual sins were commonly practiced among Gentiles.)

Circumcision/Mosaic Law Not Necessary for Salvation

Gentiles Abstain from Offensive Practices

James had a reputation for piety, but he was more tolerant than many other Christian Jews. James referred to Amos 9:11-12 to prove that Gentiles could become believers without having to follow Jewish laws and practices (Acts 15:16-18). His statement removed all obstacles to Paul's mission to the Gentiles. Speaking practically, James urged Gentile Christians to avoid sexual immorality. He also called on Gentiles to show respect for Jewish scruples by avoiding food used in the worship of idols, avoiding animals thtat were strangled, and also the consumption of blood.

The apostles sent Judas and Silas back to Antioch to deliver the decision of the council (15:22-29). The presentation of the decision caused great joy among the Gentiles (15:31).

Three important results came out of the Jerusalem Council. First, the church decided that circumcision and obeying the Mosaic law were not necessary for salvation. Second, the church affirmed that Gentile Christians ought to abstain from certain practices for the sake of Jewish-Gentile relationships within the church. Third, the church maintained a unity which gave credibility to its witness of the gospel.

Fill in the blanks to answer this question: What were three results that came from the Jerusalem Council?[12]

1. Circumcision and obeying the Mosaic law were not necessary

   for _____

2. Gentile Christians were to abstain from certain practices for the sake

   of _____ - _____ relationships within the church.

3. The church maintained a _____ that gave credibility to its witness of the gospel.

RESPONDING TO GOD'S WORD

Think back over Paul's first missionary journey and his involvement in the Jerusalem Council. List as many examples of opposition and difficulty as you can.

_____

_____

How did Paul respond to these experiences? What is God saying to you through this Scripture? Write your answer here.

_____

In response to what God is saying to you, answer Him in prayer. Summarize your prayer here.

_____

_____

---

12. Answers: 1-salvation; 2-Jewish-Gentile; 3-unity.

Day 4 *Spread the Gospel in Gentile Areas*

UNIT 8

Paul's Second Missionary Journey (16:36–18:22)

Paul began his second missionary journey with Silas as his companion. Barnabas and Mark left to work together on the island of Cyprus (15:36-41). Paul traveled through the same cities of Asia Minor (Antioch, Iconium, Lystra, and Derbe) he had visited on his first journey (16:1-5).

Region of Mysia
City of Assos
City of Pergamum
City of Troas

Paul followed a roundabout route to Troas in the region of Mysia where he received a call to cross the Aegean Sea and minister in the region of Macedonia. This signaled a significant step, for in crossing the Aegean Sea, Paul carried the gospel to Europe (see map on p. 121). He spent time in important cities of Macedonia such as Philippi and Thessalonica, briefly visited Berea, and preached a notable sermon in Athens. He spent 18 months in Corinth for his longest stay in a single location during this journey (18:11). After leaving Corinth, Paul traveled to Ephesus for a brief stay and then proceeded on to Antioch where the second journey ended (18:22). The most dramatic experience on this trip occurred at Philippi.

The Macedonian Call

Region of Macedonia
City of Berea
City of Dion
City of Philippi
City of Thessalonica

Read Acts 16:11-12,16-40 and match the following questions on the left with the correct answers on the right. Write the correct letters in the blanks. Answers may be used more than once.[13]

____ 1. What kind of city was Philippi?

A. With anger

B. Lust

____ 2. What was wrong with the slave girl?

C. Greed

Jailed at Philippi

____ 3. What motivated the owners of the slave girl?

D. How to find peace

____ 4. How did Philippi's judicial system treat Paul and Silas?

E. A seaport

F. Released all prisoners

18 Months in Corinth

____ 5. How did Paul and Silas respond to mistreatment?

G. By the book

H. With compassion

____ 6. What damage did the earthquake cause to the prison?

Region of Achaia
Athens
Corinth
Sparta

I. Keep the commandments

____ 7. What was the jailer's question?

J. With faith

____ 8. What was Paul's answer?

K. Cost many lives

L. A Roman colony

____ 9. How was the jailer's household to be saved?

M. Possessed by a spirit

N. How to be saved

13. Answers: 1-L, 2-M, 3-C, 4-G, 5-J, 6-F, 7-N, 8-O, 9-O.

O. Believe in Jesus

PAUL'S SECOND MISSIONARY JOURNEY

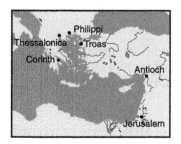

God preserved Paul and Silas through an earthquake and brought about the conversion of the jailer (16:25-34). In Corinth God appeared to Paul in a vision to assure him of safety despite difficulty (18:9-11). Paul also received a favorable judgement from the Roman governor Gallio who refused to call him a lawbreaker and rejected Jewish complaints against him (18:12-17).

🌿 **In the margin trace Paul's second missionary journey. Put a check here when you have done so. ❑ You may consult the map on page 121.**

Put a star by the city in which Paul ministered the longest on this journey.[14]

Paul continued to display boldness on this journey just as he had shown on the first. He met Priscilla and Aquila, whose friendship over the years encouraged and assisted him (18:2-3, 18-19; Rom. 16:3-4).

God protected Paul as he traveled through many situations filled with danger. He faced threats, imprisonments, and constant opposition. No one inflicted a hurt on Paul which God's grace could not overcome (2 Cor. 12:1-10).

Paul's Third Missionary Journey (18:23–21:16)

🌿 **Read Acts 18:23; 19:1,8-10,17-20; 20:17,31 and check the correct answer for each of the following questions.**[15]

1. In what areas did Paul spend most of his third missionary journey?
   ❑ a. Cities and provinces where he had never preached.
   ❑ b. Cities and provinces where he had founded churches.
   ❑ c. Cities and provinces where he earlier had failed.

Three Years at Ephesus

2. Where did Paul spend most of his time on his third missionary journey?
   ❑ a. Corinth   ❑ b. Miletus   ❑ c. Ephesus

3. How would you describe the Ephesians' response to the gospel?
   ❑ a. Good   ❑ b. Excellent   ❑ c. Phenomenal

Demetrius Led Protest

4. How long did Paul serve in Ephesus on this third missionary journey?
   ❑ a. 1 year   ❑ b. 3 years   ❑ c. 5 years

Acts contains less explicit information about Paul's third journey than it does about the other two journeys. Paul apparently passed through Asia Minor or Galatia as he began the third journey and visited some of the same churches he had seen on his first two journeys (18:23). He then journeyed to Ephesus where he spent nearly three years (19:8,10; 20:31), his longest stay at a single location in his ministry.

As Christianity spread rapidly in Ephesus sales of shrines of the goddess Artemis dropped off. This undercut the spiritual and economic influence of the worship of Artemis. Demetrius, head of the local silversmiths guild, led a public protest against the teaching of Paul. God delivered Paul from harm in this uprising (19:30-31).

After the time at Ephesus he journeyed into Macedonia where he stayed briefly. Then he traveled into Greece, likely Corinth, where he remained three months (20:3). Then he returned through Macedonia and visited Troas and Miletus.

---

14. Answer: Corinth.
15. Answers: 1-b, 2-c, 3-your response: you probably chose b or c; 4-b.

Farewell Sermon at Miletus

Arrested at Jerusalem

Paul preached to the elders of the Ephesian church in the town of Miletus, 60-70 miles from Ephesus. He shared a moving warning against greed (20:35) and a challenge to keep watch over the Ephesian congregation as God's overseers (20:28). He left Miletus and visited some of the Greek islands before landing at Tyre, Ptolemais, and Caesarea (20:3-5,17-28; 21:1-8). He was arrested abruptly in Jerusalem (21:27-36). After this arrest Paul spent two years in prison at Caesarea before he traveled to Rome for imprisonment and an appearance before Caesar (24:27).

Read Acts 21:17-36. Mark the following statements *T* (true) or *F* (false).[16]

___ 1. Thousands of Jews had become Christians in Jerusalem.
___ 2. The Jerusalem Council (Acts 15) had laid to rest the Christian Jews' prejudices against Gentile believers.
___ 3. Paul was perceived as teaching against Scripture.
___ 4. The Jerusalem elders believed the best way to lay false rumors to rest is to live them down.
___ 5. Paul had taught salvation by grace and had passed on the conclusions of the Jerusalem conference, but he had not renounced Judaism.
___ 6. The plan for Paul to participate in some rites of Judaism showed the Jews that Paul had not renounced Judaism.
___ 7. The Jews responded warmly to Paul.
___ 8. The Romans arrested Paul because they misunderstood the celebration in which he was participating.

Wrote 1–2 Corinthians

Wrote Romans

On this third journey Paul wrote 1 Corinthians during his three-year stay in Ephesus. He later wrote 2 Corinthians from Macedonia. He wrote Romans from Corinth during his three-month stay there. His three-year stay in Ephesus resulted in the spread of the gospel throughout the province of Asia (19:10). The seven churches mentioned in Revelation 2—3 probably arose from the preaching and teaching of believers in those areas during this time of Paul's ministry.

Trace on the map Paul's third missionary journey. Put a check here when you have done so. ❏ Consult the map on page 121 if needed.

Put a star by the city in which Paul ministered the longest on this journey.[17]

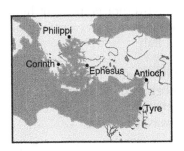

PAUL'S THIRD MISSIONARY JOURNEY

RESPONDING TO GOD'S WORD

Have you ever been terribly misunderstood? Falsely accused? The victim of a malicious rumor? Circle the words that describe how you felt: angry   bitter   tense   indifferent   calm   betrayed
Who cares?   What's the use?   I will quit.   I'm a failure.

Write here what you did about it: _____

Write here what Paul did about others' terrible treatment of him (if you know), or what you think he did in light of the Scripture in Acts.

_____

What is God saying to you? Talk to Him about it.

---

16. Answers: 1-T, 2-F, 3-T, 4-T, 5-T, 6-F, 7-F (depending on your definition of *warmly!*), 8-F.
17. Answer: Ephesus.

Day 5   *Paul's Final Years*

UNIT 8

Not Persuaded (26:28)

In Acts 26:27 Paul addressed a direct question to Agrippa and caused the king some embarrassment. Agrippa's response indicates his discomfort, "Do you think that in such a short time you can persuade me to be a Christian?" (v. 28). Whatever Agrippa thought about Paul's message, he was too prideful to commit himself in public to a movement which Festus had just called "insane" (26:24).

Agrippa Never Believed

We have no evidence that Agrippa ever became a believer. Since his time, however, we have much evidence that our faithful sharing of the gospel with others will bring lost people to Jesus. For some it requires a brief time, and for others it demands a longer time. The response of those who believe shows that God brings about spiritual changes through preaching salvation through the cross of Jesus (1 Cor. 1:18).

✍ **Mark the following statements *T* (true) or *F* (false).**[18]

    ____ 1. The way to determine whether one's witness about Jesus is effective is by immediate response of people who hear the witness.
    ____ 2. Most Christians were converted the first time they heard the gospel.
    ____ 3. Witnessing is largely a waste of time.
    ____ 4. Once a Christian has witnessed to a person, the Christian should not witness to that person again.
    ____ 5. God uses the message of the cross of Jesus to bring salvation to people.

Paul's Voyage to Rome (27:1-44)

Paul Appeals to Caesar

After Paul appealed for a trial before Caesar, the Roman governor Festus sent him to Rome. The voyage began in Caesarea when Festus put Paul in the custody of a Roman centurion aboard a vessel which sailed toward Italy.

Navigation on the Mediterranean was dangerous for sailboats after mid-September, and it was considered virtually impossible from October through February. The "fast" which had passed was the Day of Atonement celebrated in late September or early October. Sailing on the Mediterranean already was dangerous.

The ship Paul had boarded at Myra (27:5-6) fell into a storm which mercilessly pounded the helpless boat for two weeks (27:27). To keep the ship afloat, the sailors reinforced it with ropes to prevent it from breaking up (27:17). They threw overboard some of the cargo and disposed of the ship's tackle (27:18-19). Most of the passengers gave up hope of surviving the storm (27:20).

God gave a special revelation to Paul that He would preserve the ship and its passengers. Paul announced this to the crew and said, "I have faith in God that it will happen just as he told me" (27:25). Paul emerged as a leader to give direction to the crew and passengers who were caught up in despair.

Eventually the ship came to rest on an island and broke apart under the pounding of waves (27:39-41). All the crew, soldiers, and passengers survived.

---

18. Answers: 1-F, 2-F, 3-F, 4-F, 5-T.

🖋 **Read Acts 27:27-41 and check the correct ending for each of the following statements.[19]**

1. The ship had been pounded by the storm for:
   ❑ a. two weeks
   ❑ b. ten days
   ❑ c. a week

2. When the sailors realized they were approaching land, they:
   ❑ a. were joyful
   ❑ b. were fearful
   ❑ c. were relieved

3. The centurion's actions showed that he had begun:
   ❑ a. to be fed up with Paul's advice
   ❑ b. to believe that Paul knew what he was talking about
   ❑ c. to believe in Christ

4. Paul's advice during the crisis of storm was:
   ❑ a. practical
   ❑ b. spiritual
   ❑ c. both practical and spiritual

5. The ship's occupants reached shore safely:
   ❑ a. because the centurion helped them
   ❑ b. by the skin of their teeth
   ❑ c. just as Paul had prophesied

Stay on Malta

The ship came to rest on the island of Malta. The entire passengers spent the remainder of the fall and winter there and left in the spring for Rome. During Paul's stay on the island God used him in providing healing for many of those on the island (28:7-10). Paul's experience illustrates that God is often at work in some of our darkest moments to bring good and spiritual benefit out of the experience.

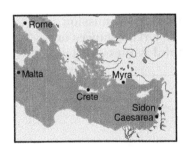

🖋 **Read Acts 27:1–28:16 and trace Paul's journey to Rome on the map in the margin. Check here when you have done so. ❑ You may consult the map on page 121 if necessary.**

Paul in Rome (28:17-31)

Paul lost no time after his arrival in Rome in making contact with Jews in the city. Three days after his arrival he called together leaders of the Jews and explained to them his desire to talk further about Jesus' fulfillment of the messianic hope of Israel (28:20).

PAUL'S TRIP TO ROME

The Jewish leaders did not want to involve themselves with Paul's legal problems, but they indicated a willingness to meet with Paul for a discussion about Christianity.

🖋 **Read Acts 28:23-31 and fill in the blanks in the following sentences.[20]**

1. On the appointed day, Paul proclaimed the gospel to a large number of _____.

2. Paul used the _____ to prove that Jesus was the Christ.

3. Some of Paul's hearers _____, and some of them did not _____.

---

19. Answers: 1-a, 2-b, 3-b, 4-c, 5-c (you could have checked a, b, or c).

4. Paul quoted the prophet _____ to rebuke unbelieving Jews and

to announce that the gospel was being sent to the more receptive _____.

5. Paul continued under house arrest for at least _____ years, and he

continued to proclaim _____.

✒ SUMMARY REVIEW

To review this unit, see if you can mentally answer the following questions. You may want to write the answers on a separate sheet of paper. Mark your level of performance on the left: circle *C* if you can answer correctly and circle *R* if you need to review.

C R   1. Describe Paul's conversion and early years as a Christian.

C R   2. When was the gospel first preached to the Gentiles? Who was the first Gentile convert?

C R   3. Briefly describe Paul's three missionary journeys, and identify those who accompanied Paul on each journey.

C R   4. Where did Paul usually proclaim Christ first in the cities he visited?

C R   5. Why is the Jerusalem Council important to us today?

C R   6. What ended Paul's public ministry, and how did he get to Rome?

Review this week's material to find the answers.

RESPONDING TO GOD'S WORD

As you recall how Paul continued to be faithful to his mission of sharing Christ with lost people regardless of the circumstances or the response, ask God to help you be a more faithful witness for Jesus Christ.

---

20. Answers: 1-Jews; 2-Scriptures; 3-believed, believe; 4-Isaiah, Gentiles; 5-two, Christ or the gospel.

Unit 9 The Writings of Paul, Part 1 (Romans)

Reading Through the New Testament

❏ Romans 1–4
❏ Romans 5–8
❏ Romans 9–12
❏ Romans 13–16
❏ Galatians
❏ 1 Thessalonians
❏ 2 Thessalonians

UNIT LEARNING GOAL: The study of this unit should help you understand Paul the person and the writing of his letters. You will be able to:
• Identify two ways Paul influenced the world.
• List several characteristics of Paul's personality.
• Describe the three sources Paul used in writing his letters.
• Explain the arrangement of Paul's letters to churches and individuals.
• Write the theme of the Book of Romans.
• Divide the Book of Romans into three major sections.

You will learn more about the life of Paul, and discover his personality traits in this unit. Also you will receive an introduction to his letters and give special attention to their sources and arrangement.

In addition, you will study the Book of Romans, which contains the most systematic statement of Christian belief in the New Testament.

Characteristics of the Letters of Paul
• Average 1,300 words in length; private letters averaged 90 words.
• Written on a papyrus sheet (about size of ordinary notebook paper)
• Written by a scribe, known as an *amanuensis*
• Always began with a petition for God's blessings on readers
• Included a greeting, main body, and farewell
• Usually concluded with lines written by his own hand
• Delivered by Paul's coworkers

Day 1 Paul's Life and Letters

UNIT 9

Paul's Uniqueness

Some persons influence life more by their writings than by their character. The writings of Karl Marx are an example of this effect. On the other hand, Jesus is a primary example of someone who made more contributions by His character and actions than by what He wrote. Jesus left no writings of His own for us to study. His actions and life have changed world history. Paul is a good example of someone who has influenced the world by both his life and his writings.

A. Fill in the blanks.[1]

1. _____ influenced the world by his writings alone.

2. _____ influenced the world by His life.

3. _____ influenced the world by his life and his writings.

B. In light of your recent study in *Step by Step*, in what Bible book would

you find much information about Paul? _____

Paul's writing style was unique. He wrote about personal beliefs he developed from real life situations. He also became personally involved with his audience in his letters. His emotions flowed onto the pages (Phil. 3:1-11). Some of his Greek sentences are very long and complex (Eph. 1:3-14 is a single sentence in Greek).

Paul's Personality

Paul's personality was as varied and sparkling as a multifaceted diamond. In matters of doctrinal importance he could be as unbending as hardened steel. In debatable issues he was pliable as rubber. His relationships with his churches alternated between sensitive love and strong rebuke.

Paul's love for his converts shines brilliantly in each of his letters. He compared his gentleness to that of a mother caring for her children (1 Thess. 2:7) and his firmness to that of a father (1 Thess. 2:11). He wrote the Philippians a thank-you note from prison (Phil. 4:10-20). He showed compassion and love for even the worldly Corinthian believers (2 Cor. 7:8-12).

Paul's will could be unyielding under pressure. He was not easily discouraged nor did trials fill him with self-pity. The Christlike character that graced his life was not merely the product of steadfast willpower. It sprang from the work of the Holy Spirit within him (1 Cor. 15:10; Gal. 5:22-24).

Paul also had unusual physical stamina. In Lystra of Asia Minor he was stoned, dragged out of the city, and left for dead by his attackers. However, the next day he left for Derbe with Barnabas (Acts 14:19-20). In 2 Corinthians 11:23-29 he listed an unbelievable variety of hardships he had personally suffered. His ability to withstand this variety of rigorous experiences testifies to his resilience and durability.

---

1. Answers: A1-Marx, A2-Jesus, A3-Paul. B-Did you answer the Book of Acts? You are absolutely correct!

Paul also possessed unusual emotional stamina. He had learned how to be content in the extremes of both poverty and plenty (Phil. 4:12-13). He could function tactfully in various delicate situations, as when he was discussing giving with the Corinthian Christians (2 Cor. 8–9). His flexibility did not indicate weakness, but he attempted to understand the viewpoint of the other person. In his personal relationships Paul maintained his principles without showing deceit (2 Cor. 4:2).

Paul aimed his most fierce outbursts at those who tried to mislead his converts. He fired a vehement rebuke at Jewish legalists who tried to trick Christians into following all aspects of the Law as a means of salvation (Gal. 1:9). He spoke forcefully and firmly to any who willfully tried to turn young Christians from their commitment to Christ (Gal. 5:12; Phil. 3:2-3).

🌿 **Check the following statements that you believe are true of Paul.[2]**

❑ 1. Paul's personality was simple and easily understood.
❑ 2. Paul was gentle and never took a dogmatic stand.
❑ 3. Paul had no patience with immature believers.
❑ 4. Paul's sensitivity often led him to change his mind.
❑ 5. Paul probably was sickly.
❑ 6. Fortunately, Paul generally was able to avoid hardships.
❑ 7. Because he lived out Christ's love, Paul never scolded or harshly rebuked anyone.

RESPONDING TO GOD'S WORD

Read again Philippians 2:25-30 noting the description of Epaphroditus. Can your church leaders use any of those terms about you?
❑ Yes ❑ No **Should they be able to do so?** ❑ Yes ❑ No
What would have to change in your life for those terms to fit you?

_____

In prayer offer yourself anew to serve the Lord, regardless of sacrifice.

Day 2 *Events in Paul's Life*

UNIT 9

We can better understand the letters of Paul by first understanding Paul the man of God. The history of Paul's life and his personality are keys to our understanding. The following paragraphs provide a quick review of Paul's life. Also, we will look at some general information about Paul's letters, and try to relate them chronologically to Paul's life. Be sure to do all the suggested activities.

Paul's Early Years

Born in Tarsus

Paul was born in Tarsus, in the Roman province of Cilicia (Acts 21:39; 22:3).

---

2. Answers: If you checked any of the above, read again the section "Paul's Personality." None are true of Paul.

🌿 **Draw a circle around Cilicia on the adjoining map.**

Although the city had a university of significant importance, Paul probably did not study there. However, he no doubt absorbed much of the Greek culture of the city.

As a Jew Paul came from the tribe of Benjamin (Phil. 3:5), but he was also born a Roman citizen (Acts 22:25-29). Paul obtained an education in Jewish law (Acts 23:6). He studied in Jerusalem under the great rabbi Gamaliel (Acts 22:3). He dedicated himself to the study of the law and demonstrated zeal for God (Acts 26:5). His persecution of Christians proved his fervor for Judaism (Acts 22:4-5; Phil 3:6).

Paul's Conversion

From Enemy to Apostle

Three Years in Arabia/ Damascus

Unexpectedly, Paul's conversion on the Damascus Road changed his life (Acts 9:1-9). The encounter with Christ transformed him from Christ's enemy to His apostle. Immediately after his conversion Paul began to preach (Acts 9:20). During his three years in Arabia and Damascus (Gal. 1:17-18), Paul's experience with Christ shaped his life and theology. At one time in those early years he met such opposition from the Jews that he fled to Jerusalem (Acts 9:23-26). He later returned to Tarsus where he remained for several years (Acts 9:26-30).

🌿 **Answer the following questions.[3]**

1. Paul was converted on the road to what city? _____

2. After his conversion, what did Paul do in that city? _____

3. Where did Paul spend three years? _____

4. What happened in Paul's life during those years? _____

_____

5. What precipitated Paul's return to Jerusalem? _____

6. Where did Paul spend the years immediately after leaving Jerusalem?

_____

Barnabas Brings Paul to Antioch

Later Barnabas became involved in a growing Christian work in Antioch and sought Paul's assistance (Acts 11:22-26). The pair toiled with great success in Antioch. After a year of ministry in the city the Christians there sent Paul and Barnabas to Jerusalem with an offering for famine-stricken believers (Acts 11:27-30).

Paul's First Missionary Journey

Paul and Barnabas returned to Antioch after ministry in Jerusalem and brought John Mark with them (Acts 12:25). This three-man team later left on the first missionary journey to Cyprus and Asia Minor (Acts 13–14). Mark left the team in the middle of the journey (Acts 13:13), but Paul and Barnabas continued their ministry and planted churches throughout the largely Gentile territory. After completing the journey, they returned to Antioch for a lengthy visit and report to the church (Acts 14:27-28).

---

3. Answers: 1-Damascus; 2-preached Christ; 3-Arabia and Damascus; 4-Paul's life and theology were reshaped through His relationship with Christ; 5-Jewish opposition; 6-Tarsus.

Paul's Galatian Letter

The Jerusalem Council

The first journey produced some questions about the relationship of Gentiles to the law of Moses. Paul's letter to the Galatians, which probably was written after the first missionary journey, deals with this potentially explosive problem. The church at Antioch sent Paul and Barnabas to Jerusalem for a conference to help settle this question. The decision of the council called for Gentiles to respect Jewish scruples about diet and avoid immorality. However, it recognized their freedom from the Mosaic law as a means of salvation (Acts 15:23-29).

🌿 **Check the correct ending for each of the following statements.[4]**

1. Paul's direct involvement in Christian ministry was due to the efforts of:
   ❏ a. John Mark ❏ b. Barnabas ❏ c. Peter

2. Paul served with his Christian friend in:
   ❏ a. Cilicia ❏ b. Tarsus ❏ c. Antioch

3. Paul went on a mission of mercy to
   ❏ a. Cyprus ❏ b. Jerusalem ❏ c. Damascus

4. Paul's companions on his first missionary journey were:
   ❏ a. Barnabas and Luke ❏ b. Silas and Titus
   ❏ c. John Mark and Barnabas

5. One who did not complete the missionary journey was:
   ❏ a. John Mark ❏ b. Silas ❏ c. Luke

6. The reason for Paul's next journey to Jerusalem was:
   ❏ a. to bring aid to famine victims
   ❏ b. to convince the church leaders he truly was saved
   ❏ c. to settle questions concerning Gentiles and the law

Paul's Second and Third Missionary Journeys

Silas, Not Barnabas

Timothy, Not John Mark

1–2 Thessalonians

After returning from Jerusalem to Antioch, Paul took Silas on a second missionary journey through Asia Minor, Macedonia, and Greece (Acts 15:36–18:22). Timothy became a part of the group as they passed through Asia Minor (Acts 16:1-3). Paul used his helpers (1 Thess. 3:1-3; Acts 18:5) and letters (to the Thessalonians) to maintain contact with the developing young churches.

Ephesus for Three Years

1–2 Corinthians, Romans

Paul's third missionary journey also originated in Antioch of Syria. During this trip, Paul remained in Ephesus, where he wrote 1 Corinthians, for nearly three years (Acts 20:31). On a later trip to Macedonia he sent 2 Corinthians to Corinth. During a three-month visit in Greece (Acts 20:1-3) he wrote Romans.

🌿 **List three letters Paul wrote on his third missionary journey.[5]**

1. _____

2. _____

3. _____

---

4. Answers: 1-b, 2-c, 3-b, 4-c, 5-a, 6-c.
5. Answers: 1 and 2 Corinthians and Romans.

After he had concluded his third missionary journey, Paul returned to Jerusalem with a collection for the poor (Acts 21:1-15; Rom. 15:25-27). Here Jewish pilgrims wrongly accused him of bringing a Gentile into the temple, and he was arrested (Acts 21:26-36).

Paul's Arrest, Imprisonment, and Death

Framework of Paul's Life

- Death, Resurrection of Christ—A.D. 29

- Conversion of Paul— A.D. 32

- First Missionary Journey —A.D. 47-49

- Council in Jerusalem (Acts 15)—A.D .49

- Second Missionary Journey—A.D. 50–52

- Third Missionary Journey —A.D. 53–57

- Arrival at Rome—A.D. 61

- End of First Roman Imprisonment—A.D. 63

- Second Roman Imprisonment? —A.D. 66–67

- Martyrdom—A.D. 67

The Romans took Paul to Caesarea, where the governor Felix left him in prison for two years (Acts 24:27). Paul presented moving defenses of his innocence of the Jewish charges before Felix and his successor Festus. Despairing of receiving justice from Roman representatives, he used his Roman citizenship to request a trial before Caesar himself (Acts 25:1-12). Festus sent Paul to Rome on what proved to be a near-fatal journey (Acts 27:1-44). After arriving in Rome, Paul remained imprisoned for two additional years (Acts 28:30-31). He used his time of Roman imprisonment to engage in bold preaching to all who visited him. During his stay, he also wrote the prison letters; Philippians, Colossians, Ephesians, and Philemon.

Write your response to the following.[6]

1. Explain why Philippians, Colossians, Ephesians, and Philemon are called the Prison Letters.

_____

2. Where was Paul when Luke finished writing the Book of Acts?

_____

Evidence from Paul's Pastoral Letters and from the early church fathers suggests that the Romans eventually released Paul from this initial imprisonment. During this release he wrote 1 Timothy and Titus and visited Crete, Asia Minor, and Macedonia. During a second Roman imprisonment Paul wrote 2 Timothy. He likely was executed under Nero during this imprisonment.

Check the following Bible books that are included in Paul's Pastoral Letters.[7]

- ❑ 1. Colossians
- ❑ 2. 1–2 Corinthians
- ❑ 3. Ephesians
- ❑ 4. Galatians
- ❑ 5. Philemon

- ❑ 6. Philippians
- ❑ 7. Romans
- ❑ 8. 1–2 Thessalonians
- ❑ 9. 1–2 Timothy
- ❑ 10. Titus

RESPONDING TO GOD'S WORD

Read Acts 20:22-24 and spend a few moments meditating on verse 24. What principles in this verse would be worthy life goals for you to adopt? Talk to the Lord about that in prayer right now.

---

6. Answers: 1-They were written during Paul's imprisonment in Rome; 2-In prison in Rome.
7. Answers: 9 and 10.

Day 3

Sources and Arrangement of Paul's Letters

U N I T   9

Paul's Sources

In 2 Timothy 3:16 Paul said, "All Scripture is God-breathed."

🌿 **Read 2 Timothy 3:16 and answer the following questions.**[8]

1. What does this verse say about all Scripture?_____

2. List the four things Scripture is useful for:

A. _____   B. _____

C. _____   D. _____

3. What is the goal of using Scripture for these purposes?

_____

God Spoke

God speaking through the Holy Spirit was the ultimate source of Paul's writing and theology. Paul knew that God had given him special revelation and authority for teaching in the churches (Acts 26:19-20; Gal. 1:11-17; Eph. 3:2-7). Even the Apostle Peter designated Paul's writings as Scriptures (2 Pet. 3:16).

Holy Spirit's Guidance

The Holy Spirit guided Paul in his writing and doctrine. The Holy Spirit evidently led Paul to draw on at least three sources in writing his letters:
• The doctrinal teachings of the early church
• The Old Testament
• Special revelation through the Holy Spirit

First, Paul received some of his teachings from the doctrines of the early church. Scholars have concluded that early Christians even expressed some of their doctrinal statements in songs. Possibly such sections of Paul's writings as Philippians 2:6-11; Colossians 1:15-17; and 2 Timothy 2:11-13 originally were hymns. Christians also expressed their beliefs in statements of faith. A statement of faith probably served as the source of Paul's teaching in 1 Corinthians 15:1-7 and Romans 10:9-10.

Old Testament

Second, Paul used the Old Testament as a source of teaching and writing. He interpreted some Old Testament passages in the light of Christ's person and work (see Eph. 4:8). He occasionally strung together passages from various parts of the Old Testament to support an argument he made. In Romans 3:10-18 Paul cited several passages from the Psalms and one from Isaiah to buttress his statement that human beings were sinful.

🌿 **Read Ephesians 3:1-7 and answer the following question.**[9]

How did Paul learn of God's grace to the Gentiles?_____

---

8. Answers: Compare your answers with mine—1. It is God-breathed or inspired; its source is God. 2-A, teaching truth, B, rebuking wrong, C, correcting behavior, D, training in doing right. 3-To be equipped or ready to take advantage of every opportunity to do good.
9. Answer: God's Spirit revealed it to him.

Special Revelations

The special revelations God gave him through the Holy Spirit constituted the third source of Paul's teaching and writing. God revealed to Paul the place of the Gentiles in His plan (Eph. 3:1-7), explained the justifying, redeeming, and reconciling work of Christ (Rom. 3:21-26; 5:10-11; Gal 3:13, 14), and gave him a knowledge of the order of resurrection when Jesus returns (1 Thess. 4:13-18).

Fountainhead of Theology

Paul was not, as some would claim, merely a mouthpiece who passed along the traditions of the church. He served as a Christ-called and Christ-centered fountainhead for the theology of the early church under the inspiration of the Holy Spirit.

Arrangement of Paul's Letters

In Order of Length

The translated New Testaments we have generally present Paul's letters in accord with their length. The order of appearance is not chronological. Romans is Paul's longest letter, and it stands first in the collection. Philemon is the shortest and stands last.

Nine Letters to Churches

First in the collection of Paul's letters are nine letters to seven churches (Romans, 1–2 Corinthians, Galatians, Ephesians, Philippians, Colossians, 1–2 Thessalonians).

Four Letters to Individuals

These nine letters are followed by four letters to three individuals (1–2 Timothy, Titus, and Philemon).

A. Mark the following statements *T* (true) or *F* (false).[10]

____ 1. Paul's letters in the New Testament are in chronological order.
____ 2. Paul's letters in the New Testament are arranged according to importance.
____ 3. Paul's letters in the New Testament are arranged according to length.
____ 4. The longest of Paul's letters is 1 Corinthians.
____ 5. The shortest of Paul's letters is Philemon.
____ 6. The shortest of Paul's letters is Titus.
____ 7. The longest of Paul's letters is Romans.
____ 8. The New Testament contains nine letters written by Paul to nine churches.
____ 9. The New Testament contains 13 letters written by Paul.

B. Fill in Paul's nine letters to churches on the rules in the margin. Also fill in Paul's four letters to individuals.

CHRONOLOGICAL ARRANGEMENT OF PAUL'S LETTERS

1. At the end of the first missionary journey: Galatians
2. During the second missionary journey: 1–2 Thessalonians
3. During the third missionary journey: Romans, 1–2 Corinthians
4. During Paul's first Roman imprisonment: Philippians, Ephesians, Colossians, Philemon
5. Before and during Paul's last Roman imprisonment: 1–2 Timothy, Titus

---

Paul's Galatian Letter

The forceful letter to the Galatians probably was written at the end of Paul's first missionary journey (though scholars sometimes disagree concerning the date). The letter clarified the meaning of the gospel Paul had preached (Gal. 1:6-17).

10. Answers: A-1,F; 2,F; 3,T; 4,F; 5,T; 6,F; 7,T; 8,F; 9,T. B-See above paragraph.

1–2 Thessalonians

Paul wrote 1–2 Thessalonians during his second missionary journey. The occasion was the completion of a visit to Thessalonica. Paul instructed the growing young congregation about affliction (1 Thess. 3:1-5), morality (1 Thess. 4:3-8), and the return of Christ (1 Thess. 4:13-18; 5:1-11; 2 Thess. 2:1-10).

Romans

1–2 Corinthians

Paul wrote his major letters of Romans and 1–2 Corinthians during this third missionary journey. Romans clarifies our understanding of Jesus' death (Rom. 3:21-26). All three letters cover an amazing variety of local church problems along with the solutions proposed by Paul (Rom. 14:1-10; 1 Cor. 5:1-8; 2 Cor. 8:1–9:15).

🌿 Fill in the blanks.[11]

1. Paul wrote Romans and 1 and 2 Corinthians while on his_____

2. The basic thrust of Romans is to clarify the meaning of_____

3. The letters to Corinth speak to a variety of_____

Philippians, Ephesians, Colossians, Philemon

We designate Paul's fourth group of letters as the Prison Letters (Philippians, Ephesians, Colossians, Philemon). They were written during Paul's first imprisonment in Rome. The writings contain vivid proofs of the strength God gave Paul during the pressure of imprisonment (Phil. 1:12-18). They present Christ as the Lord of both the universe and the church (Eph. 1:20-23; Col.1:14-18). The letter to Philemon contains a marvelous appeal for Christian love toward a former slave, Onesimus.

1–2 Timothy and Titus

Paul's final group of writings is called the Pastoral Letters (1–2 Timothy, Titus). They were written before and during his second and final imprisonment in Rome. Most scholars believe that Paul wrote 1 Timothy and Titus during a period of release. He wrote 2 Timothy when he faced the possibility of death (2 Tim. 4:6-8). He wrote all of these letters to provide direction in dealing with the problem of heresy in the churches at Ephesus and on the island of Crete.

🌿 Draw a line from the period on the left to the letter Paul wrote during that period on the right.[12]

1. End of first journey	a. Colossians
	b. 1–2 Corinthians
2. Second journey	c. Ephesians
	d. Galatians
3. Third journey	e. Philemon
	f. Philippians
4. First imprisonment	g. Romans
	h. 1–2 Thessalonians
5. Release/second imprisonment	i. 1–2 Timothy
	j. Titus

---

11 . Answers: 1-third missionary journey, 2-Christ's death, 3-church problems.
12. Answers: 1-d, 2-h, 3-b, g, 4-a,c,e,f, 5-i, j.

RESPONDING TO GOD'S WORD

Read Ephesians 4:25 at least four times. The first time stress the word *each* in the verse. The second time stress the word *falsehood*. The third time stress the word *truthfully*. The fourth time stress the word *neighbor*. Write below some of the insights that came to you.

_____

_____

_____

Thank the Lord for speaking to you through this part of Paul's letter.

Day 4   *Introduction to Romans*

UNIT 9

Most Doctrinal

Most Important

Doctrine of Justification

Romans is the most doctrinal letter and the most important document that Paul wrote. Unlike many of his other writings, it was not written just to address church problems. Paul wanted to prepare his Roman friends for a visit (Rom. 15:22-24) by building up the believers in their knowledge and by encouraging Jewish and Gentile believers to work together for the spread of the gospel. Paul's chief subject in Romans concerned the doctrine of justification by grace (in this book you will find the most systematic treatment in the New Testament of this doctrine), and the theme of this book is salvation by faith in Jesus Christ.

What was Paul's chief theme in the Book of Romans?[13]

_____

11 Chapters of Doctrine

Five Chapters on Christian Living

The first 11 chapters of Romans contain an outline of important features of Paul's theology. The final five chapters feature an application of these truths in daily living. This arrangement shows that Christianity is more than a collection of facts to be believed. It is also a lifestyle we must follow. Our own actions must reflect that Christianity is both a system of truth and a right response in obedience to that truth.

Date and Place of Writing

A. Read 1 Corinthians 16:1-4 and 2 Corinthians 8:1-7; 9:1-2. About what was Paul writing in those verses? Check your answer.[14]

❑ 1. The importance of tithing
❑ 2. Methods of planned giving
❑ 3. The collection for the poor in Judea
❑ 4. The way to get rich
❑ 5. Sacrificial giving

---

13. Answer: You may have written something like "salvation by faith in Jesus Christ," or "justification by grace through faith in Jesus Christ."

B. Read Romans 15:25-26. Based on the Scriptures you read in the previous question, check the correct statement among the following.

    ❑ 1. Romans was written after 1 Corinthians but before 2 Corinthians.
    ❑ 2. Romans was written after 1–2 Corinthians.
    ❑ 3. Romans was written before 1–2 Corinthians.
    ❑ 4. Romans was written about the same time as 1–2 Corinthians.

In 1 Corinthians 16:1-4 and 2 Corinthians 8–9 Paul urged the Corinthian church to collect funds for the poor believers in Jerusalem. By the time Paul wrote Romans the church had finished this task (Rom. 15:25-26). Paul was about to start his journey to Jerusalem with the gifts for the Jewish Christians there. These facts show that Romans was written after 2 Corinthians.

Written from Corinth

In Acts 20:3 we learn that Paul spent three months in the region of Greece after having visited the region of Macedonia. He likely wrote Romans from Corinth around the year A.D. 57. Additional evidence for writing from Corinth is the mention of Gaius (Rom. 16:23), who may be the same Gaius as is mentioned in 1 Corinthians 1:14. In Romans 16:1 Paul introduced Phoebe to his readers. The fact that she was from the city of Cenchrea near Corinth and likely was heading to Rome shows again that Corinth is the probable place for writing the letter.

Theme and Purpose

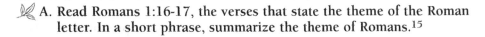 **A. Read Romans 1:16-17, the verses that state the theme of the Roman letter. In a short phrase, summarize the theme of Romans.**[15]

_____

B. Read Romans 1:11-15 and 15:22-24. Mark the following statements *T* (true) or *F* (false).

    ____ 1. Paul wrote to the Romans because he had no plans to travel there.
    ____ 2. Paul wanted to make a spiritual contribution to the believers in Rome.
    ____ 3. Paul believed the believers in Rome could be a blessing to him.
    ____ 4. Paul wanted to lead Gentiles in Rome to faith in Christ.
    ____ 5. Paul wanted the Romans to help him in his missionary efforts.

To Prepare for His Visit

The chief aim for Paul's writing Romans was to prepare the people for his first visit there. He long had intended to visit the city, but circumstances had prevented it (1:13; 15:22-24). Paul's writing in anticipation of his visit was part of an effort to strengthen the Roman Christians in their faith (1:11-15).

Theme of Romans: Salvation Through Faith in Jesus Christ (1:16-17)

Outline

Introduction (1:1-17)
  I. God's Plan of Salvation (1–8)
  II. God's Plan for Israel and the Gentiles (9–11)
 III. God's Plan for Christian Living (12–15:13)
Personal Plans and Greetings (15:14–16:27)

Paul sought to strengthen his readers by outlining God's plan of salvation (1–8) and by showing how Jews and Gentiles fitted into that plan (9–11).Based on God's

---

14. Answers: A-3; B-2.
15. Answers: A-the gospel of salvation by faith in Jesus Christ; B-1-F, 2-T, 3-T, 4-T, 5-T.

gracious plan of salvation, he urged his readers to live lives of holiness, harmony and service (12–16). Paul's wrote to strengthen his readers in their knowledge of the faith, encourage them to cooperate as fellow Christians, and to seek their prayer support for the difficulty of his coming journey to Jerusalem (15:30-32).

🌿 **Write a three-point outline of the Book of Romans using the following divisions.**[16]

1. Chapters 1–8: _____

2. Chapters 9–11: _____

3. Chapters 12–16: _____

Special Issues in Romans

Founding the church at Rome. We know very little about the beginning of Christianity in Rome. Acts 18:2 records that the Roman emperor Claudius had banned Jews from Rome. The date of his decree is around A. D. 49-50. The Roman writer Suetonius stated that the reason for the expulsion order was the unrest caused by the instigation of Chrestus. Many Bible students see a similarity between the names Chrestus and Christus (Christ) and feel that the preaching of Jesus as the Messiah had aroused the Jews to riots and unrest. This would be external evidence that Christianity was already in Rome before the middle of the first century.

Some visitors from Rome were present at the Day of Pentecost in Jerusalem (Acts 2:10). Perhaps some of the converts from this experience carried the gospel back to their native city. Many trade and communication links existed between Rome and Antioch. It is also possible that Christians from Antioch brought the gospel to Rome.

Peter Did Not Begin Church

Did Peter found the Roman church? It is hardly likely. Acts places Peter in Palestine up to and including the time of the Jerusalem Council in A.D. 50. In the mid-50s Paul mentioned that Peter was in the east engaged in missionary work (1 Cor. 9:5). Since Paul did not include a greeting to Peter in the Roman letter, it is unlikely that he was there when Paul wrote his letter. Statements in 1 Peter 5:13 suggest that Peter was in Rome in the sixties, but Christianity had already come to Rome by this time.

Peter and Paul Later Martyred in Rome

Church tradition suggests that both Peter and Paul were later martyred in Rome. Both apostles might have become martyrs making an effort to build up and develop the Roman church. The church had been founded at an earlier time, but Peter and Paul may have given their lives in an attempt to promote its spiritual growth.

🌿 **Read Galatians 2:9. According to this verse, the major target group**

of Paul's ministry was to be the _____.[17]

Both Jewish and Gentile Believers

Jews and Gentiles in the church. Romans contains references to the Old Testament, which may be evidence that the Christian church there was largely Jewish. Paul's lengthy discussion about the future of Israel in Romans 9–11 also supports this view, as does his reference in 1:16 "to the Jew first" (phrase found only in Rom.). Paul, however, felt that his unique labor was among the Gentiles. It is not likely that he would have written this letter to a chiefly Jewish congregation (Gal. 2:9). The best supposition is that the church was a mixture of both Jewish and Gentile "house

---

16. Answer: Your response.
17. Answer: Gentiles.

churches" (see Rom. 16). Paul's statement in 1:13 refers to "other Gentiles" and suggests that he was writing some words to Gentiles in the Roman church. His reference to himself as "the apostle to the Gentiles" in 11:13 also suggests that the Roman church had a sizable number of Gentile members.

Answer the following questions.[18]

    1. What indicates that the Roman church had a number of Jewish members?

    _____

    2. What indicates that the Roman church had a number of Gentile members?

    _____

Personal greetings. One of the unusual features of Romans is the long list of greetings to friends and acquaintances in Romans 16. The list is unusually long for a city Paul had never visited. He may have sent this lengthy list to establish friendly relationships with people there. The letter to the Christians at Colosse, another city Paul had never visited, also contained a list of hearty welcomes.

RESPONDING TO GOD'S WORD

    Read the benediction in Romans 16:20. Meditate on those words. Is God speaking to you through this verse about some particular circumstance in your life? Write the message here.

_____

Read the doxology in 16:25-27. Pray for God to establish you more firmly on the foundation of the gospel of Christ that God has revealed to you.

Day 5   *Overview of Romans*

U N I T   9

Outline

Theme of Romans: Salvation Through Faith in Jesus Christ (1:16-17)

Introduction (1:1-17)
  I. God's Plan of Salvation (1:18–8:39)
    A. All Have Sinned (1:18–3:20)
    B. God's Redemption in Christ (3:21–5:21)
    C. God's Life-Changing Power (6–8)
 II. God's Plan for Israel and the Gentiles (9–11)
III. God's Plan for Christian Living (12–15:13)
Personal Plans and Greetings (15:14–16:27)

---

18. Answers: 1-You may have written that Romans has many Old Testament references or that chapters 9—11 focus on the future of Israel; 2-You may have cited Romans 1:13 or Paul's reference to himself as the apostle to the Gentiles in 11:13.

Salvation: A Deliverance

Righteousness: A Gift

Faith: A Total Response

The theme of Romans is *righteousness through faith in Jesus Christ* (1:16-17). Three words that are parts of that theme will become significant in Paul's discussion throughout the book. To Paul *salvation* was a deliverance from the past penalty of sin (Eph. 2:8), the present power of sin (Phil. 2:12-13), and the future presence of sin (Heb. 9:28). Paul considered *righteousness* both a conformity to an unchanging standard (unattainable by human effort alone, Rom. 14:17) and a gift of right standing with God by faith in Jesus Christ (Rom. 5:1). *Faith* was a response of the whole person to God's revelation in Christ. It included the understanding of the intellect, the depth of the emotions, and the commitment of the will.

Read Romans 1:16-17 and underline the words *salvation, righteousness,* and *faith.* **Define those words here.**[19]

A. Salvation: ———————————————————————

B. Righteousness: ———————————————————————

C. Faith: ———————————————————————

All Have Sinned (Rom. 1:18–3:20)

Wickedness and Immorality (1:18-32)

After the key verses (1:16-17), Paul demonstrated that all Gentiles (both Greeks and barbarians) lacked this righteousness (1:18-32) and were condemned for their sinful attitudes and behavior before a holy God. To prove this, Paul pointed out that heathen religion involved a rejection of the revealed truth of God and a substitution of idolatry (1:18-25). This rejection led to the production of wickedness and immorality (1:25-32).

Read Romans 1:18-25 and answer the following questions.[20]

1. How do people suppress God's revealed truth?———————————

2. How has God revealed His power and nature to all people? ———————

3. What did people choose to worship rather than God? ———————

Jews Also Guilty (2:1–3:8)

Paul also showed the guilt of the Jews. In 2:1-24 he presented God's judgement on the Jews. Both morally and religiously the Jews failed to meet divine standards (2:17-29). Although the Jews had the advantage of God's word (3:1-8), they had failed to believe and obey it; and they found themselves facing the vengeance of God.

All Stand Guilty (3:9-20)

Paul collected a mosaic of Old Testament Scriptures to show that the human tongue, lips, mouth, eyes, and feet were inclined toward sin. All flesh, both Jew and Gentile, stood guilty before God (3:9).

God's Redemption in Christ (Rom. 3:21–5:21)

Righteousness for All (3:21–5:21)

From 3:21 through 5:21 Paul demonstrated that God had provided righteousness through the death of Jesus so that all people could experience forgiveness by faith in Christ. In 3:21-31 Paul used three key words that relate to the role of Christ in preparing the way of righteousness.

Read Romans 3:21-31 and underline the words *justified, redemption,* and *atonement* **if they are in the translation you use.**

---

19. Answers: A-deliverance from the past penalty of sin; B-conformity to an unchanging standard and a gift of right standing with God by faith in Jesus Christ; C-response of the whole person to God';s revelation in Christ.

20. Answers: Your answers should contain these ideas, though you may have expressed them differently; 1-By their wickedness; 2-Through His creation; 3-Things that God created.

Atonement—Christ Turned Aside God's Wrath

Redemption—Christ Purchased Our Freedom

Justification—Believers Declared Righteous

The term translated *atonement* (3:25) teaches that the blood of Christ has met the demands of a holy God to punish sin, and turned aside God's wrath against us. Christ's sacrificial death provides the basis for our reconciliation to God. *Redemption* (3:24) is a term borrowed from the practice of slavery in that day. It teaches that Christ has paid the price to purchase freedom for believers from the penalty and practice of sin. *Justification* (3:24) teaches that in Christ each believer is declared righteous by God when the believer puts his faith in Jesus Christ.

🌿 **Match the words on the left with the correct definitions on the right.**[21]

___ 1. Justification   A. Turned aside God's wrath against sin
___ 2. Redemption   B. Declared to be righteous
___ 3. Atonement   C. Deliverance from slavery of sin

God's Salvation Is Just (3:21-31)

God's salvation is just or fair because it is apart from the law (3:21) and available for all through faith in Jesus Christ (3:22).

🌿 **Read Romans 3:21-26 and check the following statements that accurately reflect the teachings in this passage of Scripture.**[22]
   ❑ 1. Righteousness comes from God apart from law.
   ❑ 2. Righteousness comes through faith in Christ.
   ❑ 3. All have sinned.
   ❑ 4. All are justified (declared to be righteous).
   ❑ 5. All who believe in Jesus are justified.
   ❑ 6. God was unjust because He had not punished sins.

Abraham Justified by Faith (4:1-25)

In 4:1-25 Paul answered the question of how Old Testament believers received righteousness. He used the example of Abraham to show that God's way of salvation had always been by grace through faith. Abraham's righteousness was by faith (4:11) and independent of all contact with the Law of Moses (4:13). God's reception of Abraham by faith is an example of the way He receives all believers.
In 5:1-11 Paul showed the effects of justification in the life of the believer.

🌿 **Read Romans 5:1-11. Underline the benefits of justification.**[23]

Effects of Justification (5:1-11)

This justification produces peace with God (5:1) and is provided by the love of God (5:8). Because God loved us when we were sinners, He will continue to impart His love and life to us as His children (5:9-10).

Christ the Second Adam

In 5:12-21 Paul described Christ as the Second Adam and contrasted the opposite results of the acts of these two Adams. By a single act Adam produced death for all mankind (5:12). In a single act of righteousness Christ obtained righteousness for all who have believed (5:17). Where sin was present because of the work of Adam, grace superabounded in the gracious work of Christ (5:21).

God's Life-Changing Power (Rom. 6–8)

From 6:1 through 8:39 Paul unfolded the power of God's righteousness in transforming individual Christians. He demonstrated that a life of righteousness was a life filled with holiness (chap. 6), free from the law (chap. 7), and made possible by the work of the Holy Spirit (chap. 8).

---

21. Answers: 1-B, 2-C, 3-A.
22. Answers: Did you check 1, 2, 3, 5? Excellent! If you checked 4 and 6, read the passage again.
2. 3Answers: You could have underlined the following: peace with God, access (to God), rejoice in the hope of the glory of God, rejoice in our sufferings, God has poured out his love into our heart, Holy Spirit whom he has given us, reconciled to (God), saved from God's wrath, saved through (Christ's) life, rejoice in God.

Read Romans 6:1-4. Explain here the meaning of being baptized.[24]

_____

Baptism Shows ...

Death to Sin

New Life in Christ

In the act of baptism Christians demonstrate their death to sin and new life in Christ (6:4,6,11). Because of these changes all believers must recognize their new position in Christ and present themselves in service to God (6:12-13). Freedom from sin does not produce careless living under free grace, but it promotes righteous service to God (6:18). Christians also have received freedom from the sin-arousing influence of the law (7:1-6). Even though the law can stimulate sin (7:9-11), Paul found victory in Christ Jesus to overcome the enticing effect of the law (7:25).

 Read Romans 8:1-4 and check the correct ending for each of the following statements.[25]

1. People who are in Christ Jesus are those who
   ❏ a. are church members
   ❏ b. have received Christ into their lives by faith
   ❏ c. have been baptized

2. People in Christ
   ❏ a. don't have to worry about sinning anymore
   ❏ b. are not condemned for their sins
   ❏ c. no longer commit any sins

3. Knowing the law is not enough to produce righteous living because
   ❏ a. we can never know all of it
   ❏ b. we tend to explain away parts of it
   ❏ c. we have a sinful nature

4. God has given people who believe in Jesus His Holy Spirit so that
   ❏ a. they will be able to live righteous lives
   ❏ b. they will feel spiritual
   ❏ c. they can sin without feeling guilty

Holy Spirit Indwells Each Believer

This victory in Christ comes through the Holy Spirit who indwells and provides power for each believer (8:1-17). The Holy Spirit will conform perfectly each believer to Jesus Christ at the time of the future resurrection (8:23). Nothing can separate us from a God who loved us enough to take us from the darkness of sin to the brightness of His presence (Rom. 8:38-39).

God's Plan for Israel and the Gentiles (Rom. 9–11)

Jews' Rejection of God's Messiah (9:1-29)

In 9:1–11:36 Paul defended and explained God's dealings with the nation of Israel. He began with a discussion of God's absolute sovereignty (9:1-29). Some were claiming that God had rejected His people, but Paul pointed out that it was Israel who had rejected the Messiah. He further stated that God was not unrighteous in His dealings with Israel (9:14-24).

Jews' Rejection by God (9:30–10:21)

In 9:30–10:21 Paul showed the Jewish responsibility for rejection by God. In 9:30–10:13 he pointed out that the Jews had willfully ignored God's way of righteousness and had attempted to establish their own method of righteousness.

_____

24. Answer: Your response could be something like this: Baptism signifies that our old life is dead and buried and that we live a new life in the strength of the risen Christ.
25. Answers: 1-b, 2-b, 3-c, 4-a.

🌿 **Read Romans 9:30–10:4.**[26]

    1. Write the names of the two groups of people discussed in this passage.

        A. _____ B._____

    2. Write the two approaches to righteousness discussed in this passage.

        A. _____ B._____

    3. Write the means God has chosen to provide righteousness:_____

**Future Glory of Israel
(11:1-32)**

In 10:16-21 Paul stated that the Jews were without excuse because they had rejected the gospel they had heard. He discussed the future glory of Israel in 11:1-32. He indicated that the rejection of the Jews was partial and not complete (11:1-10).

🌿 **Read Romans 11:1. What argument did Paul use to show that God had not rejected His people, the Israelites?**[27]

_____

**Future Conversion
of the Jews**

Paul's own position as a believer showed that not all Jews were unbelievers. He also showed the rejection of the Jews was temporary and not final (11:11-15). Paul stated that a repentant Israel could be brought back into God's program (11:16-24) and expressed confidence in the future conversion of the Jews (11:25-32). He concluded with a passionate outburst of praise (11:33-36).

God's Plan for Christian Living (Rom. 12:1–15:13)

Put Faith into Practice

Paul called his readers to put their Christian faith into practice in 12:1—15:13. After a stirring appeal for self-consecration (12:1-2), he outlined duties to God and other Christians (12:3-21), described responsibilities to the state and others (13:1-14), and outlined the relationships between weak and strong Christians (14:1—15:13).

🌿 **Read Romans 12:1-2 and fill in the blanks in the following statements.**[28]

    1. Paul urged believers to offer themselves as living sacrifices because

       of the _____ God has shown to them.

    2. Christians are not to _____ to the pattern of _____ but

       are to be _____ by the renewing of their _____.

    3. Those who carry out God's will find that it is _____, and _____.

Love for Neighbors

Paul outlined relationships between believers in society (12:3-21) and between Christians and their governments (13:1-7). He appealed for Christians to demonstrate love for all of their neighbors (13:8-10).

In 14:1 through 15:13 Paul discussed Christian liberty in matters of moral uncertainty. As an example, Paul presented a "strong" believer and a "weak" believer.

---

26. Answers: 1A-Gentiles, 1B-Israelites; 2A-works, 2B-faith; 3-Faith in Christ.
27. Answer: Your answer should reflect that Paul was an Israelite whom God had not rejected.
28. Answers: 1-mercy; 2-conform, this world, transformed, minds; 3-good, pleasing, perfect.

Strong and Weak Believers

Paul urged both the weaker and the stronger brother to respect the other (14:3). He urged both groups to be persuaded in their own minds (14:5) and he directed the "strong" brother not to place a temptation in the path of a "weaker" brother (14:20).

🌿 **Read Romans 14:13-21 and check the statements with which you agree.**[29]

❑ 1. Christians should concentrate on not doing things that may lead others astray rather than on passing judgment on one another.
❑ 2. Christians should avoid practices that they think are wrong, even if other Christians see no harm in those practices.
❑ 3. God is pleased when Christians avoid practices that other believers see as wrong, even if those practices are not wrong in themselves.
❑ 4. If a Christian views a practice as wrong when actually it is not wrong, other Christians should encourage that person to become involved in the practice in order to learn that it is not wrong.
❑ 5. Christians' actions are to be governed by the principles of peace and mutual edification, not by the principle of personal rights.

Personal Plans and Greetings (Rom. 15:14–16:27)

In his conclusion (15:14–16:27) Paul explained his plans and purpose for his ministry (15:14-33) and sent personal greetings to Roman Christians (16:1-23).

🌿 **SUMMARY REVIEW**

To review this unit, see if you can mentally answer the following questions. You may want to write the answers on a separate sheet of paper. Mark your level of performance on the left: circle C if you can answer correctly and circle R if you need to review.

C R   1. List two pagan religions existing during New Testament times, and give the major emphasis of each.
C R   2. What are two ways in which Paul has influenced the world?
C R   3. List two characteristics of Paul's personality.
C R   4. What three sources did Paul use in writing his letters?
C R   5. How are Paul's letters arranged in the New Testament?
C R   6. What is the theme of the Book of Romans?
C R   7. How would you divide the Book of Romans into major sections?

RESPONDING TO GOD'S WORD

🌴 Read Romans 15:14-16. In one word, what did Paul say that his letter was designed to do for the Roman Christians? Write that word in the following blank: _____

List here some means that God has used in your life to remind you of truths you had learned previously.

_____

Ask God to make you more sensitive to hearing and responding to His reminders to you.

---

29. Answers: Probably you checked all except 4. If so, you understand what Paul wrote in 14:13-21.

Unit 10 The Writings of Paul, Part 2 (1 Corinthians–Ephesians)

**Reading Through
the New Testament**

❑ 1 Corinthians 1–4
❑ 1 Corinthians 5–8
❑ 1 Corinthians 9–12
❑ 1 Corinthians 13–16
❑ 2 Corinthians 1–4
❑ 2 Corinthians 5–9
❑ 2 Corinthians 10–13

> **UNIT LEARNING GOAL:** The study of this unit should help you understand the background and writing of several of Paul's letters. You will be able to:
> • Divide 1 Corinthians into two broad divisions.
> • Summarize three problems in the Corinthian church.
> • Explain why Paul wrote Galatians and identify its major doctrinal teaching.
> • Explain why we call some letters Paul's Prison Letters.
> • Write the theme and basic emphasis of Ephesians.

First Corinthians

Paul's first letter to the Corinthians is the most practical letter he wrote. The spectrum of problems he confronts includes both moral and theological failure plus a breakdown of personal relationships and a crumbling of family life. Paul also dealt with the position of women in the church and the practice of speaking in tongues.

Second Corinthians

Second Corinthians provides an example of a Christian response to opposition and misunderstanding. It features Paul's defense of his ministry and reveals some of the sources of Paul's incredible endurance. It is a reminder that the grace of God always is sufficient in our lives.

Galatians

In Galatians Paul gives a determined defense of the doctrine of salvation by grace through faith. The letter contains a strong attack against the "gospel" of salvation by works.

Ephesians

Paul's Ephesian letter has an almost meditative quality about it. In common with Colossians, it was written in prison and emphasizes the church as the body of Christ. In Ephesians Paul emphasized the gifts given to God's people, including their new position as saints, and the spiritual motivation for serving God effectively. He described the privileges of the Gentiles as fellow-heirs of God's promises, and the commitments expected from God's people because of the new calling God had given them.

Day 1 Paul's First Letter to Corinth

UNIT 10

An Immoral City

Acrocorinth and Aphrodite's Temple

1 Corinthians Written A.D. 54

Doctrines of Crucifixion, Resurrection, Holy Spirit

The City of Corinth

Corinth was the largest and most prosperous city of Greece. It had a population of several hundred thousand and was located on an isthmus that linked northern Greece with the Peloponnesian Peninsula. Corinth was an immoral city that attracted many whose purposes for visiting included illicit pleasure. The name of Corinth was synonymous with living a debauched and licentious lifestyle.

The most impressive physical feature of Corinth was the massive plateau known as the Acrocorinth, which rose nearly two thousand feet from the surrounding plain. At the foot of the craggy peak the city of Corinth grew and flourished. Atop its flat summit some one thousand sacred priestesses made their services available as cult prostitutes in a temple dedicated to Aphrodite, goddess of love.

Occasion and Date of 1 Corinthians

On Paul's third missionary journey, he returned to Ephesus where he remained for nearly three years (Acts 20:31). Since Paul had been in Corinth (for 18 months during his second missionary journey), spiritual conditions in the church had greatly deteriorated. He may have received reports about this from friends in the church. While Paul was in Ephesus, he likely wrote the Corinthians a letter mentioned in 5:9 (which we do not have) warning them not to associate with the immoral and the wicked.

From members of Chloe's house (1:11) Paul learned that the Corinthian church had divided into factions. He also received an inquiry from Corinth requesting his advice and guidance on certain questions of interest to the church (7:1). It is possible that a delegation composed of Stephanas, Fortunatus, and Achaicus may have brought these questions to Paul (16:17). On the basis of the reports and the request, Paul wrote 1 Corinthians during the later part of his stay in Ephesus (probably A.D. 54) and sent it to the church.

Overview and Content of 1 Corinthians

This book is important both theologically and practically. Theologically, Paul presents many vital truths dealing with the crucifixion and resurrection of Christ and the role of the Holy Spirit in spiritual gifts. Practically this letter demonstrates the personal abilities and character of Paul as a pastor and church leader. It demonstrates his wisdom and concern for the congregations, and provides principles for us to follow as we deal with problems in our own churches. First Corinthians demonstrates that Paul was not an ivory-tower theologian but an intense pastor deeply interested in the holiness, testimony, and development of his flock.

Outline

Theme of 1 Corinthians: A Gifted and Worldly Church

I. Paul Responds to Problems (1–6)
   A. Division in the Church (1:10–4:21)
   B. Moral Problems in the Church (5:1–6:20)
II. Paul Answers Questions (7–16)

Paul Responds to Problems (1 Cor. 1–6)

🌿 Read 1 Corinthians 1:4-7 and answer the following question: How had God's grace blessed the Corinthian church?[1]

_____

Paul began his first letter to Corinth with an introduction in 1:1-9. He gave the church a Christian salutation (1:1-3) and expressed thanksgiving for the grace of God that had provided spiritual gifts to the Corinthians (1:4-7). He also praised God for His faithfulness (1:9).

🌿 Read 1 Corinthians 1:10-12. In light of these verses, what do you think was happening in the Corinthian church? Check your answers.[2]

   ❏ 1. The Corinthian Christians were robbing one another.
   ❏ 2. The Corinthian Christians were disagreeing with one another.
   ❏ 3. The Corinthian Christians were united.
   ❏ 4. The Corinthian Christians had adopted different spiritual "heroes."

Problem of Factions (1:10–4:21)

Paul then dealt with the problem of factions in the church (1:10–4:21). Servants from the household of Chloe had brought Paul reports of divisions in the church (1:11). These divisions developed around personalities (1:12). Paul passionately responded that mere human leaders never could replace the leadership of Christ. He pointed out that he had not baptized to recruit disciples for himself (1:14-17).

🌿 Read 1 Corinthians 2:1-5. Check the following words that describe what many Corinthians expected a meaningful message or messenger to demonstrate.[3]

   ❏ 1. Eloquence   ❏ 2. Superior wisdom   ❏ 3. Weakness   ❏ 4. Fear
   ❏ 5. Trembling   ❏ 6. Persuasiveness   ❏ 7. Crucified Christ

> **Reasons for Factions in the Church**
>
> A Misunderstanding of the Christian Message (1:18–3:4)
>
> A False Concept of the Ministry (3:5–4:5)
>
> Puffed Up with Human Pride (4:6-13)

Paul outlined three reasons for the persistence of factions in the church. First, he insisted that the Corinthians had misunderstood the Christian message (1:18–3:4). They emphasized clever, oratorical presentations as an indication of human wisdom, but Paul insisted that the preaching of the cross showed the emptiness of human wisdom (1:18-25). The Corinthians also emphasized the importance of important personalities in their group, but Paul insisted that God often worked through weak, despised people rather than with the rich and prominent (1:26-31). Further, Paul indicated that the life-changing message of the gospel had demonstrated its power as God's wisdom (2:1-5). He discussed the Spirit's ministry in the life of the believer and contrasted natural and spiritual persons. Bluntly, he charged the Corinthians with an immaturity that hindered their grasp of the truth (3:1-4).

A second reason for the presence of factions in Corinth was the false conception of the Christian ministry that the Corinthians held (3:5–4:5). The Corinthians viewed Paul, Apollos, and other ministers as competitors, but Paul insisted that they were all laborers with God (3:5-9). Paul outlined his own role as that of a master builder. Christ, and not some human being, was to serve as the foundation of the church (3:10-17). He warned the Corinthians against glorying in men (3:21), and he presented himself as a servant of Christ and a trustee of divine truth (4:1).

_____

1. Answer: By generously giving spiritual gifts to the members.
2. Answers: You should have checked 2 and 4.
3. Answers: You could have checked 1, 2, and 6.

Read 1 Corinthians 4:6-7 and check the correct answer for each of the following questions.[4]

1. What was Paul's purpose in writing about Apollos and himself?
   - ❑ a. He wanted to emphasize their importance in God's work.
   - ❑ b. He was building up his own ego.
   - ❑ c. He was teaching the folly of taking pride in one person over another.

2. Who makes you different from anyone else?
   - ❑ a. God who made you.
   - ❑ b. Your environment and upbringing.
   - ❑ c. Your heredity.

3. What do you have that you did not receive?
   - ❑ a. The ability to choose
   - ❑ b. A developed intelligence
   - ❑ c. Nothing

4. Of what can you legitimately boast?
   - ❑ a. Your achievements
   - ❑ b. Your use of opportunities
   - ❑ c. Nothing

Limited Liberty

Moral Problems (5:1–6:20)

Human pride constituted a third reason for the presence of factions in the church (4:6-13). Paul warned his readers against conceit and indicated that God's grace had given them all they needed. Calling them his spiritual children, he appealed for reconciliation (4:14-21). Paul confronted moral problems in the Corinthian church: the church's refusal to discipline immorality, Christians' practice of suing one another in the pagan courts, the abuse of Christian freedom, and the general practice of immorality.

A member of the church had committed gross immorality; and the church, rather than quickly confronting the offender, actually ignored the affair (5:1–6:20). Paul bluntly addressed the church and directed the members to handle the immorality by disciplining the person who continued to practice it (5:1-13).

Church Discipline

By church collectively

For offender's good

For the church's good

For the good
of their witness

Paul stressed that discipline in the church was not like a policeman arresting a criminal, but rather like a father correcting his son. Discipline was to be handled by the church collectively. It was for the good of the offender, for the good of the church, and for the good of their witness.

Lawsuits Against Fellow Christians

In chapter six Paul directed Christians who brought lawsuits against one another to settle them among themselves or to take a loss (6:1-8). While it is often difficult to apply specific situations from the first century to specific situations two thousand years later, the principle is clear. A Christian should care more about the loss of spiritual stature than the loss of money. Also, an action a Christian takes is wrong if it results in a loss of witness or in disgrace to the name of Christ.

Abuse of Christian Freedom

Paul concluded chapter 6 by warning his readers against their abuse of the principle of Christian freedom and by applying this principle to the general practice of immorality (6:9-20). Paul then reiterated that Christ has freed us, not to sin but, that we might have the power to serve Him (vv. 12-13). Christ does not free us from the *ability* to sin (thus robbing us of choices that make us distinctively human, created in the image of God), but He is determined to free us from the *appetite* for sin.

---

4. Answers: 1-c, 2-a, 3-c, 4-c.

Our Bodies Belong to Christ

Paul applied this principle to sexual immorality by reminding the Corinthians that our bodies belong to Christ (vv. 15,19-20). We may not use them as we please, nor abuse them and thus disgrace our Lord (vv. 15-16). Sexual immorality is a sin against our own bodies and defiles the temple where the Holy Spirit lives (vv. 18-19).

RESPONDING TO GOD'S WORD

Read 1 Corinthians 6:12-20. According to Paul, why is sexual immorality such a serious sin for the believer?

_____

Pray that God will guard you from immorality and keep your life pure for Him.

Day 2   *Paul's Letters to Corinth*

UNIT 10

Outline

Paul Answers Questions from the Corinthians (7–16)
Theme of 1 Corinthians: A Gifted and Worldly Church

I. Paul Responds to Problems (1–6)
II. Paul Answers Questions (7–16)
   A. Marriage (7:1-40)
   B. Christian liberty (8:1–11:1)
   C. Public worship (11:2–14:40)
   D. Resurrection (15:1-58)
   E. Giving (16:1-9)

Marriage Is Normal

Singleness Is an Option

In a second division of the letter (7:1–16:9), Paul made replies to questions raised in a letter he had received from Corinth. Paul believed that marriage was the normal condition of men and women, but he indicated that commitment to Christ made singleness a real option (7:32-35).

Paul indicated that Christians ought to limit their liberty to eat offending foods if the practice harmed others (8:1-13). He also indicated that individuals should limit their liberty in eating offending foods out of concern for the progress of the gospel (9:19-23). Paul was willing to surrender any of his rights that hindered the spread of the gospel. Paul also pointed out the importance of a believer limiting his liberty in Christ so as not to inhibit his own individual spiritual development (9:24–10:22). If engaging in any practice harmed him spiritually, he should stop the practice. He urged all of his readers to seek the glory of God and not merely their own individual rights and privileges (10:31).

The Corinthians also asked Paul questions about proper styles in worship. They raised questions about the veiling of women in worship and about the Lord's Supper (11:2-34). Concerning the first question Paul urged women to conceal their heads with a veil or some type of covering. Paul made this appeal in order to emphasize the importance of following established social custom in the churches. He also urged the women to use their new freedom responsibly in showing respect for their husbands as well as respect for church custom (11:5,16). In observing the

Lord's Supper, Paul urged the Corinthians to avoid gluttony and drunkenness and develop a community of fellowship (11:17-22). He urged Christians to examine their spiritual condition before sharing in the Lord's Supper.

Questions About Spiritual Gifts (12:1-31)

Questions about the proper use of spiritual gifts also affected the Corinthian church. Corinthians seemed to be attracted to the more sensational gifts of the Spirit, and they emphasized them rather than the teaching and service gifts. To help their misunderstanding, Paul gave a general survey of spiritual gifts.

🌿 **Read 1 Corinthians 12:4-11 and mark the following statements *T* (true) or *F* (false).**[5]

____ 1. Christians have the same spiritual gifts.
____ 2. Spiritual gifts are given to bless those who receive them.
____ 3. Spiritual gifts are given to those who deserve them.
____ 4. The Holy Spirit decides who receives which spiritual gifts.
____ 5. Chapter 12 in 1 Corinthians lists all God's spiritual gifts.

Diversity of Gifts

Paul discussed the diversity of gifts in the church and used the illustration of the human body to show that Christians were mutually dependent on those with differing spiritual gifts (12:1-31). He emphasized that a response in love to one another was the only manner of preserving fellowship and unity (13:1-13).

Gift of Prophecy More Important

Decency and Order Also Important

Paul affirmed that the gift of prophecy was more important and significant than the practice of speaking in tongues (14:1-25). He concluded by providing directions for the proper experience of worship in the Corinthian church (14:26-40). In this section he gave specific instructions for the church to practice whenever some spoke in tongues. He admonished some wives to avoid creating disturbances in the church, and he appealed for all types of worship to be carried out decently and in order.

Question About the Resurrection

A theological question that the Corinthians asked of Paul concerned the resurrection of Christ. Because of certain philosophical ideas some Corinthians were skeptical of the possibility of resurrection. Their skepticism led to a denial of the possibility of Christ's resurrection. Paul responded to this theological heresy by insisting on the importance of the resurrection of Christ. He defended the resurrection as a part of the gospel (15:1-11) and as fundamental to our salvation (15:12-19).

In 15:29-58 Paul discussed the resurrection. He also indicated that Christ's resurrection was the pattern of our own future resurrection (15:20-28). In 15:29-58 he discussed the resurrection of believers. He showed that a belief in the resurrection had a practical effect on individual behavior (15:29-34). He discussed the nature of the resurrection body (15:35-49) and outlined the future victory Christians could anticipate when they experienced resurrection (15:50-58). Paul presented the resurrection of Christ and the future resurrection of believers with such force that they provide us an incentive to labor always for God (15:58).

Giving

Paul showed the breadth of his pastoral concern when he discussed the issue of receiving an offering from the Corinthians for poverty-stricken Jerusalem believers (16:1-4).

---

5. Answers: Number 4 is true, the others are false.

🌿 Read 1 Corinthians 16:1-4 and check the words that describe the offering Paul instructed the Corinthians to take.[6]

❑ 1. Regular   ❑ 2. Occasional   ❑ 3. Proportional
❑ 4. Set amount   ❑ 5. Voluntary   ❑ 6. Mandatory

The expression of the benediction is important because it contains the Aramaic word *Maranatha*. The word means literally "Our Lord comes." Aramaic likely was the dialect in which believers first expressed their beliefs. The expression of a hope for Jesus' return in this language shows that the hope was a part of the original beliefs of the church.

Paul's Second Letter to Corinth

Previously Paul had written the Corinthians a letter mentioned in 1 Corinthians 5:9 (which we do not have) warning them not to associate with the immoral and the wicked. After this, Paul returned to Ephesus on his third missionary journey and wrote 1 Corinthians. Apparently Paul followed this letter with a visit to Corinth which is not mentioned in Acts. This visit, described in 2 Corinthians 2:1, is what scholars call the painful visit. Paul made this visit in order to work out a means of reconciliation with those Corinthians who were opposing and questioning his ministry. Apparently the visit did not bring Paul and his accuser together, and Paul returned to Ephesus.

There he probably wrote another letter, now lost, which some have called the "severe" letter (2 Cor. 2:4). In this letter Paul expressed his love for the Corinthians, but he also used strong words to call them to repentance (2 Cor. 7:8-12). After sending this letter by Titus, Paul left Ephesus for Macedonia. Titus later brought word to Paul in Macedonia that the strong appeals of Paul's letter had led the Corinthians to repentance so that once again they were eager to see and talk with him (2 Cor. 2:12-13; 7:5-7). After receiving the words form Titus, Paul wrote 2 Corinthians and later followed with a visit. This later visit of Paul to Corinth is suggested in Acts 20:2-3. During this visit Paul wrote the letter to the Romans.

🌿 A. Mark the following statements *T* (true) or *F* (false).[7]

____ 1. The Book of 1 Corinthians was Paul's first letter to the Corinthians in Corinth.
____ 2. Sometime after Paul wrote 1 Corinthians, he apparently made a visit to Corinth that is not recorded in the Book of Acts.
____ 3. Paul's visit to Corinth mentioned in 2 Corinthians 2:1 was not a happy experience.
____ 4. Paul probably wrote at least four letters to the believers in Corinth, and we have the second and fourth (1 and 2 Cor.).

Date and Purpose

2 Corinthians Written A.D. 56

Paul wrote 2 Corinthians somewhere around A.D.56, approximately a year after the collection of money for poor Jerusalem Christians referred to in 1 Corinthians 16:1. Paul opened up his emotions and conscience in 2 Corinthians more than in any other of his writings, with the possible exception of 2 Timothy. His writing the letter accomplished several goals. First, his explanation of the greatness of the ministry

---

6 . Answers: 1, 3, 5.
7. Answers: 1-F, 2-T, 3-T, 4-T.

God had given him (2:14–7:16) let his opponents know his motivation and incentive for ministry. No finer statement of the nature of ministry appears in the New Testament. Second, he appealed to the Corinthians to complete their giving to the needs of the Jerusalem Christians (2 Cor. 8–9). Third, he defended his apostleship by referring to his divinely-given authority for sharing in the ministry of Jesus Christ (2 Cor. 10–13).

The Unity of 2 Corinthians

In 2 Corinthians 1 through 9 we can detect a tone of happiness (see 2:14), but in 10 through 13 Paul switched to a posture of self-defense (see 10:11). Some students of the New Testament argue that the difference in content is so noticeable that they cannot believe that they were originally a part of the same writing. Also, in 2 Corinthians 7:16 Paul asserted that he had unlimited confidence in the Corinthians. However, in 2 Corinthians 10 through13 he expressed reservations about them.

Majority Addressed in 1–9

Minority Addressed in 10–13

One explanation of the different attitude is that in chapters 1 through 9 Paul spoke to the majority of the church who had repented of their past opposition to Paul. In chapters 10 through 13 he spoke to a minority who stubbornly resisted him. No manuscripts of 2 Corinthians appear without the letter existing as a unit. It seems clear that we should see this book as a unity in which Paul directed his message to different groups in different sections of the writing.

RESPONDING TO GOD'S WORD

At the beginning of today's study, the outline of 1 Corinthians listed five questions the Corinthians asked Paul (about marriage, Christian liberty, public worship, the resurrection, and giving). With which question do you most closely identify?

_____

What did Paul say to the Corinthians that you can apply to this problem in your life?

_____

Day 3   *Overview of 2 Corinthians*

U N I T   1 0

Outline

Theme of 2 Corinthians: The Ministry of Reconciliation

I. Paul Explains His Actions (1:1–2:13)
II. Paul Exalts His Ministry (2:14–7:16)
III. Paul Appeals for Generosity (8:1–9:15)
IV. Paul Defends His Authority (10:1–13:14)

Paul began this letter with an outburst of thanksgiving for God's strength and protection to him (1:3-11). He explained a difficult trial he had faced in Asia. God faithfully had given Paul consolation even as he suffered. Paul also dealt with charges that he was guilty of fickle conduct (1:12–2:13).

> **Read 2 Corinthians 1:12 and underline the words below that you feel best summarize Paul's behavior toward the Corinthians.[8]**

Honest   Pragmatic   Sincere   Upright   Selfish   Godly

In 1 Corinthians 16:5-9 and 2 Corinthians 1:15-16 Paul explained his plans to visit Corinth. However, he had not followed through on his plans. Someone in Corinth called this type of behavior unstable and fickle. Paul insisted that he had not practiced deceit with the Corinthians (1:18) and that the reason for his failure to visit them was his desire to spare them a painful encounter (1:23–2:4). He defended his integrity (1:12) and consistency (1:17). He expressed pardon to an opponent in Corinth and called on the church to show forgiveness to him (2:5-11).

In 2:14–7:16 Paul balanced the difficult experiences he had faced (affliction, criticism, personal pain, and uncertainty) with a description of the power and glory of the ministry. Paul stood convinced that God always enabled him to carry on an effective ministry despite the difficulties.

Grandeur of the Ministry

In the first section he described the triumph and grandeur of the ministry (2:14–4:6). A part of his triumphant experience came from the conversions he had seen in Corinth (3:2-3). Paul also triumphed in that he worked with the life-giving power of the new covenant that gave him spiritual liberty (3:4-6,17-18).

God's Love Was Paul's Motivation

In his second section he outlined the glory of the ministry despite its hardship (4:7–5:11). Despite the presence of trials God had given Paul hope (4:16-18). As he faced the possibility of death, he looked for the joy of ultimate presence with the Lord (5:6-8). In the third section he described his motive for ministry and manner of conducting ministry (5:12–6:10). God's love for Paul (5:14) was a motivation to declare the message that Christ had paid for the consequences of sin (5:21). Such a deep motivation gave Paul stamina as he met hardship (6:1-10).

> **A. Read 2 Corinthians 6:3-10.[9]**
> How can God's servants show themselves to be genuine servants of God?

_____

_____

> **B. Read 2 Corinthians 6:14—7:16.**
> What do you think being "yoked together with unbelievers" means today?

_____

_____

Reconciliation Brings Joy

In 7:2-16 Paul elaborated on his experience of reconciliation with the Corinthians. This section explains a reason for the exuberance Paul had expressed in 2:14. The repentance of the Corinthians had given Paul an occasion of joy. The obvious joy of Titus at his reception by the Corinthians proved to be a contagious delight for Paul (7:13-16). No Christian can read Paul's presentation in 2:14–7:16 without developing an excitement about the privilege of ministry for the Lord.

---

8. Answer: You may have underlined any except pragmatic and selfish.
9. Answers: A-Compare your answer to mine: By facing life's hardships and slanders with faith and godly living. B-Be prepared to discuss your answer in the small-group session this week.

Generosity Promotes Unity

Paul now discussed the challenge of receiving a collection for the needs of Jewish Christians in Jerusalem. Judean Christians had been hit hard by outbreaks of famine during the reign of the emperor Claudius. In Acts 11:27-30 the largely Gentile church in Antioch had sent relief through Paul and Barnabas to their Christian brothers and sisters in Jerusalem. Realizing that generosity here could promote deep Christian unity, Paul urged the Corinthian Christians to give generously. He had made his first request for giving in 1 Corinthians 16:1-4. The Christians had lagged in their giving. He now renewed the request.

To spur the Corinthians to excellence in giving, Paul cited the example of generous giving of the Macedonians (8:1-7). He used the example of Christ's unselfishness as an added incentive for giving (8:8, 9). He made some sound preparations for honest delivery of the funds so as to meet any accusations of financial mismanagement (8:16-24). He appealed for generosity in 9:6-15 by describing God's blessings on the generous, and he described the unity and gratitude to God which were a result. In his final major section Paul responded to a minority of the church who continued to oppose him (10:1–13:14).

Read 2 Corinthians 10:1-6.[10]

What evidence in these verses supports the idea that chapters 10–13 were addressed to people in the church at Corinth who opposed him?

_____

First, Paul defended his use of authority in his relationships with the Corinthians (10:1–11:15). He insisted that he had been consistent in his use of authority (10:10-11). He had been careful to mention only what God had accomplished through him, not what he had accomplished independently (10:17-18). Paul had a jealous desire that the Corinthians give complete obedience to God (11:2-3).

Read 2 Corinthians 11:4-6,12-15 and check the correct ending for each of the following statements.[11]

1. Apparently the Corinthians
   - ❏ a. had been reverting to pagan worship
   - ❏ b. had been listening to false Christian teachers
   - ❏ c. had been ignoring Christian worship

2. The teachers who had come into Corinth
   - ❏ a. claimed superiority to Paul
   - ❏ b. were not effective speakers
   - ❏ c. were rejected by the Corinthian believers

3. Paul identified the teachers who had come into Corinth
   - ❏ a. as fellow workers
   - ❏ b. as people who were ill informed
   - ❏ c. as servants of Satan

In 12:14–13:10 Paul prepared his readers for his coming third visit to them. He expressed hope that when he arrived they would have repented of such sins as strife, immorality, and greed (12:19-21). He warned that he might need to take strong action (13:1-14) and concluded with a reference to the trinity in 13:14.

_____

10. Answer: Evidently some people were saying that Paul was bold when absent from them but timid when present, and that he lived by the world's standards. (See 10:11, also).

11. Answers: 1-b, 2-a, 3-c.

RESPONDING TO GOD'S WORD

Read 2 Corinthians 4:7-12. What principles for Christian service to others did Paul express?

_____

_____

Ask the Lord to enable you to live in such a way that the life of Jesus will be seen in you.

Day 4   *Paul's Letter to the Galatians*

UNIT 10

Readers, Date, and Occasion

The term *Galatia* was used in two different ways in the New Testament period. Used as an ethnic term, it referred to an area of central Asia Minor in which people of Celtic background from Gaul came to live. In 25 B.C., the Romans took control of the area and combined the original territory of the Galatians with new land reaching into the southern part of Asia Minor. This political Galatia included Pisidian Antioch, Iconium, Lystra, and Derbe.

To which Galatia did Paul write, the area originally inhabited by the Galatians, an area in the northern part of Asia Minor, or to the larger areas including some new territory in the south? If he wrote to churches such as Derbe, Lystra, and Iconium, he used the term *Galatia* in a political sense. Several arguments support the "Southern" Galatian theory, and this theory seems more compelling.

Galatians Written A.D. 49/50

The date for writing Galatians follows more easily after one decides the identity of the "churches of Galatia." If one had followed the North Galatian theory, Paul would have written Galatians in the mid or late fifties (A.D. 55-57) from either Ephesus or Macedonia. However, following the South Galatian theory, Paul wrote the letter perhaps from Syrian Antioch as early as A.D. 49 or 50.

Locate on the adjoining map the probable geographical area in which the recipient of Paul's letter to the Galatians lived. Put a check here when you have done this: ❑

In light of Galatians 1:7; 4:17; and 6:12-13, briefly describe the reason Paul wrote Galatians.[12]

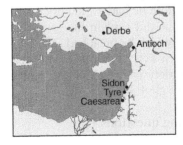

ASIA MINOR

Paul wrote this letter after he received information that Judaizers had spread false teaching through the churches of Galatia (1:7; 4:17; 6:12-13). These Judaizers taught the same ideas as those mentioned in Acts 15:1, although the identity of the two groups is not necessarily the same. Paul wrote Galatians to call his Christian friends back to the grace of Christ (1:6).

---

12. Answer: Check your response by the following paragraph.

Overview and Content of Galatians

Theme of Galatians: Paul's Defense of the Gospel of Grace

Outline

  I. Paul's Personal Argument for Grace (1:1–2:14)
 II. Paul's Theological Argument for Grace (2:15–4:31)
III. Paul's Practical Argument for Grace (5:1–6:18)

Paul's salutation (1:1-5) served notice that he intended to defend the divine origin of his apostleship. Compare Paul's description of himself in 1:1 with a more peaceful letter such as Philippians 1:1.

Read Galatians 1:6-10. Summarize the message of these verses.[13]

_____

Paul came straight to the point of the theological problem facing the church. After the salutation Paul described the occasion and the theme (1:6-10). He denounced those who were troubling the churches with their willful tampering with the truth.

To defend God's gospel of free grace, Paul presented a biographical argument (1:11–2:14). He argued that his preaching came as a revelation from God.

Read Galatians 1:11–2:14 and mark the following statements *T* (true) or *F* (false).[14]

___ 1. Paul received the gospel he preached from believers in Damascus.
___ 2. After his conversion, Paul hurried as fast as possible to Jerusalem to consult with the apostles there.
___ 3. The Jerusalem trip mentioned in 2:1 was probably the same as that mentioned in Acts 9:26-29.
___ 4. The other apostles affirmed Paul's call from God to preach the gospel to the Gentiles.
___ 5. Jewish believers had little difficulty in recognizing Gentile believers as brothers and sisters in Christ.

Paul's purpose was to show the divine origin of his message. Paul first stated that he received his gospel directly from God. It was not his own composition (1:12). Second, he suggested that none of the other apostles had contributed to the content of his gospel. Three years passed after his conversion before he had even a brief visit with any of the other apostles (1:18-24). Third, when he did explain his gospel to his friends, they accepted him and accredited the gospel which he preached (2:1-10). Finally, he pointed out that he was able to rebuke even Peter without having his ideas rejected (2:11-14). This fact supported the propriety of his rebuke to Peter. Paul also provided a theological argument in 2:15 through 4:31.

Read Galatians 2:15-21 and answer the following questions.[15]

  1. What is the difference in how Gentiles are saved and how Jews are saved?

_____

  2. How are people saved?_____

---

13. Compare your answer to mine: There is but one true gospel; hold to it!
14. Answers: 1-F, 2-F, 3-F, 4-T, 5-F.

3. Explain how Christians can live godly lives. (2:20)

Justification Comes Through Faith in Christ

Paul also offered a theological argument, showing the spiritual failure of legalism to lead anyone to salvation (2:15–4:31). He began with the statement that justification came through faith in Christ without the works of the law (2:15-21). Paul pointed to the personal experience of the Galatians for their recognition that they had received the Holy Spirit by a faith response to the gospel (3:1-15). He also referred to the true intent of Old Testament teaching to show that the children of faith receive the blessing of Abraham (3:16-18).

 Read Galatians 3:6-14 and Genesis 12:1-3. How does Galatians define the blessing mentioned in Genesis 12:2?[16]

The Law Prepared for the Gospel

Paul pointed out that the purpose of the law was to prepare the recipients for the gospel (3:19-29). In 4:6-11 he contrasted the benefits of responding to God by faith with the drudgery of approaching God by legalistic prescriptions. He made a personal appeal to the Galatians as his spiritual children in 4:19-20. Here he showed feelings for them and expressed concern for their spiritual condition.

Living in Christian Liberty (5–6)

Kind Treatment

Finally, he provided a practical argument (5:1–6:18). He demonstrated the positive effects of living under the standards of Christian liberty. Those who followed legalism were cutting themselves off from the sphere of grace. They were bogged down in legalism (5:1-12). True sanctification would triumph over envy and strife (5:25-26), demonstrate mercy and sympathy toward those caught in sin (6:1-5), practice liberal giving (6:6), and reap the benefits of life in the Spirit (6:7-10).

Fruit of the Spirit

Love, Joy, Peace, Patience, Kindness, Goodness, Faithfulness, Gentleness, Self-Control

---

 Read Galatians 5:16-26 and check the correct answer for each of the following questions.[17]

1. How can Christians overcome the desires of the sinful nature?
   - ❑ a. By going to church regularly
   - ❑ b. By trying harder
   - ❑ c. By walking in the Spirit

2. What conclusion can you draw about people who practice a lifestyle characterized by the acts and attitudes mentioned in Galatians 5:19-21?
   - ❑ a. They are not Christians.
   - ❑ b. They may be Christians who have backslid.
   - ❑ c. They will enter the kingdom of God.

3. What conclusion can you draw about people who practice a lifestyle characterized by the things mentioned in Galatians 5:22-23?
   - ❑ a. They are walking in the Spirit.
   - ❑ b. They are hypocrites.
   - ❑ c. They are out of touch with reality.

---

15. Answers: 1-None. 2-By faith in Christ. 3-By faith in the Christ who lives in them.
16. Compare your answer to mine: The blessing is salvation in Christ which is received with the faith Abraham demonstrated.
17. Answers: 1-c, 2-a, 3-a.

In a concluding section in 6:11-18 Paul questioned the motives of his opponents and exulted in the cross of Jesus. He added a benediction to his Galatian friends.

The gospel of salvation by grace through faith is a Christian truth that many believers neglect and misunderstand. Paul's clear presentation of this truth in Galatians underscores its importance and provides a practical application of its relevance.

RESPONDING TO GOD'S WORD

Ask God to help you walk in the Spirit by faith today. Remind yourself of the fruit of the Spirit from the previous page. Pray for the Lord to produce consistently the fruit of the Spirit in your life.

Day 5
Introduction to the Prison Letters and Ephesians

UNIT 10

We name Ephesians, Philippians, Colossians, and Philemon the Prison (Captivity) Letters because Paul was in prison when he wrote them. All of these letters make some reference to Paul as a prisoner (Eph. 3:1; 4:1; 6:20; Phil. 1:7,13-14: Col. 4:3, 10,18; Philem. 9-10,13,23). They fit well into the background of Acts 28:16-31, when Paul endured imprisonment in Rome for two years.

List the four letters commonly called the Prison Letters.

1. _____ 2. _____

3. _____ 4. _____

Date of Prison Letters

Ephesians, Colossians, Philemon, 61–62 A.D.

Most scholars date Paul's first Roman imprisonment in the early 60s. A common date is A.D. 61–63. During this imprisonment Paul penned Ephesians. The mention of the name of Tychicus in both Ephesians 6:21-22 and Colossians 4:7-9 implies that he was the carrier of the letters. In addition, the mention of Onesimus in both Colossians 4:9 and Philemon 10 implies that he accompanied Tychicus in carrying the letters. This information suggests that these three Prison Letters were written generally about the same time.

None of these three letters suggests that Paul expected a release from prison soon. In Philippians, however, we find evidence that Paul anticipated a release in which he might see his friends in Philippi (Phil. 1:24-26; 2:24). This suggests that Ephesians, Colossians, and Philemon were written earlier in Paul's imprisonment, perhaps in A.D. 61 or 62. Philippians was written near the time of Paul's release from this first imprisonment.

Introduction to Ephesians

300,000 Inhabitants

The city of Ephesus was situated on the west coast of what is now Asiatic Turkey. It was located at the mouth of the Cayster River between the mountain ranges and the sea. In New Testament times it had perhaps a quarter of a million inhabitants.

Temple Dedicated to Diana

The city had a glorious history. Its harbor had allowed it to serve as an import/export center. A magnificent road, 70 feet wide and lined with elaborate columns, ran through the city to the harbor. The city had theatres, public baths, libraries, and streets paved with marble. It contained a temple dedicated to the fertility goddess, Diana (also called Artemis). The temple became known as one of the wonders of the ancient world. Local tradition held that the temple contained an image of the goddess which had fallen from heaven. During New Testament times the city also served as a center of worship of the Roman emperor.

Paul Arrived in A.D. 51 or 52

Paul first arrived at Ephesus after he left Corinth near the end of his second missionary journey (Acts 18:18-21). The date was in A.D. 51 or 52. Later Paul returned to Ephesus on his third missionary journey (Acts 19:1), and he remained there between two and three years (Acts 19:8,10; 20:31). During this time his preaching and powerful ministry won a hearing for the gospel (19:10-12).

After his nearly three-year stay in Ephesus, Paul left for a visit to Macedonia and Greece (around A.D. 56/57). He later returned to the vicinity of Ephesus and asked elders from the church to meet him in nearby Miletus, a distance of about 40 or 50 miles. He demonstrated his concern and love for the church in a moving appeal to these elders (Acts 20:17-38).

🌿 **The following information is related to Paul's ministry at Ephesus. Match the statements with their answers.[18]**

____ 1. The time of Paul's arrival at Ephesus.

____ 2. The most likely date of Paul's stay in Ephesus.

____ 3. The scriptural reference to Paul's first visit.

____ 4. The scriptural reference to Paul's second visit.

____ 5. The scriptural reference to Paul's final visit to Ephesus.

____ 6. The date of Paul's ministry in Macedonia.

____ 7. The date of Paul's first Roman imprisonment.

____ 8. The person who carried, or delivered, the Books of Ephesians and Colossians.

a. Acts 18:18-21

b. A.D. 56 or 57

c. Near the end of his second missionary journey

d. Tychicus

e. A.D. 61–63

f. A.D. 51 or 52

g. Acts 20:17-38

h. Acts 19:1

Outline

Overview and Content of Ephesians

Theme of Ephesians: We Are Heirs of God's Blessings

I. God Blesses us in Christ (1:1–3:14)
II. God Requires us to Live for Christ (4:1–6:24)

---

18. Answers: 1-c; 2-f; 3-a; 4-h; 5-g; 6-b; 7-e; 8-d.

Unlimited Divine Resources

In Ephesians 1:3–2:10 Paul outlined spiritual blessings (all given "in Christ") which have affected persons chiefly in their relationship to God. After a salutation he outlined personal spiritual blessings such as:
• God's election of believers (1:4-6)
• redemption in Christ Jesus (1:7-8)
• the revelation of God's will (1:9-10)
• the giving of the Holy Spirit (1:13-14).

Paul followed this discussion with a prayer that Christians might have a full understanding of the unlimited divine resources available for them (1:15-23). He asked that Christians have an expectant attitude, a knowledge of the wealth of their inheritance in Christ, and an experience of divine power. In 2:1-10 Paul described the new life in Christ as transporting a believer from a position of spiritual death to an earthly experience of heavenly life. All of this becomes available by God's grace through Jesus Christ (2:8-10).

God's New Society

In 2:11–3:21 Paul outlined the new society God had created by extending His blessings to both Jews and Gentiles. God had abolished the contempt existing between Jews and Gentiles, reconciled them both to Himself, and given them personal access into His presence (2:14-16). Gentiles had become citizens of God's kingdom indwelt by the Holy Spirit (2:19-22).

God's Grace to Gentiles

In 3:1-13 Paul elaborated on the grace God had shown to the Gentiles. Through the gospel God had made Gentiles sharers of His promises in Christ. These blessings made Gentiles heirs of God's grace along with the Jews (3:6). Paul marveled that God had entrusted him with the task of proclaiming this good news (3:8-9). In 3:14-21 Paul prayed that his readers would be strengthened with the might of God's Spirit and know the dimensions of divine love. These thoughts led him to burst into spontaneous praise (3:20-21).

A New Walk

In chapters 4–6 Paul called for a practical response to the blessings he had outlined in the first three chapters. He called on his readers to demonstrate a new walk in their ministry in the church (4:1-16). Their walk was to show unity (4:3), a proper use of spiritual gifts (4:7-11), and maturity (4:12-16).

New Relationships

Paul also urged believers to show a new relationship to one another (4:17-32). Christians were to banish all dishonesty in word and deed, and practice forgiveness to one another (4:25-32) and walk in love and light (5:1-21).

A New Home

The new life affected the Christian home (5:22–6:9). Paul outlined how the new walk of the Christian changed the relationship between husbands and wives (5:22-33), parents and children (6:1-4), and servants and masters (6:5-9).

🌿 **Read Ephesians 5:22—6:9 and complete the activity below. Circle a number, 1 being poor and 5 being excellent, which indicates the quality of your family life and your work relationship.**

Family	1	2	3	4	5
Work Relationships	1	2	3	4	5

Record one action you will take to make improvement in each area.

1. Family life: _____

2. Work relationships: _____

Armor for Spiritual Warfare

Paul was aware that Christians still faced a deadly enemy. In 6:10-24 he urged his readers to prepare for spiritual warfare by arming themselves with righteousness, faith, and prayer in order to meet the temptations of Satan. In 6:21-22 he mentioned the role of Tychicus as the bearer of the letter. He concluded with a benediction in 6:23-24.

✍ SUMMARY REVIEW

To review this unit, see if you can mentally answer the following questions. You may want to write the answers on a separate sheet of paper. Mark your level of performance on the left: circle *C* if you can answer correctly and circle *R* if you need to review.

C R 1. Give the two broad divisions of 1 Corinthians
C R 2. Describe three problems in the Corinthian church.
C R 3. Write the emphasis of 2 Corinthians in a sentence.
C R 4. Why did Paul write Galatians? What is its major doctrinal teaching?
C R 5. Why do we call some letters "Paul's Prison Letters"?
C R 6. What is the theme and basic emphasis of Ephesians?

Review this week's material to find the answers.

RESPONDING TO GOD'S WORD

As you conclude your work today, record the six parts of the armor of the Roman soldier.

1. _____   4. _____

2. _____   5. _____

3. _____   6. _____

Choose one of the pieces of armor to use as an object lesson in your quiet time tomorrow. Ask God to show you how this Scripture passage can help you experience victory over Satan.

Unit **11** The Writings of Paul, Part 3 (Philippians–Titus)

Reading Through the New Testament

❑ Ephesians 1–3
❑ Ephesians 4–6
❑ Philippians
❑ Colossians
❑ Philemon and
  1 Timothy 1–2
❑ 1 Timothy 3–6
❑ 2 Timothy and Titus

UNIT LEARNING GOAL: The study of this unit should help you understand the background and writing of the rest of Paul's letters. You will be able to:
- Explain the theme and basic emphasis of Philippians.
- Write the theme of Colossians.
- Identify the problem Paul discussed in Philemon.
- List what Paul remembered about the Thessalonian Christians.
- Interpret Paul's view of the day of the Lord in 2 Thessalonians.
- Explain why the Pastoral Letters were written.
- Identify the themes of 1 Timothy, 2 Timothy, and Titus.

This unit will deal with three of Paul's Prison Letters, the Thessalonian Letters, and Paul's Pastoral Letters (1–2 Timothy and Titus).

Fill in Paul's letters.

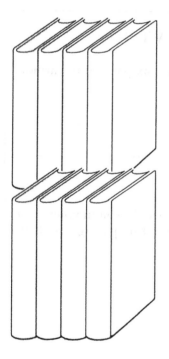

Philippians

Philippians is Paul's most joy-filled letter, though it was written from prison. It is a letter of gratitude for a gift from the Philippians and a challenge to further Christian growth and service.

Colossians

Paul's letter to Colossae emphasized a proper understanding of the person of Christ to meet the threat of heresy. Colossians shows that Christ is the solution to every practical and theological problem that plagues churches and individuals.

Philemon

Paul's letter to Philemon is the shortest and most personal of all his letters. It was a plea for one of Paul's converts, Onesimus, Philemon's runaway slave who had become a brother in Christ.

1 Thessalonians

Paul wrote 1 Thessalonians to encourage a church facing severe persecution and plagued by doctrinal misunderstanding, especially concerning the Lord's coming.

2 Thessalonians

Shortly after writing 1 Thessalonians, Paul learned that false teaching had spread in the Thessalonian church, and he wrote 2 Thessalonians to correct this. He stressed God's future judgment, explained the order of some end time events, and urged the Thessalonians to avoid idleness and careless behavior.

The Pastoral Letters

Students of Paul's writings have used the term *Pastoral Letters* for the Books of 1–2 Timothy and Titus. Paul wrote these letters later in his ministry to provide guidance in dealing with false teaching for Christians in Ephesus and on the island of Crete.

Day 1   *Paul's Letter to the Philippians*

UNIT 11

The Philippian Church

Philippi was a city of the province of Macedonia and a Roman colony, which gave its citizens special rights and privileges. A small Jewish community existed in Philippi before Paul visited the city (Acts 16:13). The Jewish faith appealed to women such as Lydia, a native of Thyatira and a Gentile. The story of the founding of the church appears in Acts 16:12-40. The church was founded in a city where such practices as occult activities, religious intolerance, and opposition from local citizens was common.

The opposition led to Paul's imprisonment, but a miraculous deliverance during an earthquake showed God's control of all events. Paul left Philippi after his release from prison and completed his second missionary journey (Acts 20:1-2). The Philippian letter suggests that Paul had frequent contact with the church (Phil. 4:14-16).

> 🌿 **Read the accounts of Paul's ministry in Philippi in Acts 16:12-40; 20:1-2; and Philippians 4:14-16. Check here when you have completed these passages:** ❑

Most of the members of the Philippian church seem to have been Gentiles. Although Lydia was a Jewish proselyte (a convert to the Jewish religion), the names of church members in the letter (Phil. 4:2-3) are the names of non-Jews. The Philippians were esteemed and admired by Paul, so that he could call them his "joy and crown" (Phil. 4:1). They gave him financial help so that he was not dependent either on his own working or on other churches (2 Cor. 11:8-9; Phil. 4:14-18). The response of the Philippians to Paul provides an example for churches today to use in helping others by sacrificial Christian service.

Dates, Occasion, and Purpose

Written A.D. 62 or 63

Paul was still imprisoned in Rome in A.D. 62 or 63 when he wrote this letter (see discussion in unit 10, day 5).

A Letter of Appreciation

The Philippians had aided Paul repeatedly in the past and had most recently sent Paul a financial gift through Epaphroditus. Epaphroditus became ill, and Paul sent him back to Philippi along with this letter of appreciation (2:25-30).

Warning Against Divisiveness and Judaizers

In addition to expressing gratitude for this gift, Paul also warned against divisiveness in the Philippian church (2:2; 4:2) and against Judaizers. He prepared the Philippians for approaching visits from Timothy and hopefully from Paul himself (2:19-24).

Overview and Content of Philippians

Theme of Philippians: God's Word to a Healthy Church

Outline

I. Paul's Commendation and Advice (1–2)
II. Paul's Warnings (3—4)
  A. Against Judaizers (3:1-21)
  B. Against Disunity (4:1-18)

Presence of Strife

After expressing greetings to the Philippians, Paul offered a prayer that they might grow to a maturity of love (1:3-11). The presence of strife in the church made his prayer necessary. Paul urged the Philippians to abound in love (1:9).

🌿 **Read the prayer appearing in Philippians 1:3-11, and then circle the words below that accurately describe the spirit of Paul's prayer.[1]**

Thankfulness   Joy   Confidence   Vision   Affection   Concern

Paul discussed his imprisonment (1:12-26) by first mentioning its effect on other Christians (1:12-18). Christians who had observed Paul's witness in prison had become bold in their witness. Paul developed the confidence that God would allow him to live so that he might continue to minister among the Philippians (1:19-26).

🌿 **Briefly describe an adverse experience in your past which you now can see God has used to build your confidence in Him.**

_____

_____

How do you believe God could use your experience to help someone else?

_____

As Paul examined the lives of the Philippians, he saw many spiritual needs (1:27–2:18). He urged his friends to practice steadfastness so that they might not be unsettled by the attitudes or actions of those who opposed them. He also presented the example of Christ's humility as an incentive for the Philippians to develop the same trait in their own relationships (2:1-11). He urged them to work out their spiritual problems by following the directives he had given them (2:12-13).

> "Your attitude should be the same as that of Christ Jesus: Who being in very nature God, did not consider equality with God something to be grasped, but made himself nothing, taking the very nature of a servant, being made in human likeness."
>
> —Philippians 2:5-7

🌿 **Read Philippians 2:5-16 and answer the questions related to the Scriptures.[2]**

1. What attitude were the Philippians to adopt?
  ❏ a. Determination   ❏ b. Obedience   ❏ c. The same as Christ

2. Whom did Paul say was working within them to enable them to live

  the Christian life? _____

3. What were to be the indicators that the Philippians were following the

  example of Christ? _____

4. What do you think it means today to "work out your salvation with fear

  and trembling"? _____

Paul reserved one of his highest commendations for Timothy, who truly cared for the Philippians (2:19-24). He also commended the sacrificial service of Epa-

---

1. Answer: All the words are descriptive of the prayer in Philippians 1:3-11.
2. Answers: 1-The same as Christ (v.5). 2-God Himself (v. 13). 3-Obedience (v. 12). Harmony in their relationships and blameless lifestyles (v. 14), 4-Your response. Hopefully, your answer will include living in obedience to Christ by trusting in His strength daily.

phroditus, who had risked his life to bring a gift from Philippi to Paul (2:25-30). Paul was sending him back to Philippi with an expression of appreciation for a job well done (2:29).

Paul had a great concern about the effect of Judaizers on his Philippian friends (3:1-21). These legalists had emphasized their own attainments (3:1-7), and would pervert the church from the gospel (3:2).

Focus on Growth in Jesus

Paul urged his readers to focus on their growth in the knowledge of Jesus and regard all else as insignificant (3:8-16). He called on them to imitate his own example, not that of the legalists (3:17-21).

Finally, Paul mentioned the Philippian problem of strife in the church and urged his readers to be in unity (4:1-3). He shared his own prescription for anxious care (4:6-13) and expressed gratitude to the Philippians for their generous care (4:14-20). He concluded with greetings and a benediction (4:21-23).

The joyful tone of this letter could give you the impression that Paul is enjoying a free life in Christ. In fact, we learn almost incidentally in Paul's discussion in chapter 1 that he is a prisoner. The presence of this attitude of boundless joy shows the power of Christ's presence in Paul's life. It encourages us not to bog down in our trials but cast all our cares and anxieties on Him.

RESPONDING TO GOD'S WORD

"Whatever was to my profit I now consider loss for the sake of Christ" (Phil. 3:7). What does this statement mean to you?

_____

Essentially, Paul meant that those things on which he had depended were of no use in his salvation, and that they had hindered him in knowing God. Is there anything on which you are depending that is useless? If so, will you pray now to reaffirm your dependence on Christ alone?

Day 2

Paul's Letters to the Colossians and Philemon

UNIT 11

The Church at Colosse

Colosse was the least significant of the cities to which Paul wrote a letter. We have no record of his ever visiting the city. The original evangelization of the city probably took place during Paul's stay in Ephesus (Acts 19:10). Epaphras (1:7; 4:12) may have founded the church.

Philemon, Onesimus Members

Philemon and his slave Onesimus were members of this church (Philem. 2,10-11; Col. 4:9). Epaphras may have brought Paul information about the church during Paul's Roman imprisonment (Acts 28:30). This information may have led Paul to rebuke the errors he learned about and call his readers back to a full commitment to Christ.

Date, Occasion, and Purpose

The date for writing this letter has been discussed under the date for Ephesians. Paul wrote the letter from Rome in his first Roman imprisonment.

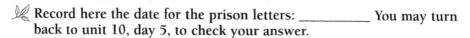 **Record here the date for the prison letters:** _____ **You may turn back to unit 10, day 5, to check your answer.**

The mention of Epaphras in 1:7 suggests that he and Paul had some contact in which Paul may have learned about problems in the church. Two purposes are apparent in Paul's writing the letter.

Christ's Preeminence for Doctrine

• First, Paul found in Colosse a heresy concerning Christ's person. This heresy devalued the person of Christ and led Paul to emphasize Christ's preeminence (1:15-19). The heresy also emphasized speculative human philosophy (2:8) and contained some elements of Judaism (2:11,16; 3:11). Paul gave a positive presentation of the true nature of Christ and His work.

Christ's Power for Daily Living

• Second, Paul emphasized the application of Christ's power for daily practice. He urged his readers to experience transformation in their relationships with one another, especially in the home (3:12,18-25).

Check the correct responses to complete the following activity.[3]

1. The characteristics of the Colossian heresy.
   ❑ a. It devalued the person of Jesus Christ.
   ❑ b. It emphasized attainment of worldly significance.
   ❑ c. It emphasized speculative human philosophy.

2. The nature of Paul's response to the problem at Colosse.
   ❑ a. An emphasis on the supremacy of Christ
   ❑ b. A charge to practical daily living
   ❑ c. An exhortation to live in transformed relationships as a result of knowing Christ

Overview and Content of Colossians

Theme of Colossians: Christ Has First Place

Outline

I. Christ is First in His Person (1:1–2:23)
II. Christ Must Be First in Our Conduct (3:1–4:18)

Read Colossians 1:9-14. As you read the Scriptures, check the statements that describe the apostle's prayer for the Colossian Christians.

❑ To be filled with the knowledge of God's will.
❑ Have spiritual wisdom and understanding.
❑ Live a life worthy of the Lord in every way.
❑ Bear fruit in every good work.
❑ Grow in their knowledge of God.
❑ Be strengthened with His might.
❑ Live with patience and endurance each day.
❑ Joyfully give thanks for their inheritance in Christ.

---

3. Answers: 1-a, c. 2-a, b,c.

All are characteristics of the apostle's prayer. If you had to choose two of these to be in your life, which would you ask someone to pray for you?

_____

_____

Christ the Hope of Glory

A discussion of doctrine about Christ's person and work began in 1:15 and continued through 2:23. In this passage Paul explained the preeminence of Christ in creation, redemption, and the church. He explained that Christ living in each person provided the hope of glory (1:27). He presented Christ as the Sum of all the wisdom and knowledge of the Father (2:3).

A. **Read Colossians 1:15-20. As you read the Scriptures, record in the space below words or phrases that describe the person of Christ.**[4]

_____

_____

B. **Put in your own words what these truths about Christ mean to you.**

_____

Christ the Answer to False Teaching

Christ Is Fully God

In 2:4-23 Paul explained how Christ provided the answer to the false teaching which vexed the church. A deep personal relationship to Christ provided a buffer against the deceitful words of the false teachers (2:6-7). Since all that God is and has dwells in Christ, Paul's readers were not dependent on the vain philosophies of human beings (2:8-10). In 2:20-23 Paul showed that a human-imposed self-discipline left the root cause of moral problems untouched. Union with Christ provided freedom from this misunderstanding about sin.

Christ Changes Conduct

In the second section Paul called his readers to a relationship with Christ's person that would change their conduct (3:1–4:18). He expected their growth to lead to a renunciation of sin and the practice of righteousness. He explained that their experience with Christ could bring victory over the church problems (3:1–4:6).

Read Colossians 3:1–4:6 and circle the words that describe the type of problems you think were in the church at Colosse.[5]

worldly mindedness	morality	passion	greed
kindness	gentleness	anger	patience
malice	slander	forgiveness	vulgar talk
marital problems	deceit	love	unity
child-rearing issues	laziness	faithfulness	

New Life in Christ

Paul celebrated his readers new life in union with Christ Jesus (3:1-4) and called on them to mortify deeds of wickedness and immorality (3:5-6). He wanted his readers to seek the traits of forgiveness, humility, mercy, and kindness (3:12-17). He wanted their new life in Christ to affect the home (3:18-25). New relationships between husbands and wives, parents, and children, and servants and their masters were to spring out of this new commitment to Christ.

4. Your answer should have included such descriptive terms as: the image of the invisible God, firstborn over all creation, creator, the head of the church, the first born from the dead.
5. Answers: Probably the church at Colosse—like many churches—had a mixture of many of these. There are references in the reading that would indicate the presence of both good and bad in the church.

Paul discussed the application of holiness in prayer and relationships to others in 4:2-6. Christians were to use their time wisely and respond with grace in all their behavior.

Paul's Personal News

Paul's conclusion in 4:7-18 contained personal news. He commended Tychicus (4:7-9). He delivered greetings from some of his friends such as Mark, Epaphras, and Luke (4:10-14). He included instructions for sharing this letter with others in 4:16 and gave a benediction in 4:18.

Paul's words to his Christian friends in Colosse give an effective example of the use of commendation and rebuke. He commended Epaphras (4:12) for his fervent prayer life. He challenged Archippus to carry out the ministry God had appointed for him (4:17).

Personalities in Philemon

Philemon

Philemon was a resident of Colosse and had become a Christian through Paul's ministry (v. 19). His conversion was probably a product of Paul's ministry in Ephesus. A church met in Philemon's home.

Onesimus

Onesimus, whose name means *profitable*, had fled from Philemon with some of his master's money or other belongings. His conversion through contact with Paul had led him and Paul to the conviction that he should return to his master. In Onesimus' day runaway slaves could be severely beaten or condemned to death if caught. Paul returned Onesimus to Philemon with his letter in hand. He journeyed in the company of Tychicus, who carried Ephesians and Colossians (Col. 4:7-9; Eph. 6:21-22).

Paul's Letter to Philemon

Number the statements below to correctly reflect the order of events surrounding the Book of Philemon.[6]

____ A. Onesimus became the slave of Philemon.
____ B. Paul wrote a letter to Philemon on behalf of Onesimus.
____ C. Philemon received a letter asking him to take Onesimus back as a brother in Christ.
____ D. Onesimus stole something from his master Philemon and fled to Rome.
____ E. Onesimus became a believer.
____ F. Onesimus met Paul and told his story.

Date, Place, and Significance of Writing

Paul penned only four letters to individuals: 1 and 2 Timothy, Titus, and Philemon. This letter is the most personal and intimate of Paul's letters to individuals. Philemon is also one of Paul's prison letters. It was written from Rome during the early sixties (A.D. 61-62). (See unit 10, day 5, for additional information.)

This letter is useful in describing Paul's approach to slavery which was a vexing social problem of his day. In his appeal to Philemon, Paul urged slaves to respect their masters. He called on masters to give kind, merciful treatment to their slaves (see Col. 3:22–4:1). His appeal to Philemon was for a voluntary response (v. 21).

---

6. Answers: A-1, B-5, C-6, D-2, E-4, F-3.

He did not order him to release Onesimus, but he left the decision to Philemon. As an incentive to release Onesimus Paul appealed to the common bonds of Christian brotherhood between Onesimus and Philemon (v. 16). He reminded Philemon of the spiritual debt he owed Paul (v. 19).

Paul's words brought slavery to the place in which it could only wither and die. His description of the relationship between Philemon and Onesimus as "brothers" sounded the death knell for slavery. When an owner began to view his slave as a brother in Christ, it would be hard to abuse him and difficult to retain him as mere property. The development of the recognition of brotherhood in Christ contributed to the demise of the practice of slavery.

Overview and Content of Philemon

Theme of Philemon: The Worth of the Individual

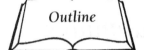

Outline

I. Our Worth Is in Christ (1–11)
II. Our Decisions Are Voluntary (12–25)

Paul's gracious words in verses 1-7 showed the significance of Philemon's role in the church at Colosse. Philemon was a convert of Paul (v. 19). He had shown generosity to other believers in Colosse (v. 5). His love had encouraged other Colossian believers (v. 7). He hosted the Colossian church in his own home (v. 2). The mention of the names of Apphia and Archippus in close relation to that of Philemon has led some to feel that they are his wife and son.

Paul made his request for Philemon graciously to receive Onesimus back (vv. 8-16). Paul expressed his plea for Onesimus in the form of a courteous request. He acknowledged the past failures of Onesimus (v. 11), but he pointed out that he was now useful to both Paul and Philemon. Onesimus' conversion had changed his character (v. 11). Paul had considered retaining Onesimus to serve with him, but he did not want to do anything without the full understanding of Philemon (vv. 13-14). He urged Philemon to receive Onesimus back as a beloved brother (v. 16).

✍ **Read Philemon 1-16. Check here when you have finished:** ❏

> **A. Record in the following space three words you think might describe how Philemon felt when he saw Onesimus enter his home with Tychicus.[7]**
>
> 1. _____, 2. _____, 3. _____.
>
> **B. If you were Philemon, what Christian response would you make to Onesimus's return?**
>
> _____

Promises and Pledges

Paul supported his request by promises and gracious pledges to Philemon (vv. 17-25). Paul urged Philemon to treat Onesimus as he would treat Paul (v. 17). He promised to repay any debt of Onesimus (vv. 18-19), He did not stipulate the exact action he wanted Philemon to take, but he hinted strongly at emancipation (vv. 20-21). Paul expected to see Philemon soon after an anticipated release from prison (v. 22). He concluded with greetings from Christian friends and a benediction (vv. 23-25).

---

7. Answers: A-Your response. I think Philemon may have felt anger, confusion, relief, and disappointment. Certainly he was curious at the turn of events. B-Your response. Be prepared to share your answers in the group session.

RESPONDING TO GOD'S WORD

Read Colossians 4:17. This was Paul's word of encouragement to Archippus to complete the work God had assigned him. Think for a few moments on the ministry God has assigned to you. Are you working diligently in it?
❏ Yes   ❏ No

What will it take to complete it? _____

Pray and ask the Lord to strengthen you to do the work (Col. 1:28-29).

Day 3 | *Paul's Letters to the Thessalonians*

UNIT 11

The Thessalonian Church

In New Testament times Thessalonica was an important naval center. Politically it was a free city, and the capital of Macedonia. It was located on an important Roman road through Macedonia known as the Egnatian Way.

Paul's First Visit

Acts 17:1-9 narrates Paul's first visit to Thessalonica on his second missionary journey. The city had enough Jews to found a synagogue, and Paul spent three weeks reasoning with them from the Scriptures. Paul's message to the Thessalonians declared the resurrection and messiahship of Jesus. He received a limited response among both Jews and proselytes, but unbelieving Jews stirred up opposition and set the city into turmoil. A mob led by Jews attacked the home of Jason in which Paul was staying. They accused Paul of claiming that Jesus was a king and a rival of Caesar. After the uproar, Christian friends helped Paul and Silas flee to Berea.

Further Visits?

Paul doubtless returned to Thessalonica on his third journey, but only a general ministry is mentioned in Acts 20:1-3. In his first imprisonment Paul expressed a hope that he might visit Macedonia again (Phil. 1:25-26; 2:24), and he may have visited the city again during the release (1 Tim. 1:3; 2 Tim. 4:13).

PAUL'S SECOND MISSIONARY JOURNEY

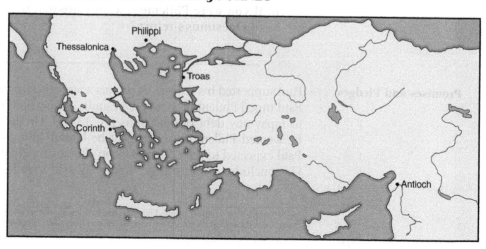

Date, Occasion, and Purpose of the Thessalonian Writings

🖋 On the map on page 180, trace the path of Paul's second missionary journey. Note in particular his visit to Thessalonica.

1–2 Thessalonians, A.D. 51

Paul left Thessalonica and journeyed to Athens (Acts 17:14-15). Silas and Timothy later joined him there, but he sent Timothy back to Thessalonica to minister (1 Thess. 3:1-2). Timothy later joined Paul in Corinth (Acts 18:5; 1 Thess. 3:6). Paul then wrote both Thessalonian letters from Corinth around A.D. 51.

Paul wanted to encourage the persecuted Thessalonians (1 Thess. 2:14; 3:1-4). Paul also defended himself against criticisms he had received (1 Thess. 2:1-12). He appealed for holiness and love in the church (4:1-12) and answered questions about loved ones who had died before the return of Christ (4:13-18).

Paul commended the Thessalonian church for their demonstration of faith, hope, and love. In the face of great affliction they had shown stability and commitment to Christ. Nevertheless, he urged his Christian friends to grow in their expression of holiness and love, and in their understanding of the events of Jesus' life.

🖋 Check the statements below that are reasons for Paul's writing 1 Thessalonians.[8]

❑ 1. To encourage his Thessalonian friends
❑ 2. To defend himself against criticism
❑ 3. To appeal to the church to live in love and holiness
❑ 4. To answer questions related to those who died prior to Christ's return
❑ 5. To urge the Thessalonian Christians to live in such a way as not to be ashamed of themselves at Christ's return

Immature Attitudes and Actions

After writing 1 Thessalonians, immature attitudes and actions still continued in the church. Severe persecution spurred their belief in the immediacy of Christ's return (2 Thess. 1:3-10). Some had quit their jobs in this anticipation (2 Thess. 3:10-13).

A Need to Understand Christ's Coming

To help them better understand God's will for them in this crisis situation, Paul wrote the Thessalonians that their suffering was preparing them for life in God's kingdom (2 Thess. 1:4-5). He explained that a falling away from God and the manifestation of a wicked one (usually called the Antichrist) would precede Christ's return (2 Thess. 2:3, 8-10). Finally, he urged them not to practice idleness but to live a life of work as their service to God (2 Thess. 3:12-13).

🖋 In the following pairs of statements, check those that most accurately reflect the teachings of 2 Thessalonians 3.[9]

❑ 1a. Pacify the idle and disobedient lest your faith be ill spoken of.
❑ 1b. Avoid those who are idle and do not live in obedience to the gospel so outsiders will know you do not approve of their disobedience.

❑ 2a. Follow the apostle's example in living the Christian life.
❑ 2b. The apostle's example led to the idleness in the church at Thessalonica.

❑ 3a. "If a man will not work, he shall not eat."
❑ 3b. Feed those who will not work because Jesus would.

---

8. Answers: All the statements were reasons given for the writing of 1 Thessalonians.

❑ 4a. Exercise discipline of unruly members by not associating with.
❑ 4b. Never tire of doing what is right.

Overview and Content of the Thessalonian Writings

Theme of 1 Thessalonians: Encouragements for the Christian

Outline of 1 Thessalonians

I. We Are Encouraged by Past Remembrances (1–3)
II. We Are Encouraged by Future Hope (4–5)

🌿 **Read 1 Thessalonians 1:1-5 and complete the following statements.**[10]

1. In his prayers for the Thessalonians, Paul remembered their _____

    produced by faith, _____ prompted by _____, and endurance

    inspired by their _____ in the Lord Jesus Christ.

2. Paul believed God had chosen them because the gospel came to them not

    simply with _____, but also with _____, the _____

    Spirit, and deep _____.

Power of the Gospel

Paul described the power of the gospel in Thessalonica (1:1-10) and emphasized the productive ministry God had given him (2:1-16). However, he had met opposition. He defended himself by pointing out the gentleness and care he had shown them (2:7-8). He insisted that he had not exploited them nor lived at their expense (2:9). Paul exhorted them as a father giving attention to his children (2:11).

Paul assured these young Christians how much he longed to see them and his encouragement at their stamina for Christ (2:18-20; 3:9-10). He prayed that he soon would see them (3:11). He was encouraged by their steadfastness (3:6-8).

Despite his encouragement, Paul had learned of several problems among the Thessalonians. He urged them to control their bodies in holy behavior, and warned that God would avenge all sexual misbehavior (4:3-6). Paul expressed appreciation for their demonstration of love, but he insisted that they need to continue their growth in love (4:10-12) and in holiness (4:1-12).

🌿 **Check the statements that accurately reflect the teaching of 1 Thessalonians 4:3-12.**[11]

❑ 1. Live holy lives by refraining from immorality.
❑ 2. Control your body instead of your body controlling you.
❑ 3. Christians have a responsibility to help one another be disciplined.
❑ 4. The Lord will punish the disobedient in these matters.
❑ 5. Rejection of these scriptural teachings is rejection of God Himself.
❑ 6. God expects Christians to love one another.
❑ 7. It is all right for Christians to be busybodies.
❑ 8. The Lord expects His people to be hardworking and industrious.
❑ 9. Our conduct will affect our testimony before the world.

---

9. Answers: The accurate statements are 1-b, 2-a, 3-a, 4-a & b.
10. Answers: 1-work, labor, love, hope. 2-words, power, Holy, conviction.
11. Answers: Statements 1-6 and 8-9 are true. Statement 7 is false. The Lord wants His people to live harmonious, quiet lives, minding our own business as we serve Him.

Misunderstandings About Christ's Return

Paul provided instruction about errors in their understanding of Christ's return (4:13–5:11). The Thessalonians had a serious misunderstanding about their loved ones who had died before the return of Christ. They were sorrowing as if those who had died might miss the opportunity for fellowship with Jesus in eternity. Paul assured them that deceased believers will be raised to meet the Lord in the air and will be with Him for eternity. Living believers will be taken to meet Jesus with them after deceased believers' transformation (4:13-18). The unexpectedness of the Lord's return should cause us to live as children of light who daily demonstrate our spiritual commitment to Jesus (5:1-11).

Need to Respect Leaders

Paul provided instructions for ministry to one another (5:12-28). He emphasized the need to respect their leaders and keep harmony within their fellowship (5:12-13). He also urged them to put aside all ideas of retaliation and maintain an openness to the working of the Holy Spirit (5:15,19).

> 🌿 **Read 1 Thessalonians 5:12-15 and answer the following questions.**[12]
>
> A. What negative things can result from disobedience to the Lord's will in how we relate to those in leadership in the church?
>
> _____
>
> B. What positive things can occur as a result of obeying the Scriptures just read?
>
> _____

Outline of 2 Thessalonians

Theme of 2 Thessalonians: God's People Stand Corrected

    I. Corrections Concerning Persecution (1:1-12)
    II. Corrections Concerning Prophecy (2:1-17)
    III. Corrections Concerning Perseverance (3:1-18)

In writing his second letter to the Thessalonians, Paul began with an expression of gratitude for the faith and love of his readers (2 Thess. 1:3). He acknowledged the seriousness of the afflictions they faced and indicated that their steadfast endurance showed that they were worthy of inheriting the divine kingdom (1:5). Paul taught that the return of Christ would bring tribulation on their persecutors and reward for those who were in Christ (1:6-7). Unbelievers would be punished with everlasting destruction from the Lord's presence (1:9).

Coming Day of the Lord

The Thessalonians had shown continued misunderstanding of the events surrounding the return of the Lord. Someone had convinced them that the day of the Lord had already come (2:2-3). Paul reminded them of some events that would occur before the day arrived. He pointed out that a falling away from God would lead to the revealing of the man of sin (2:3). He described the man of sin as one who exalted himself and fought against all of God's purposes (2:4).

The Wicked One's Appearance

Paul indicated that this wicked one had not yet appeared but would at the proper time (2:7). When he appeared he would produce signs and wonders that would deceive many and lead them to believe a lie (2:9-11). He reminded his readers that, because they were God's children, they had no cause to worry about future judgment and urged them to stand fast (2:13-15).

---

12. Answers: A-Your response could include setting a poor example for others, discouraging new believers, or causing strife and division in the church. B-Positive things that could occur is setting a good example for those in and outside the church, promoting peace in the body of Christ, and building and strengthening the fellowship of the church.

Practical Instructions

Paul encouraged the church to show stamina in their prayer life and diligent work in their daily activities (3:1-18). He urged his friends to pray for him (3:1-5). He warned them to avoid the internal division which had characterized them and to begin or resume sober, industrious habits of daily work (3:6,12). He warned them against fellowship with those who disobeyed his instructions (3:14).

RESPONDING TO GOD'S WORD

Read 1 Thessalonians 5:12-13. Can you think of ways you can show appreciation for your pastor? Record one action you will take.

_____

Read 2 Thessalonians 1:3-12 and then answer this question: If I knew Jesus were to return today, what steps would I want to take so that I would be unashamed to meet Him face-to-face?

_____

_____

Day 4

Introduction to Pastoral Letters, 1 Timothy

UNIT 11

Introduction to the Pastoral Letters

🌿 **Answer the following questions.**[13]

A. Which letters are known as the Pastoral Letters? _____

B. Why did Paul write these letters? _____

Timothy Serving in Ephesus

Paul appointed Timothy as his representative to deal with problems in Ephesus and urged him to take the necessary steps to correct them. The difficulties were within the church (1 Tim. 1:3-7, 18-20). Paul warned against the lifestyle of these false teachers. Paul wrote forcefully to Timothy because Timothy needed to overcome his hesitancy and act firmly in dealing with the false teaching in Ephesus.

Titus Serving in Crete

Paul also wrote with vigor to Titus and urged him to combat the doctrinal and moral heresy among Christians on the island of Crete. Paul's words provide us a pattern for dealing with similar doctrinal and moral disobedience today.

🌿 **Check the following statements with which you agree:**[14]

❑ 1. Paul wrote Timothy and Titus to guide them in dealing with false doctrine in the churches at Ephesus and Crete.

---

13. Answers: A-1 & 2 Timothy and Titus. B-to help the young pastors and to provide Christians in Ephesus and on the island of Crete guidance in dealing with false teachings.

❑ 2. Members or leaders within the churches at Ephesus and Crete were rejecting sound doctrine.

❑ 3. It is all right to believe wrong doctrine as long as you keep it to yourself.

❑ 4. False doctrine will cause problems in the church.

❑ 5. We are not to judge others even when they are teaching false doctrine.

❑ 6. It is necessary to deal directly and forcefully with those espousing false teaching.

❑ 7. Paul's instruction to Timothy and Titus give us an example of how we are to face such issues.

Date, Place, and Purpose

First Roman Imprisonment, A.D. 61-63

Freedom, A.D. 63-65, Wrote 1 Timothy and Titus

Paul's Prison Letters indicate that he anticipated release from his Roman imprisonment (Phil. 1:25-26; Philem. 22). Most scholars believe that he received freedom to do additional mission work during the years A.D. 63-65. It is concluded by many that he wrote 1 Timothy and Titus during this period of freedom. His words in 1 Timothy 1:3 suggest that he wrote the letter from somewhere in Macedonia. He likely wrote Titus from Nicopolis on the western shore of Greece (Titus 3:12).

Imprisoned Again, Wrote 2 Timothy

Paul later suffered a second arrest and subsequent martyrdom. During this time he wrote 2 Timothy. This letter appears to have been written when Paul faced the imminent possibility of death (see 2 Tim. 4:6-8). He was probably in Rome and had faced some type of court appearance just before he wrote (2 Tim. 4:16). The date is in the middle or late sixties.

Urged Timothy to Be Bold

Paul's chief purpose in writing the Pastoral Epistles was to urge Timothy and Titus to deal effectively with the problems of heresy and immoral behavior in the churches. Paul wrote to Timothy to urge him to charge the Ephesians not to give heed to heretical ideas (1 Tim. 1:3-4). He also wanted Timothy to outline how the Ephesians were to live as members of God's family (1 Tim. 3:14-15). In writing 2 Timothy, Paul urged Timothy to overcome his timidity and boldly proclaim the gospel, even if it caused him pain and suffering (2 Tim. 1:6-8). He gave Timothy instructions to come quickly to him in Rome (2 Tim. 4:9).

Urged Titus to Be Firm

Paul instructed Titus to deal firmly with unrest in the church on Crete (Titus 1:10-13). Paul reminded Titus of the details of his responsibility and explained that behavior expected of different groups in the church (Titus 2:1-10). He called Titus to meet him in Nicopolis on the west coast of Greece (Titus 3:12).

🌿 **What was Paul's main purpose in writing the Pastorals?**[15]

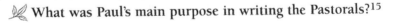

Overview and Content of 1 Timothy

Theme of 1 Timothy: God's Standards for Church Conduct

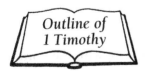

Outline of 1 Timothy

I. God's Standards for Doctrine and Worship (1:1–2:15)
II. God's Standards for Service and Living (3:1–4:16)
III. God's Standards for Church Ministry (5:1–21)

---

14. Answers: 1-Agree, see 1 Timothy 1:3-7; Titus 1:5. 2-Agree, see 1 Timothy 1:18-20; Titus 1:9-14. 3-Disagree. Sorry— I know this one is tricky. But what we believe guides how we act and thus the example we set for those around us. Being a responsible disciple calls for both sound doctrine and behavior. 4-Agree. 5-Disagree. The idea that Christians have no right to make judgments as to right and wrong, or sound or false doctrine is false doctrine itself. 6-Agree. 7-Agree.

15. Answer: Paul's purpose was to deal with the problems of heresy and immoral behavior in the churches at Ephesus and Crete.

Warning About Heresy

After a brief salutation, Paul emphasized the authoritative nature the call of God had given him and the corresponding authority to speak firmly to his readers (1:1-2). Paul warned Timothy about the heresy he face in Ephesus and explained his task in opposing it (1:3-20). Timothy was to warn the Ephesians to avoid false doctrine and help them produce genuine love from a pure heart (1:3-5).

🌿 **Read 1 Timothy 1:3-5. What words characterize the heresy at Ephesus.**[16]

_____

A Call to Prayer and Holy Living

Requirements for Leaders

From 2:1 through 6:19 Paul outlined some emphases that would accomplish this task. First, he urged Timothy to call all the Ephesians to prayer and holy living (2:1-15). Second, because leaders in the church had contributed to the problem, Paul also outlined requirements for leaders (3:1-13).

🌿 **Read 1 Timothy 3:1-13. Check here when you complete that reading:** ❑
This passage commonly is used to apply to those in the office of pastor and deacon. Does it apply to other leaders in the church?[17]   ❑ Yes   ❑ No

Evidently, the church in Ephesus was susceptible to heresies. In 1 Timothy 4 Paul explained in some detail how Timothy was to carry out his task of opposing the false practices in the church (4:1-16). The false teachers in Ephesus were proud, greedy, and contentious (6:3-10). Timothy was to resist them and make sure that his own life set an example for the believers (4:12). Paul urged Timothy personally to avoid these errors and to pursue godliness, faith, and love (6:11).

Organize Church Life

The church in Ephesus had demonstrated concern for all ages and sexes within it. Paul provided directions for:
• the church's ministry to widows (5:3-16). He urged the church to assist widows whose needs were evident and whose moral commitment was beyond reproach.
• recognizing and appointing elders to places of leadership (5:17-25). The church was to reject unfounded charges brought against its leaders, but it was to be quick to rebuke those who sinned. In no instance were they to be hasty in appointing untested leaders to office.

Paul encouraged those who were rich to use their wealth for good works (6:18). He warned against trusting in their own resources and urged them to place their confidence in the living God (6:17). Paul warned Timothy to keep the task given him and avoid the empty chatter the false teachers called "knowledge." Those who followed these ideas would miss the mark of the Christian faith (6:20-21).

RESPONDING TO GOD'S WORD

Read 1 Timothy 4:6-16. Now, answer the following questions. **What was the most significant truth you found in the passage?**

_____

What action will you take that will strengthen your walk with the Lord

as a result of knowing this? _____

---

16. Answer: Did you include words such as false doctrine, devotion to myths and genealogies, and promoting controversy?
17. Answers: That was somewhat tricky, but the answer is yes. All the Word of God speaks to His people.

Day 5 2 *Timothy and Titus*

UNIT 11

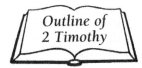
Outline of 2 Timothy

Overview and Content of 2 Timothy

Theme of 2 Timothy: Serving as God's Minister

I. God's Minister Must Be Strong (1:1–2:26)
II. God's Minister Must Stand Strong (3:1–4:22)

Paul described to Timothy some of the obstacles he would face in his efforts to deal with the heresy in Ephesus (1:1—2:26). After a salutation to Timothy Paul expressed his gratitude to God for fellowship with Timothy (1:3-5). Remembering Timothy's deep attachment to him filled Paul with joy. He referred to Timothy's tears (v. 4) and timidity (v. 7). Paul challenged Timothy to "fan into flame the gift of God" especially given to him (v. 6).

🌿 **Did the example of a Christian leader or friend encourage you during**

a difficult time? Record his/her name here. _____

You may want to write the person a note to tell what his/her walk with God has meant in your life.

Qualities Needed in Ministry

To prepare Timothy for obstacles in his ministry, Paul outlined the qualities he would need in ministry (1:6-18). These included:
• the demonstration of courage (1:6-7)
• a willingness to suffer (1:8-12)
• a performance of faithfulness in ministry (1:15-18)

Lifestyle Needed in Ministry

Paul urged Timothy to live a separated lifestyle. He cited examples from daily life that provided instruction for effectiveness in ministry (2:1-7). Timothy was to show the commitment of a faithful teacher, the single-mindedness of a soldier, the discipline of an athlete, and the endurance of a farmer.

As an incentive for endurance Paul reminded Timothy of the content of his gospel (2:8) and the example of his own suffering (2:9-10). He proclaimed the certainty of reward for those who served the Lord with endurance (2:11-13). He urged Timothy to resist the false teachers by separating from their influence (2:14-19).

🌿 **Paul advised Timothy in quarreling over certain issues with certain people. What is the difference in a healthy examination of what one believes and a destructive discussion of ideas?[18]**

_____

This separation did not demand a rupture of all contacts, for Timothy was to show gentleness and patience as he gave instructions (2:24-26). Paul warned Timothy that he could expect much difficulty in future experiences of testing (3:1–4:22). To prepare Timothy for this, Paul reminded him of the stubborn character of human beings and urged him to claim strength from his obedience to Scripture.

---

18. Answer: A healthy examination of your faith will lead to a stronger faith. A destructive discussion will attempt to turn you away from faith. It is important to discern the motive of those who initiate such discussions.

In meeting such opposition Timothy would find help from Paul's example (3:10-13) and by continuing to apply Scripture (3:14-17).

Diligence in Ministry

Paul gave Timothy a personal charge to demonstrate diligence in ministry (4:1-5). Paul shared his own experience with Timothy (4:6-8). He felt that his time of ministry was rapidly ending, but he anticipated receiving a reward from the Lord for the obedience of his life.

Paul concluded with personal appeals and requests to Timothy (4:9-13). Paul wanted Timothy to come quickly before winter weather made crossing the Mediterranean impossible (4:9, 21). He expressed his loneliness and asked Timothy to bring a cloak to protect him against the dampness of his confinement. He warned Timothy against the deceitful behavior of Alexander. He expressed greeting to friends who were with Timothy and gave information about mutual friends (4:19-22). His final words included a benediction for Timothy.

Overview and Content of Titus

 To overview the Book of Titus, read the following passages to refresh your memory of who Titus was: Galatians 2:1-10 and Titus 1:4.

Theme of Titus: Correction of Church Problems

I. Correction by Sound Doctrine (1:1-16)
II. Correction by Godly Living (2:1–3:15)

Outline of Titus

 **Read Titus 1:1-4 and complete the following sentences.**[19]

A. The knowledge of the truth of Christ is to lead to _____

B. Our faith and knowledge rests on the _____ of _____ life.

Characteristics of Sound Leaders

Paul had left Titus on Crete with the responsibility of correcting disorders in the church. He described characteristics that sound leaders must have (1:5-9). Paul wanted church leaders to demonstrate virtues of obedience and commitment that would be obvious. He demanded an exemplary life in the home and a patience in teaching the truth to those who opposed the content of the gospel.

Paul described the deep-rooted stubbornness of the troublemakers in the church (1:10-16). Using the words of a Cretan poet, he pictured them as dishonest, savage, and shiftless (1:12). He urged Titus to rebuke troublemakers and encourage Christians to ignore the empty teaching to which they were listening (1:13-14).

 **In the following pairs of statements, check those that most accurately reflect the teaching of Titus 1:10–2:1.**[20]

❑ 1a. Many rebellious and deceitful people were in the church at Crete.
❑ 1b. The church at Crete was dominated by godly, doctrinally sound people.

❑ 2a. Rebellious and deceitful people are not to be allowed to disrupt the soundness and fellowship of the church.
❑ 2b. The church and its leadership has no right to control the actions and teaching of its members.

---

19. Answers: A-godliness. B-hope, eternal.

❑ 3a. The purpose of rebuking one engaged in teaching error is to show the soundness of the church leadership.

❑ 3b. People who pervert the gospel are to be rebuked for their error in hope that they will then listen to sound doctrine.

❑ 4a. Those who claim to know God, but live in disobedience, actually deny their relationship with Him.

❑ 4b. Living in disobedience is all right as long as one can give testimony of having been baptized.

Godly, responsible living would provide an antidote for the problem the church faced (2:1-15). Paul gave specific directives to younger and older men and younger and older women for behavior that would be a testimony of the Christian faith (2:1-8). He also called on slaves to obey their owners and avoid dishonesty and thievery (2:9-10).

Paul supported his appeal for holy living by reminding them of the grace of God and the return of Christ (2:11-15). God's grace promoted disciplined, godly living. The return of Christ encouraged hope and separation from selfish lifestyles.

In a closing chapter Paul outlined some good works calculated to convince the unsaved world of the power of Christianity (3:1-15). Paul called for his readers to obey the authorities, avoid quarrelsome behavior, and show gentleness and self-control before all men. He directed them to avoid foolish questions that only led to empty discussions. Paul gave Titus instructions to meet him at Nicopolis and urged him to bring some special friends with him. He concluded with a benediction in 3:15.

❧ SUMMARY REVIEW

To review this unit, see if you can mentally answer the following questions. You may want to write the answers on a separate sheet of paper. Mark your level of performance on the left: *C* if you can answer correctly and circle *R* if you need to review.

C R 1. What is the theme of Philippians?
C R 2. What does Colossians emphasize about Christ?
C R 3. What is the problem Paul discussed in Philemon?
C R 4. What did Paul remember about the Thessalonian Christians?
C R 5. What was Paul's view of the day of the Lord in 2 Thessalonians?
C R 6. Why were the Pastoral Letters written?
C R 7. What are the themes of 1 Timothy, 2 Timothy, and Titus?

Review this week's material to find the answers.

RESPONDING TO GOD'S WORD

Read Titus 2:1-10; 3:1-2. Spend a few moments reflecting on the impact the actions of your church make on its community. Ask the Lord to give your church and its leaders wisdom to know how to live so the desired results described in Titus 2:1-10 will happen in your community.

---

20. Answers: 1-a, 2-a, 3-a & b, 4-a.

Unit **12** *The General Letters (Hebrews–Jude)*

**Reading Through
the New Testament**

❏ Hebrews 1–5
❏ Hebrews 6–9
❏ Hebrews 10–13
❏ James
❏ 1 Peter
❏ 2 Peter and Jude
❏ 1–3 John

> **UNIT LEARNING GOAL:** The study of this unit should help you understand the background and writing of the general letters. You will be able to:
> • Explain why Hebrews was written and state its theme.
> • Describe the theme and emphasis of James.
> • Identify from 1 and 2 Peter the various ways Christians witness to the world.
> • Cite from John's letters the evidences of true faith and how to walk in truth.
> • Explain from Jude the importance of contending for the faith.

In this unit you will study the General Letters of the New Testament. Scholars use the term *General Letters* for these writings because in most instances the author refers to the location of the readers with general terms rather than with a specific location.

Hebrews

The letter to the Hebrews presented the incredible wealth of the person and work of Christ as being superior to Judaism, Old Testament prophets, angels, Moses, Joshua, and Aaron. It shows how the person and work of Christ produces faith, enduring commitment, and good works acceptable to God.

James

James called Christians to overcome trials, avoid partiality, control their tongues, and renounce worldliness. He teaches us the importance of an humble dependence on God and the value of believing prayer.

1 & 2 Peter

Peter wrote his first letter to persecuted believers who needed to respond to their affliction with obedience and stamina. His second letter was written to defeat the growing influence of heresy within the church.

1, 2, 3 John

In John's first letter he presented three tests he wanted his readers to use in determining genuine Christianity. In his second letter John warned against false teachers who were in error about the genuine humanity of Christ (v. 7). In his third letter John directed Christians in a troubled congregation to a proper response to a dictatorial leader in their body (vv. 9-10).

Jude

Jude was written to warn readers about the practices and beliefs of heretics within the church.

Day 1   *The Book of Hebrews*

UNIT 12

Introduction to Hebrews

The letter to the Hebrews spoke a warning to Jewish-Christian believers who were considering leaving their commitment to Christ and turning back to the empty rituals of Judaism (5:11–6:6). To prevent this, the writer presented Christ as superior to the Old Testament prophets, angels, Moses, Joshua, and Aaron. He showed the incredible wealth of the person and work of Christ and wove these truths into passages containing frightening warnings for apostates. He showed that the superiority of Christ produced faith, enduring commitment, and good works acceptable to God.

🌿 **A. What danger was facing the Jewish-Christian believers addressed**

in the Book of Hebrews?

B. The writer of Hebrews presented Christ as superior to _____,

_____, _____, _____, and Aaron.

To check your answer see the above paragraph.

Author—Barnabas?

The early biblical scholar Origen said, "But who it was that really wrote the epistle (Hebrews), God only knows" (Eusebius, *Ecclesiastical History Twin Brooks Series* (Grand Rapids: Baker, 1955). This important opinion has not prevented many from speculating about the identity of the author. Some Christian leaders have supported Barnabas as the author because Barnabas was a Levite (Acts 4:36) and would understand the Old Testament ritual that is so prominent in Hebrews.

Luke?

Paul?

Some have suggested Luke as the author, because he seemed capable of writing the excellent Greek that Hebrews contains. However, Luke was a Gentile, and the outlook of Hebrews is Jewish. The Christian churches in the eastern Roman Empire generally saw Paul as the author of Hebrews. However, Paul never wrote anonymously in any of his other epistles. Although we do not know the author's name, we do know that Hebrews is an authoritative writing in the New Testament. The title of Hebrews ("to the Hebrews") denotes that Jewish Christians were the original recipients of the letter. The statement in 2:3 suggests that the readers had received their knowledge of the gospel from those who had heard Jesus speak the gospel, but not from Jesus Himself.

The writing contains evidence that the author knew details about the life of the congregation (5:11-12; 6:9-10; 10:32-34; 12:4; 13:7). He described their generosity (6:10), their persecution (10:32-34), and their immaturity (5:11–6:12). He indicated that he planned to visit them soon (13:19,23). An additional fact in 13:24, "Those from Italy send you their greetings," sounds as if Italians away from Italy are sending greetings back home. If this is true, Rome likely is the destination of Hebrews. An additional fact that favors this conclusion is that a knowledge of the existence of Hebrews first appeared in the writing of Clement from Rome.

Enduring Persecution

During this period Rome regarded Judaism as a legal religion, and the government would not officially persecute those who practiced it. Christians originally received some protection when they were regarded as a part of Judaism. Later, however, this privileged exemption from persecution may have disappeared when Christianity was seen as different from Judaism (see Acts 18:12-17). The readers of Hebrews were enduring severe persecution (Heb. 10:32-34), and some of them probably considered returning to Judaism in order to avoid persecution. Hebrews was written to persuade and strengthen them concerning their Christian profession.

The language of Hebrews is elegant and difficult to translate. The difficulty of the Greek beneath the English translation is not easy to detect in translation. Most English translations strive for readability.

Hebrews lacks many of the personal references of Paul's letters. It does not begin with a special greeting from the author to the readers. Its conclusion contains references to the personal plans of the writer and to the release of Timothy from imprisonment (Heb. 13:22-25).

We must date the letter to the Hebrews before A.D. 95, when Clement referred to it in Rome. The book also contains no reference that proves the Jewish temple had been destroyed, an event that took place in A.D. 70. In fact, the present tense of the verbs in 10:11 ("performs" and "offers") suggests, but does not prove, that priests were still offering sacrifices in the temple.

Written in Late 60s

Persecution of Jews and probably Christians increased as the time of destruction of the Jewish temple in Jerusalem drew near (see 10:32-34). Timothy was still alive (13:23). The best option for the date appears to be the middle-to-late 60s before the Romans destroyed the temple.

Hebrews contains many Old Testament quotations and allusions. Most of these quotations come from the Greek version of the Old Testament, the Septuagint. The writer frequently refers to Psalms, particularly Psalm 110:1, 4. References to the Old Testament are important to provide a groundwork for the writer's presentation of his arguments.

References to Christ

"Son"—5:8
"Lord"— 2:3
"High Priest"— 2:17
"Apostle"—3:1
"Author and Perfecter
of our faith"—12:2

The writer mentioned that the old covenant was obsolete and inadequate even while it was in operation (see Heb. 8:6-13). This emphasis on change from the old order to a new order prepared the readers for the introduction of new and better promises in connection with Christ.

The letter contains clear references to the deity of Christ (4:14-16), as well as a series of warnings. The writer injected them directly into the argument of the epistle. He urged his readers not to ignore the importance of their salvation in Christ (2:1-4; 3:7–4:13; 5:11–6:20; 10:26-39; 12:15, 29).

Theme of Hebrews: The Superiority of Christ

Outline

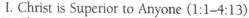

   I. Christ is Superior to Anyone (1:1–4:13)
  II. Christ is Superior to the Jewish Religion (4:14–10:18)
 III. Christ Demands Our Enduring Faith (10:19–13:16)

Overview and Content of Hebrews 1–2

Christ Superior to Prophets

To show the superiority of Christ, the author contrasted God's revelation through Christ with His revelation through the prophets (1:1-3). Through the prophets God had spoken in small parts and fragments, but through Jesus He had spoken with finality. The writer pointed out that Jesus was the Heir, Creator, Divine Reflection, Image of God, and Sustainer of the world. In redemption Christ had removed our sins, and God had seated Him on His right hand as a token of His accomplishment.

Christ Superior to Angels

Next the author demonstrated the superiority of Christ over angels (1:4–2:18). He indicated that angels were created at a point in time as God's servants who ministered to believers (1:14). By contrast, Christ was the Son of God, who received worship from the angels and had existed from eternity (1:5, 6, 10-12). Because of Christ's superior person and work the failure to believe on Him was a dangerous decision (2:1-4). The writer taught that the incarnation and death of Christ made it possible to bring believers into God's glory (2:5-13). The sufferings of Christ in temptation and affliction equipped Him to offer spiritual encouragement to His children as they faced trials and temptation (2:14-18).

"Because He Himself suffered when He was tempted, He is able to help those who are tempted."

—Hebrews 2:18

RESPONDING TO GOD'S WORD

Read Hebrews 2:18. Recall the worst temptation you have ever faced or now face. If you did not yield, how did you remain strong enough to resist temptation?

_____

What could have been the worst result if you had yielded?

_____

If you yielded to temptation, what was the result?

_____

Recall the words to the hymn "Yield Not to Temptation" and the thought expressed in verse 18. Jesus is able to help when we are tempted and to forgive us when we confess our failures. Conclude today's study with a time of prayer.

Day 2 *Overview and Content of Hebrews 3-13*

UNIT 12

Hebrews 3:1–4:13

Christ Superior to Moses (3:1-19)

In yesterday's study we concluded by noting the superiority of Christ over the prophets (1:1-3) and over angels (1:4–2:18). Beginning with chapter 3, the writer showed that Christ was superior also over Moses (3:1-19). To the Jewish mind Moses represented their best. He was their fearless leader who had led them out of captivity in Egypt. However, the writer of Hebrews reminds his readers that Moses was only a *servant* of God who *ministered in* God's household (3:5). Christ was the *son* of God who *ruled over* the household of God (3:6). Because Christ was superior to Moses, it was more important to follow Him than Moses, and also more serious to renounce Christ than to renounce Moses (3:7-19).

Christ Superior to Joshua (4:1-19)

The author also demonstrated the superiority of Christ over Joshua. The Hebrew name for *Joshua* and the Greek name for *Jesus* both mean *Savior*. Although the name of Joshua signified his ability to be a savior for God's people, and in a sense Joshua led his people into the promised land of blessing, Joshua failed to lead God's people to the ultimate place of spiritual rest (4:1-2,8). Through Jesus the people of God attain real, genuine rest (4:9-10).

Hebrews 4:14–10:18

Christ a Superior High Priest

In a lengthy section the author showed that the priestly work of Christ was superior to the priestly work of Aaron and his priests under Jewish law (4:14–10:18). He presented Christ as our great high priest who gave us the privilege to enter boldly into God's presence (4:14-16). God had appointed Aaron as a high priest to represent men before God. Because Aaron was surrounded with his own weakness, he was able to identify with the people as they faced temptation (5:1-4).

🌿 **Draw a line to match the names with their descriptions on the right.[1]**

1. Angels	A. A high priest who represented men before God
2. Moses	B. His name means salvation.
3. Joshua	C. He was a minister in God's household.
4. Aaron	D. Portrayed as God's servants who minister to believers.

"Although he was a Son, he learned obedience from what he suffered."

—Hebrews 5:8

God appointed Jesus to serve as our High Priest. However, He allowed Him to undergo trials and to learn the value of obedience by the sufferings He faced (5:5-8). The writer left his argument concerning Christ's superiority to warn his audience that their lack of growth hindered their usefulness and skillful performance for God (5:11-14). He urged his readers on to maturity (6:1-3) and discussed the seriousness of apostasy or falling away (6:4-8).

What does this teaching on apostasy mean? Some interpreters view this passage as a hypothetical warning. Their idea is that such falling away is presented as an example but is not a realistic possibility. However, the repetition of the warning here and also in 10:26-31 seems to make the possibility realistic rather than hypothetical.

Some teachers feel that this passage suggests that a Christian can lose his salvation. This interpretation could not be true, for it would contradict the clear teaching of such passages as John 10:27-29; 1 Corinthians 3:11-15; and Ephesians 1:13-14. Still others feel that readers are "near" Christians but not real Christians. They see them as close to becoming Christians but without a true response to Christ. However, it does not seem possible to designate someone who is merely close to becoming a Christian as one who has "shared in the Holy Spirit" (6:4).

Readers Are Professing Christians

The best interpretation views these readers as people who have professed Christ. The writer suggested that if they had professed Christ, they must show the reality of their faith by enduring in their commitment to Christ. If these readers fell away from Christ in order to escape persecution, it would demonstrate that they lacked genuine faith. They would show their profession of faith was only an expression of words and not genuine commitment (6:6). The work and love they demonstrated gave assurance that they were believers (6:9-12). However, he urged them to grow toward full maturity by following after God's certain promises (6:13-19).

Those who endure in their commitment to Christ show they are truly the children of God. A genuine believer cannot fall away to the loss of salvation (John 10:28). However, one who only has claimed to be a believer can fall into utter disobedience and self-centered living. God has promised to continue to produce good works in those who have genuine faith (Phil. 1:6).

A High Priest like Melchizedek (6:20–7:28)

The argument (or sermon) on Christ's superiority picks up again in 7:1. Our writer had mentioned in 5:10 that as a high priest Christ did not serve after the order of

---

1. Answers: 1-D, 2-C, 3-B, 4-A.

Aaron but followed the order of Melchizedek. Now in 7:1-28 he referred back to this Old Testament character to show the superiority of Christ's priesthood (see Gen. 14:17-20). The name *Melchizedek* meant "king of righteousness." As king of Salem, he was also king of "peace."

An Eternal High Priest

The Bible did not mention any beginning or ending for Melchizedek's life. Our writer focused on the righteousness and eternal nature of his life as a pattern that Jesus also demonstrated (7:1-3). These features of Melchizedek made his priestly ministry superior to that of the Aaronic priests. God installed Christ to be a priest after a new order, that of Melchizedek (7:17). The writer gave three reasons to explain the superiority of Christ's priesthood patterned after Melchizedek.
- First, an oath or promise of God established Christ in this priesthood (7:20-21).
- Second, Christ's priesthood was permanent. Since He served as an eternal priest, He always lives to pray for His people (7:25).
- Third, Christ' character was holy and removed from sin (7:26-28). He provided exactly the type of strength that weak, sinful believers needed. He could do for His followers what weak and sin-plagued Aaron could not.

A New Covenant (8:1-13)

In addition to beginning a new order of priesthood, Christ also had introduced a new covenant (8:1-13). The covenant He had inaugurated was a fulfillment of the new covenant Jeremiah had described (Jer. 31:31-34).

" 'This is the covenant I will make with the house of Israel after that time' declares the Lord. 'I will put my law in their minds and write it on their hearts. I will be their God, and they will be my people. No longer will a man teach his neighbor, or a man his brother, saying "Know the Lord," because they will all know me from the least of them to the greatest,' declares the Lord. For I will forgive their wickedness and will remember their sins no more.' "

—Jeremiah 31:33-34

This new covenant provided three benefits for those living under it.
- First, God put His laws into their minds and provided inner strength (8:10).
- Second, God provided a personal knowledge of Himself for all people, not just for Old Testament priests or a select few (8:11).
- Third, God offered forgiveness of sin (8:12). Christians still receive these benefits as they come to know Christ as Savior and Lord today.

🌿 **Read Hebrews 9:11-28. Check the statement in each of the following pairs that most accurately represents the teachings of this passage.[2]**

❏ 1a. Jesus entered the Holy place through a typical blood sacrifice.
❏ 1b. Jesus entered the Holy place by His own blood.

❏ 2a. Only the blood of Jesus is sufficient for our eternal salvation.
❏ 2b. The sacrifice of bulls and goats was sufficient for our salvation.

❏ 3a. The blood of goats and ashes of a heifer made the one sprinkled ceremonially clean.
❏ 3b. The blood of Christ cleanses us so we may serve the living God.

❏ 4a. Jesus is the mediator of a new covenant.
❏ 4b. Jesus validated the old covenant.

Christ Our Sacrifice

The writer also wanted his readers to understand the effectiveness of Christ's sacrifice. The sacrifices offered under the old covenant could not perfect the conscience of the worshipers. They could not produce heart religion (9:6-10). Under the new covenant Jesus sacrificed His life for our sin (9:14).

Christ's death was effective because it cleansed the conscience from the guilt of sin and produced a holy life (9:15-22). Christ's death also was effective because He represents His people in God's very presence (9:24). His death affected our relationship with God the Father. This was a relationship that truly mattered.

---

2. Answers: 1-b (v. 12), 2-a (v. 12), 3-a & b (vv. 13-14), 4-a (v. 15).

Christ's Sacrifice Was Permanent

The author concluded his argument concerning Christ's superiority to Aaron in 10:1-18, by showing that He was both Priest (v. 12) and Sacrifice (v. 10), and that the effect of His work was permanent (v. 14). The once-for-all death of Christ was an effective removal of sin (10:11-18). God accepted the sacrifice of Christ for our sin because it reflected obedience to His will (10:5-10). This sacrifice did not need repeating.

Hebrews 10:19–13:25

Spiritual Endurance Required, 10:19–12:21

Beginning in 10:19, the writer urged his readers to practice spiritual endurance. He found them drawing away from Christ and called them back to God and fellowship with one another. He urged them to draw near to God because they had experienced inward and outward cleansing (10:22) and to stimulate one another to good works by meeting together (10:24-25). The writer warned that turning away from Christ would bring them into divine judgment (10:26-31). These readers had no doubt suffered for their faith by imprisonment, ridicule, and loss of property. He called them to continue to obey God and claim the hope of reward (10:32-39).

Faith Pleases God

Heroes of Faith

The writer reminded the readers that faith gives reality to things that are invisible (11:1), and faith is pleasing to God (11:6). As an additional incentive to endurance the writer mentioned Old Testament heroes of faith (11:1-40). As examples he pointed to the patriarchs (11:1-22), Moses (11:23-28), Gideon, Samson, David, and other men and women (11:29-38). The writer saw that New Testament believers were beginning to experience the fulfillment for which Old Testament believers had hoped (11:39-40). The writer also pointed to the example of Christ as an incentive for endurance (12:1-11). Christians could find strength for endurance as they considered the example of Christ. As the readers experienced hardship, they were still under the corrective discipline of God who was seeking to produce holiness in them (12:7-11).

🌿 **Read Hebrews 12:7-11. Check the statements that accurately reflect the teachings of the passage.[3]**

❑ 1. God is treating us as His children when He disciplines us.
❑ 2. We should try to avoid discipline.
❑ 3. God disciplines us for our good.
❑ 4. The intent of God's discipline is to develop holiness in our lives.
❑ 5. The immediate effect of discipline is usually joy.
❑ 6. Discipline will produce righteousness and peace.

God's Character Encourages Endurance

The writer presented God's character as an encouragement for endurance (12:12-29). God desires that His people be holy (12:14). His presence at Sinai caused the physical effects of thunder and lightning and produced great fear among the people (12:18-21). If God's words from Sinai produced fear, how much more should His words from heaven through Jesus produce fear (12:25-29). The writer showed that Christians were heirs to an immovable kingdom. This certainty gave them the grace to serve God without compromise.

Final Exhortation, 13:1-25

In a series of final exhortations the writer urged his readers to carry out practical Christian duties and give God genuine commitment (13:1-16). He directed them to show sympathy for friends who were imprisoned (13:3), and urged them to show respect for their leaders (13:7,17). He called on them to give the spiritual sacrifices of obedience, praise, and ministry to others (13:15-16). He called for prayer and gave them some personal news about Timothy (13:18-23).

---

3. Answers: 1, 3, 4, and 6.

RESPONDING TO GOD'S WORD

Can you think of someone who needs encouragement in his/her faithfulness to the fellowship and activities of the church? What specifically can you do that would encourage him/her?

_____

Now take a moment to pray for him/her.

Day 3   *The Book of James*

UNIT 12

Introduction to James

The text of James only identifies the writer as a "servant of God," but this fact suggests an important clue to the author's identity. The writer must have been a very important James to have identified himself with so little information.

The most likely candidate for author of the Book of James is James, the Lord's brother. He probably was the oldest of Jesus' brothers, for his name appears first in the two lists of their names (Matt. 13:55; Mark 6:3). He was an unbeliever in the Lord during Jesus' earthly ministry (see John 7:2-5). The risen Christ apparently appeared to him (1 Cor. 15:7), removed his doubts, and he became a follower of Christ (Acts 1:14). References to him in Acts 12:17; 15:12-29; 21:18-25; and Galatians 1:18-19; 2:6-9 suggest that he quickly became an important leader in the early church.

James 5:14-18 presents our author as a person of prayer. The extra-biblical picture of James is that he spent such time in prayer that his knees became as hard as those of a camel. We cannot clearly prove that the Lord's brother was the author of this writing. However, he is the most likely candidate we find in the New Testament.

Many scholars feel that James is one of the earlier, perhaps the earliest, of the New Testament writings. Three features support this view. First, the language of James and that of Christ in the Synoptic Gospels bears a close similarity. The words of James are not quotations of Jesus' words, and this leads some scholars to suggest that James wrote in a period before the Gospels were written. Second, James described the economic gap between the rich and the poor. When the Jewish revolt against Rome broke out in A.D. 66, the rich endured losses, and conflict between rich and poor ceased. This observation pushes the date of James earlier rather than later. Third, the church organization in James is simple, for only "elders" are mentioned in the book (5:14). Bishops and deacons are not mentioned. All of these factors point to an earlier date, perhaps in the early 50s.

James addressed his letter to "the twelve tribes scattered among the nations" (1:1). Both the writer and his readers have a Jewish background. The term translated "meeting" in 2:2 is the Greek word for "synagogue." The usage may not indicate that Christians were actually meeting in a synagogue, but Jewish Christians were using this name to describe their place of meeting for the worship of Jesus.

Four Jameses in New Testament

1. James, the father of Judas (Luke 6:16; Acts 1:13)
2. James, the son of Alphaeus (Matt. 10:3)
3. James, the son of Zebedee, brother of John; died as martyr under Herod Agrippa (Acts 12:2)
4. James, the Lord's brother

Written in the Early 50s

Readers Have Jewish Background

James wrote to a group of Jewish Christians who faced trials and persecution. Under threat they were tempted to compromise their Christian commitment and relapse into an accommodation to the ways of the world. Wealthy, unbelieving Jews were among those who harassed them (2:6; 5:1-6). These wealthy opponents both insulted them (2:7) and brought them before public officials to accuse them (2:6). These wealthy men retained wages Christians should have received (5:4).

Persecuted Christians Need Stamina

James spoke to his friends as a pastor and urged them to develop spiritual stamina. He also spoke as a prophet to encourage those who considered compromise to deepen their faith and show evidence of its reality.

🌿 **In the following pairs of statements, check the statement that correctly expresses the occasion for the writing of James.[4]**

❏ 1a. James wrote to Jewish Christians who faced trials and persecution.
❏ 1b. James wrote to a church that was lazy because of its affluence.

❏ 2a. The persons to whom James wrote enjoyed a privileged position in the community.
❏ 2b. James' readers were being tempted to compromise their Christian commitment and relapse into an accommodation to the ways of the world.

❏ 3a. James' readers were wealthy members of the Jewish community.
❏ 3b. Wealthy, unbelieving Jews were among those harassing and causing public hardship for Jewish Christians.

❏ 4a. One problem James was addressing was Christians pilfering the belongings of their employers.
❏ 4b. The Christian readers were being taken advantage of by employers who retained wages the Christians should have received.

Once we accept James the Lord's brother as the author, we can say that he likely wrote from Jerusalem, his place of residence. He also referred to "autumn and spring rains" in 5:7. Palestine received early rains in late October or early November. The autumn rains softened the ground for planting. The latter rains came during late April or May. These rains matured the crop. This climatic peculiarity was true in Palestine but not true in many other locations. They point to the likelihood of a Palestinian origin for James' letter.

Ethical Emphasis

James makes its unique contribution to the New Testament with its strong ethical emphasis. It teaches that a faith that does not produce works is empty and useless. James does not contain detailed discussion of some important doctrines such as Jesus' person and work. He does not mention Jesus' incarnation, death, or resurrection. He seems to assume that he and his readers share these beliefs about Jesus.

James used clear, bold language. Many times he expressed his words with the imperative mood such as "Do not merely listen to the word, and so deceive yourselves. Do what it says" (1:22). He had a vivid imagination. He compared a doubting man to "a wave of the sea, blown and tossed by the wind" (1:6). He was also a keen observer of nature. He described the effects of the sun's heat (1:11) and the importance of rainfall (5:7).

Compared to Wisdom Literature

Many scholars compare this epistle with the Wisdom Literature of the Old Testament, such as Psalms and Proverbs. Both James and the Wisdom writings deal

---

4. Answers: 1-a, 2-b, 3-b, 4-b.

with such subjects as the use of the tongue, the need to control the passions, and the dangers of wealth. James often makes more radical demands of his readers than we find in some of the Wisdom writings.

Overview and Content of James

Theme of James: Practical Christian Living

Outline

I. A Pastor's Call to Endurance and Good Works (1:1–2:26)
II. A Prophet's Call to Wisdom and Obedience (3:1–5:20)

After giving a greeting in which he identified himself as a "servant of God" (1:1), James encouraged his readers in their trials by pointing out some of the benefits of testing. They should pray for wisdom to assess correctly and respond properly to their trials (1:2-11). They were also to recognize that temptation comes from within them (see James 4:1) and was not put there by God (1:12-18). James called his readers to accept responsibility for their own behavior.

Read James 1:2-8. Match the statements below.[5]

___ 1. When you face trials   A. will develop perseverance
___ 2. The testing of your faith   B. you will complete and mature
___ 3. When you have persevered   C. you must ask and not doubt
___ 4. If you lack wisdom   D. you should consider it a joy
___ 5. When you ask for wisdom   E. you should ask God who gives it generously

Dead Faith (2:14-26)

James challenged his readers to show their faith by producing works of mercy (2:14-26). He characterized faith without works as "dead" (2:17). He used Abraham and Rahab as demonstrations of a faith that produced works (2:21-26).

"What good is it, my brothers, if a man claims to have faith but has no deeds? Can such faith save him? Suppose a brother or sister is without clothes and daily food. If one of you says to him, 'Go, I wish you well; keep warm and well fed,' but does nothing about his physical needs, what good is it? In the same way, faith by itself, if it is not accompanied by action, is dead. But someone will say 'You have faith; I have deeds.' Show me your faith without deeds, and I will show you my faith by what I do."

—James 2:14-18

Read James 2:14-18 in the margin and then consider the following personal responses. You are not to write anything down and you will not be expected to share these in your group.

A. Are the people who work around you aware that you are a Christian?
B. Does your conduct in your work place show the reality of your personal faith in Christ?
C. If a committee from your church approached your co-workers or neighbors and said, "We are investigating (your name) for a leadership position in the church," would your neighbor or co-worker be able to give you a reference as a genuine believer?

James also focused on the practice of personal discipline (3:1-18). He pointed out the difficulty of controlling the tongue (3:7-8) and its inconsistency (3:9-12).

Evidences of spiritual need among the readers included worldly ways (4:1-12), which could only be overcome by submitting to God in humility and repentance (4:7-10). They also had an arrogant attitude (4:13–5:6). James reminded some who self-confidently planned their own lives without reference to God's will that their lives resembled a transitory vapor. They must admit their own limitations and seek God's will (4:14-15). James particularly denounced wealthy landowners for their greed and careless, arrogant living (5:1-6). He warned his readers that God listened to the cries of the oppressed and would judge those who practiced injustice (5:1).

---

5. Answers: 1-D, 2-A, 3-B, 4-E, 5-C.

Persistence in Devotion

The readers needed to practice a persistent devotion in their service to the Lord (5:7-12). James gave three examples of the practice of enduring devotion and commitment and urged the readers to imitate the farmer who planted and waited for rains in order to produce a crop (5:7). He mentioned the Old Testament prophets who spoke boldly for God despite their suffering (5:10). He commended Job who obeyed the Lord despite his tragic suffering (5:11).

Prayer Always Appropriate

James urged his readers to use prayer in all the times of life (5:13-18). In periods of affliction they were to pray for strength and help. In times of blessing they were to praise God (5:13). In periods of critical sickness the ill person was to summon the leaders of the church for prayer. Prayer for the sick could lead to physical healing and/or spiritual blessing (5:14-15).

Reclaiming Those Who Stray

James also showed a concern for reclaiming Christians who had strayed (5:19-20). He promised that the Christian who won back a sinner would save the wanderer from death and cover over a multitude of sins (see 1 Pet. 4:8).

James' message jolts us to attention by reminding us of actions and attitudes God demands in His people. His guidelines provide a moral compass pointing us in a direction pleasing to God.

RESPONDING TO GOD'S WORD

Read James 3:13-18. Check the boxes beside that which you wish to learn from the Lord:

❏ to be a wise and understanding Christian
❏ to practice true humility (v. 13)
❏ to admit the truth when bitter envy or selfish ambition rules (v. 14)
❏ to recognize evil practices as being from the devil (vv. 15-16)
❏ to recognize the fruit of heavenly wisdom (v. 17)
❏ to become a peacemaker (v. 18)

Day 4   *1 and 2 Peter*

UNIT 12

Peter wrote his letters to persecuted believers who needed to respond to their affliction with obedience and stamina. Peter wanted their response to earn respect from the watching world. He also wanted to defeat the growing influence of heresy within the church. He appealed for spiritual growth as an antiseptic to overcome heresy.

Introduction to Peter's letters

Authorship

During the 20th century some scholars have questioned Peter's authorship because of the refined Greek the letter contains and the nature of the persecution mentioned. However, leaders of the early church made frequent references to 1 Peter. They showed no evidence of any questions about the authorship of the book. Peter claims authorship in 1:1. We also can find support for this acceptance by recognizing the similarity between statements in 1 Peter and the speeches in Acts (compare 1 Pet. 4:5 and Acts 10:42), which seems to come from the same person.

Many more modern scholars have questioned Peter's authorship of 2 Peter. However, the author of 2 Peter also claimed to be Peter (1:1) and stated that he was an eyewitness of Jesus' transfiguration (1:16-18). He claimed to be an apostle and admitted a friendship with Paul (3:15). He obviously intended to be seen as Peter. We may confidently accept his claims as true.

In 1 Peter the apostle designated his friends as Christians living in the provinces of Pontus, Galatia, Cappadocia, Asia, and Bithynia (1 Pet. 1:1). These provinces were in the northern part of Asia Minor. (See map in margin.)

🌿 **Locate the provinces addressed in 1 Peter on the adjacent map.**

Peter's readers had been idolaters when they were unbelievers (4:3), in which case they would have come from a Gentile background. We may assume that Peter wrote to the same group in his second letter (see "my second letter to you," 2 Pet. 3:1).

Occasion and Date

Each chapter of 1 Peter contains some reference to suffering (1:6-7; 2:21-25; 3:13-17; 4:12-19; 5:10). Christian historians know that Nero brought persecution to Christians in Rome in the early sixties. The effects of his persecution caused a ripple effect that spread over into outlying provinces in northern Asia Minor. Peter wrote to give direction and encouragement to his friends in Christ who were experiencing persecution. In 2 Peter the apostle omitted any clear references to the date. He assumed that his death would be soon (1:13-15) and warned about heresy.

Place of Writing

In 1 Peter the apostle said, "She who is in Babylon ... sends you her greetings" (1 Pet. 5:13). Most scholars understand that Babylon is a reference to Rome. Second Peter contains little indication of Peter's location when he wrote.

Overview and Content of 1 and 2 Peter

Theme of 1 Peter: Living as God's Chosen People

    I. God's People are Holy (1:1–2:3)
   II. God's People Witness to the World (2:4–3:12)
 III. God's People Suffer (3:13–5:14)

Outline of 1 Peter

Peter began the first teaching section of his first letter with a discussion of the method and nature of salvation (1:1-12), and he followed it with a preaching section on holiness (1:13–2:3).

🌿 **As you read the next section, underline the three images Peter used to describe the people of God.**[6]

In a second teaching Peter used three images to portray the people of God (2:4-10). First, he saw the church as a living body giving sacrificial service to God (2:2-5). Second, he described the church as a structure founded on Christ as the cornerstone (2:5-8). Third, Peter used the language of Exodus 19:5-6 and Hosea 2:23 to present believers as a group chosen to radiate the glories of God (2:9-10).

In a second preaching section Peter presented the manner in which a Christian leaves his imprint on the world (2:11–3:12). In Peter's day Christians faced determined opposition and searing accusations from unbelievers who faulted their lifestyle. Peter called on his readers to demonstrate a distinctive, winsome commitment to convince their accusers of the genuineness of Christianity.

---

6. Answers: Did you find these images: a living body, a structure, and a special people?

Demonstrating Christianity in Society

Demonstrating Christianity in the Home

Peter urged all citizens to submit to the governing authorities (2:13-17). He encouraged servants to obey and respect their masters with the meekness Christ had shown in His crucifixion (2:18-25). Peter knew the importance of demonstrating Christianity in the home. He appealed to women to demonstrate a respect for their husbands which would attract unsaved spouses to Christ (3:1-6). He appealed to husbands to treat their wives as spiritual equals (3:7). Peter knew that all believers needed to fill their lives with mercy and forgiveness toward others (3:8-12).

🌿 **Read 1 Peter 3:8-12. Mark the following statements _T_ (true) or _F_ (false).[7]**

___ 1. Christians are to live in harmony with one another.
___ 2. A church fight where everyone "speaks his piece" can be good.
___ 3. Love should characterize the Christian.
___ 4. Christians should be known by sympathy, compassion, and humility.
___ 5. Christians may repay evil that is done against them.

Suffering and Persecution

In a final section Peter entered into an intensive discussion of suffering and persecution (3:13–4:19), confronting directly the difficult afflictions the readers were experiencing. Peter taught his audience that it was important for them to be prepared to suffer for righteous living if God's plan included suffering (3:13-17).

Peter encouraged them by showing that Christ's resurrection triumphed over suffering and death (v. 18). He urged them to arm themselves with a willingness to follow the Lord even in suffering (4:1-6). He taught that the power of God's Spirit strengthened them as they faced suffering (4:14), and he encouraged them to trust the faithfulness of God in their trial (4:19).

Assurances for Faithful Servants

Peter concluded his letter with a listing of assurances for faithful servants of God (5:1-14). He described the expected rewards from God for faithful church leaders who fed and cared for their flocks (5:1-4). He directed them to be submissive to one another and to humble themselves under the circumstances God permitted in their lives (5:5-6). He reminded them that though suffering was temporary, God was calling those who obeyed Him to "eternal glory" (5:10).

Overview and Content of 2 Peter

Theme of 2 Peter: Faith for Tough Times

Outline of 2 Peter

I. The Importance of Growing in Faith (1:1-21)
II. The Danger of False Teachers (2:1-22)
III. The Certainty of the Day of the Lord (3:1-18)

Peter's second letter was to Christian friends troubled by false teaching. He called them to spiritual growth and warned of deceitful beliefs of false teachers.

God's Provisions for Growth

Peter explained the provisions God had available for the growth of His children (1:1-21) including the power, promises, and purpose of God (1:3-11); the majestic presence of Christ in their lives (1:16-18); and the divine message God had given in Scripture (1:19-21). He stressed the necessity for spiritual growth to help his readers meet the challenge of false teaching.

Warning Against False Teachers

In 2:1-22 Peter gave a lengthy warning against the false teachers. He portrayed them as immoral and greedy (2:1-3), and he warned that certain judgment would fall on those who followed their ways (2:4-10).

---

7. Answers: 1-T, 2-F, 3-T, 4-T, 5-F.

🌿 **Read 2 Peter 2:1-10. As you read, check the characteristics of the false teachers mentioned by Peter.[8]**

❏ 1. Deny the Lord.
❏ 2. Preach fervently in the name of Jesus.
❏ 3. Live worldly lifestyles.
❏ 4. Cause reproach to come on the church and name of Christ.
❏ 5. Faithfully attend worship.
❏ 6. Exploit people for their own purposes.
❏ 7. Follow the corrupt desires of the sinful nature.
❏ 8. Despise or reject authority.

False Teachers' Evil Practices and Attitudes

To discourage any readers from giving attention to the heretics, Peter portrayed the evil practices and attitudes of their character (2:10-22). He found them to be arrogant, thoroughly corrupt, and deceitful. He warned that they had the power to enslave those who gave attention to their false teaching (2:17-19). Peter also taught that those who followed the teaching of the heretics would experience an ultimate rejection from God (2:20-22).

Certainty of Jesus' Return

Peter inspired his readers with a hope for endurance as he outlined the certainty and result of Jesus' return (3:1-18). The fact of Christ's return held true despite the ridicule of those who opposed it (3:1-4). He proved the coming return of the Lord by asserting that God controlled history (3:5-7), Christ's promise is sure (3:10), and God's faithfulness is trustworthy (3:8-9).

The knowledge of the return of the Lord should produce holy living (3:11) and an urgency in witnessing (3:12). Christians could prevent any stumbling in their lives by mature, consistent growth in Christ (3:17-18).

RESPONDING TO GOD'S WORD

🌴 Second Peter spoke of false teachers. Do they still exist today?
❏ Yes ❏ No

Peter characterized false teachers as:
• posing as Christian leaders,
• teaching falsehoods,
• living immoral lives,
• being greedy,
• attracting many to follow them.

Can Christians identify false teachers by carefully listening to what they teach and observing their lifestyle? ❏ Yes ❏ No

What about some today who widely proclaim themselves to be "Christian prophets" and call for people's time, financial support, and loyalty? Should Christians be reluctant to support such people? ❏ Yes ❏ No
Should we observe their lifestyle? ❏ Yes ❏ No

Ask God to give you discernment in this matter. Keep your eyes on Jesus. Through your church, support Christian leaders whose lives honor Him.

---

8. Answers: 1, 3, 4, 6, 7, and 8.

Day 5 *John's Letters and Jude*

UNIT 12 **Introduction to 1–3 John**

Author, the Apostle John

Such early Christian leaders as Polycarp, Papias, and Irenaeus believed that the Apostle John was the author. Evidence supporting this belief appears in the similarity between the vocabulary of the Gospel of John and the first letter. Terms such as *light* and *eternal life* appear in both writings. The author's claim in 1 John 1:1-4 that he had been an observer of Christ during His ministry on earth also points to John's authorship.

The use of the term *elder* again in 3 John is a likely reference to John the apostle. Most students of the Bible feel that the author of the three letters is one person, and the name of John the apostle is the most likely choice.

Date in 90s

We lack sufficient material for assigning a specific date to John's Letters. We know that John was a "pillar" in the Jerusalem church (Gal. 2:9), but the only biblical evidence on his later years appears in Revelation 1. Church tradition suggests that he spent the ministry of his later years in and around Ephesus. The phrases and content of the epistles resemble those of the Gospel of John, and this leads many scholars to date the writings near the time of the Gospel. Most will date the letters somewhere in the early or mid-90s.

John's first letter does not name recipients, but the apostle identifies his readers as "little children" (2:1) and as "brethren" (2:7). This suggests that John knew his readers. Perhaps they were a group of Christians from Asia Minor whom John warned as they faced false teaching (4:1-2).

2 John to Elect Lady

3 John to Gaius

John addressed his second letter to the "elect lady and her children" (v. 1). This term could describe a personal friend of John, but most scholars regard the term as a description of a local church and its members. John wrote his third letter to Gaius, but we have no specific idea of where Gaius lived.

Written Against Gnosticism

As John wrote his letters, the heresy called Gnosticism was developing within Christendom. Many of John's statements in his first letter appear to be directed specifically against false ideas that resembled the later development of Gnosticism. Gnostics taught that anything physical was necessarily evil, and they believed that Jesus was not a genuine human being. He only *seemed* to be human. Against this view John insisted that he had heard, seen, and touched Jesus (1:1-2); and he thus insisted that Jesus had a real body.

Gnostics also taught that the incarnation of Jesus had been temporary. They believed that a Christ-spirit came on Jesus at His baptism and left Him before His crucifixion. To oppose this idea, John taught that the same Jesus Christ appeared both at the baptism ("by water") and at the crucifixion ("by...blood"). The same Jesus Christ both entered His ministry at baptism and died on the cross (5:6).

🌿 **Write *G* for *Gnosticism* or *T* for *truth* next to the following statements.**[9]

____ 1. Anything physical was evil.
____ 2. Jesus was not a genuine human being; he only *seemed* to be human.
____ 3. Jesus was heard, seen, and touched.
____ 4. Jesus had a real body.

_____ 5. The incarnation of Jesus had been temporary.

_____ 6. A Christ-spirit came on Jesus at His baptism and left Him before His crucifixion.

_____ 7. The same Jesus entered ministry at baptism and died on the cross.

Purpose of 1 John

John wrote his *first letter* to promote fellowship and joy (1:3-4), to urge his readers to practice obedience (2:1), to warn against false teaching (2:26), and to provide a basis for assurance of salvation (5:13). He penned his *second letter* to provide a warning against the false teaching that misunderstood the genuine humanity of Christ (2 John 7). He wrote his *third letter* to provide guidance for a church divided by an internal dispute (3 John 9-10).

Overview and Content of John's Letters

Theme of 1 John: Evidence of True Faith

Outline of 1 John

   I. Obedience as Evidence of Faith (1:1–2:6; 2:28–3:10; 5:4-21)
  II. Love as Evidence of Faith (2:7-17; 3:11-24; 4:7–5:3)
 III. Right Belief as Evidence of Faith (2:18-27; 4:1-6)

🌿 **Read the excerpts from 1 John 1:1-4 in the margin before you continue your study.**

"That which was from the beginning ... the Word of life ... appeared: we have seen it ... and we proclaim to you the eternal life ... so that you also may have fellowship with us. ... We write this to make our joy complete."

—1 John 1:1-4

In 1:5 through 2:6 John presented the first discussion of the evidences for eternal life. He urged his readers to walk in the light of obedience to God (1:7). He urged those who stumbled in their spiritual lives to confess their sin and experience God's forgiveness (1:9). He wrote these words to discourage sin, and he presented Christ as our advocate in God's presence whenever we fall into sin (2:1-2). John indicated that those who genuinely knew God would follow His commandments (2:3).

In 1 John 2:7-17 John described the correct attitude that should characterize a believer. He pointed out that believers will love one another and not the world. The believer who loves his Christian brother walks in fellowship with God (2:10). Believers also will direct their love toward God and not toward the pleasure-centered lifestyle of the world (2:15-17).

🌿 **Read John 8:12; 13:34-35; 1 John 2:7-11. When you complete the reading choose the correct answer(s) to the statements below.**[10]

   1. Jesus has commanded us to
     ❑ a. tolerate one another
     ❑ b. love one another

   2. The one who follows Jesus will
     ❑ a. have the light of life
     ❑ b. walk around in the darkness

   3. John tells us that
     ❑ a. the one who hates his brother abides in darkness
     ❑ b. the one who loves his brother walks in the light

Believer Views Christ Correctly

John presented a third element in demonstrating the reality of eternal life in 2:18-27. A genuine believer will hold the correct view of Christ and His work. John

---

9. Answers: 1-G, 2-G, 3-T, 4-T, 5-G, 6-G, 7-T.
10. Answers: 1-b, 2-a, 3-a & b.

warned believers against those who refused to admit that Jesus was the Messiah (2:22-23). John pointed out that the teaching work of the Holy Spirit would guard against their believing the erroneous emphases of the false teachers (2:26-27).

John repeated his call for right practice in 2:28 through 3:10. He pointed out that the hope inspired by a knowledge of Christ's return produces holiness (3:1-3). He warned that a person who consistently failed to practice righteousness demonstrates that he does not belong to God (3:6,10).

In 3:11-24 John presented a more specific definition of love for one another. God had demonstrated this love in the sacrificial death of Christ (3:16). We are to show this love to others by deeds of kindness and mercy (3:17-18). Our practice of this love brings us an assurance of our standing with God (3:19).

Recognition of Spirit of Truth

In chapter 4 John emphasized the recognition of the Spirit of truth as he again stressed the importance of a proper belief in Christ in 4:1-6. A true believer must accept Jesus as God's incarnate Son (4:2-3). John warned his readers that false teaching would attract those who were gullible and worldly in their goals (4:5).

Demonstration of God's Love

From 4:7 through 5:3 John discussed the demonstration of God's love. The greatness of the divine love provided an incentive to love each other (4:11). Our practice of love for one another demonstrates that God's love has reached its goal within us (4:12). The presence of love provides confidence for believers on the day when Jesus returns (4:17-18). Our love for God also will produce a genuine concern for fellow Christians (4:19-21).

Assurance of Eternal Life

John concluded his first letter by giving further assurances of eternal life and by stressing the importance of living in God's will (5:4-21). He stressed that those who are born of God have the faith necessary to overcome the world (5:4). He taught that those who respond to God's revelation in Christ had eternal life (5:11-12). Those who live in God's will experience intimate privileges in prayer (5:14-15). Those who are in the center of God's will experience victory over the practice of sin (5:18).

 Is it possible to know that your prayer will be answered? John tells us that if we ask according to His will, "we know that we have what we have asked of him." Be prepared to discuss this in your group session.

Theme of 2 John: Walking in the Truth

In 2 John the apostle met the same type of false teaching he had encountered in 1 John. He used the term "elect lady and her children" to refer to a Christian church. He pointed out that a common acceptance of truth bound him to this church (vv. 1-2). He encouraged his readers to continue to walk in God's commandments (v. 6).

John warned that those who deny the incarnation of Christ lack true faith (vv. 7, 9). He urged his readers to give no form of assistance to those whose doctrine was in error (vv. 10-11). He also prepared them for his future visit (vv. 12-13).

Theme of 3 John: Working Together for the Truth

In 3 John, the apostle wrote to urge Christians in a congregation to deal wisely with a contentious, domineering church member. First, he commended a faithful member–Gaius–who had shown kindness and hospitality to traveling Christians (vv. 2-8). Second, he warned against the arrogant behavior of Diotrephes (vv. 9-11). Third, he gave an expression of praise to Demetrius whose behavior had

earned universal respect (v. 12). He concluded with an expression of hope that he soon would be able to visit the church (v. 14).

Match the names of the men with their description.[11]

   ___ 1. Gaius   A. He was praised because his excellent behavior had earned universal respect.

   ___ 2. Diotrephes B. He had shown kindness and hospitality to traveling Christians.

   ___ 3. Demetrius C. He was firmly rebuked for his unchristian actions and attitudes.

Introduction to the Book of Jude

Jude identified himself as a servant of Jesus Christ and a brother of James (v. 1). He was doubtless referring to James, the Lord's brother (see Mark 6:3), as his own brother. Assuming Jude was a younger brother of Jesus, we would date his birth in the early part of the Christian era. His letter would be dated later in Jude's lifetime, but no later than A.D. 70 or 80.

Pause now and read the Book of Jude. As you read, note the sections of Jude that begin with the salutation "dear friends." Circle the number of times you found the salutation "dear friends."   1   2   3   4

Readers

Jude did not give a specific address, and his reference to those who are "sanctified" and "preserved" could refer to Christians who live anywhere. Jude obviously had a specific historical situation in mind. His use of Jewish apocryphal writings (see vv. 9, 14-15) might point to a Jewish setting. His references in verses 17-18 seem to suggest that the readers had heard some of the apostles. Some have called Jude a circular letter written to warn all Christians against heresy. Others favor a Palestinian setting, but it is impossible to be firm about the location.

Jude makes reference to two non-biblical writings in the short space of 25 verses. He refers both to 1 Enoch (v. 14) and the Assumption of Moses (v. 9). His reference to these books indicates that he holds them in high esteem, but he is not suggesting that they are as important as Scripture.

Overview and Content of Jude

Theme of Jude: Contending for the Faith

Theme of Jude

Briefly in verses 3-4 Jude outlined the occasion for his writing. He had prepared to write a letter on the subject of "salvation" when he learned of the problem caused by the presence of false teachers. Jude urged his readers to show strenuous effort in their response for the faith. He wanted them to defend the gospel message and demonstrate its power by right living. He also warned against the actions of the godless heretics who denied the Lord Jesus Christ.

Heretics Trouble Christians

In verses 5-16 Jude described the heretics whose teaching was troubling his readers. He mentioned five features about the heretics. First, Jude pictured them as deserving divine judgments (vv. 5-7). Second, he warned against their arrogance (vv. 8-9). Third, he described their corrupt ways by comparing them to Balaam and Korah in the Old Testament (vv. 10-13). Fourth, he referred to 1 Enoch to describe the future punishment to which they were doomed. Fifth, he described their self-will (v. 16).

---

11. Answers: 1-B, 2-C, 3-A.

🌿 Match the features of the heretics described by Jude with the verse references describing them.[12]

___ 1. He pictured them as deserving divine judgment.

___ 2. He warned against their arrogance.

___ 3. He described their corrupt ways by comparing them to Balaam and Korah in the Old Testament.

___ 4. He referred to 1 Enoch to describe the future punishment to which they were doomed.

___ 5. He described their self-will.

A. Jude 8-9

B. Jude 10-13

C. Jude 16

D. Jude 5-7

E. Jude 14-15

Resist Heretics

In 17-23 Jude prepared his readers to resist the enticing words of the heretics. He urged his friends to pay heed to the warnings given by the apostles, perhaps in such passages as 2 Timothy 3:1-7 (vv. 17-19).

Jude also urged them to grow in their knowledge and application of the Christian faith and to pray with vigor (vv. 20-21). He encouraged them to remain in God's love by the practice of obedience and urged them to fan the flames of Christian hope by holy living in anticipation of the return of Jesus. He directed his friends to give help to straying believers by demonstrating mercy to those who were in difficulty (vv. 22-23).

Doxology to God

In verses 24-25 Jude burst into a spontaneous doxology before God. He described God as the one who alone could provide the strength needed for complete obedience. In verse 24 he pictured God as one who could provide enduring power for believers. In verse 25 he praised God for His "glory, majesty, dominion, and power" because of the work of Jesus Christ.

🌿 **SUMMARY REVIEW**

To review this unit, see if you can mentally answer the following questions. You may want to write the answers on a separate sheet of paper. Mark your level of performance on the left: circle C if you can answer correctly and circle R if you need to review.

C R 1. What is the purpose and theme of Hebrews?

C R 2. What is the theme and emphasis of James?

C R 3. Identify from 1–2 Peter three ways Christians witness to the world.

C R 4. List from 1 John 3 evidences of true faith.

C R 5. What does John say about truth in 2 and 3 John?

C R 6. What does Jude say about faith?

Review this week's material to find the answers.

RESPONDING TO GOD'S WORD

Using the doxology in Jude 24-25, spend time in personal worship and praise of God. Focus on the twin truths of the Lord's keeping power (v. 24) and our responsibility to glorify Him (v. 25).

---

12. Answers: 1-D, 2-A, 3-B, 4-E, 5-C.

Unit 13 — The Book of Revelation

**Reading Through
the New Testament**

❏ Revelation 1–3
❏ Revelation 4–6
❏ Revelation 7–9
❏ Revelation 10–12
❏ Revelation 13–15
❏ Revelation 16–18
❏ Revelation 19–22

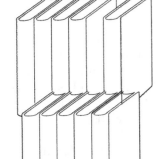

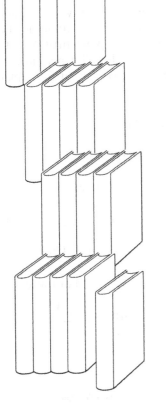

UNIT LEARNING GOAL: The study of this unit should help you understand the background and writing of the Book of Revelation. You will be able to:
- Explain the meaning of the word *Revelation* and how it was given.
- Describe the threefold purpose of Revelation.
- Interpret the various views people hold about Revelation.
- Express the theme and list the four visions of Revelation.
- Summarize the judgments of God and the end of history.
- Describe the reign of Christ and the eternal blessing of heaven.
- Testify to an expectancy for the coming of the Lord Jesus.

🌿 **Fill in the names of the New Testament books in the margin.**

Reasons You Should Be Eager to Study Revelation

A Revelation from Christ. We should be eager to study Revelation because it comes directly from our Lord, Jesus Christ. God the Father gave it to Him to reveal to us. It is the final revelation from Christ in Scripture.

Emphasizes Judgment, Redemption, Kingdom. We should be eager to study Revelation because it emphasizes some of the central themes of the Bible. Three themes strongly enunciated in Revelation are *judgment, redemption,* and the *kingdom of God.*

Filled with Songs of Praise. We should be eager to study Revelation because it is filled with magnificent songs of praise to God. These songs extol the Person and the work of God the Father and of Christ the Son.

Points to the Return of Christ. We should be eager to study Revelation because it stresses the Lord's coming. Jesus said, "Behold, I am coming soon!" (22:7,12,20). As we study this climactic book, our hearts should respond, "Amen. Come, Lord Jesus" (22:20).

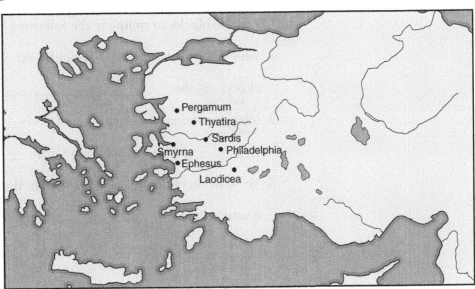

Day 1   Introduction to Revelation

UNIT 13

John

Author, Date, and Readers

The author of Revelation designated himself as John (1:1, 4, 9; 22:8) and as a prophet (22:9). No early church leader named John could be identified with so little information except the apostle John. Such leaders as Justin Martyr, Irenaeus, Origen, and Tertullian agreed that the apostle John authored the book.

Some scholars date Revelation in the time of Nero after the burning of Rome in A.D. 64. We know that Nero persecuted Christians after this event, but the persecution then was local. Revelation envisioned worldwide persecution (13:7-8). Another fact taken as support for authorship in Nero's reign is that the numerical value of the Hebrew letters for Nero Caesar (spelled "Neron Kesar") add up to 666, the number of the beast in 13:18.

A.D. 95 or 96

The early church father Irenaeus dated Revelation during the reign of the Roman emperor Domitian (A.D. 81-96). Most scholars suggest that John wrote the book in A.D. 95 or 96. We do not know details of Domitian's persecution of Christians. We do know he ruthlessly suppressed those who opposed his plans and orders. The outlook of the book is for additional persecution (see 1:9; 2:13; 3:10). John wrote the Revelation to Christians in the seven churches of Asia (see chaps. 2–3).

 Draw a circle around Ephesus, Smyrna, Pergamum, Thyatira, Sardis, Philadelphia, and Laodicea on the map on the first page of this unit.

Purpose and Style

John wrote Revelation to remind suffering believers of the sovereignty of God and the redeeming work of Christ. To provide hope for believers in Asia Minor, he emphasized the completion of God's plan of redemption at the return of Christ. Visions and symbols of Revelation provide encouragement and hope for all generations of believers. They remind us that the resurrected Lord Jesus is carrying out God's plan and will return to judge and rule the earth in righteousness.

Purpose

To remind us of—
• God's sovereignty
• Christ's redemption
• Christ's coming kingdom

 Fill in the blanks to complete the following sentences.[1]

1. John wrote the Revelation to remind suffering believers of the _____

   of God and the _____ _____ of Christ.

2. John emphasized the completion of God's _____ of _____ at the

   _____ of Christ in order to provide _____ for troubled believers.

3. The symbols of the Revelation remind us that the resurrected Lord Jesus

   is carrying out _____ _____ and will return to _____

   and _____ the earth with _____.

---

1. Answers: 1-sovereignty, redeeming work, 2-plan, redemption, return, hope, 3-God's plan, judge, rule, righteousness.

🌿 **Underline the characteristics of the three styles of literature found in Revelation as you read the following section.**

Style

The Book of Revelation contains elements of three styles of literature that appear in the Bible.

1. Prophecy. It is a prophecy, a proclamation (1:3; 22:18). It revealed God's plan for the future in such a way as to change the lives of the readers in the present.

2. Letter. It resembles a letter. Particularly in chapters 2–3 we find evidence that John wrote his book to seven specific churches.

3. Apocalyptic. Apocalyptic literature used a vivid stockpile of symbols, looked forward to the future intervention of God in history, and predicted the destruction of evil. Much apocalyptic literature outside the Bible used a false name for the author (such as Enoch in 1 Enoch), but this is not true of Revelation. The name John represented John the Apostle, and was not a pen name. The Old Testament Book of Daniel shares this literature style in common with Revelation.

The Book of Revelation stands as unique literature in the New Testament because it has characteristics of all three types of literature: prophecy, letter, and apocalyptic.

🌿 **List the names of the three styles of literature found in the Revelation.[2]**

1. _____

2. _____

3. _____

RESPONDING TO GOD'S WORD

Read 1:1-3. Meditate on the phrases "Revelation," "To show His servants," "He made it known," and "Blessed." Recognize that God wants to make the message of this book clear to you, and He has promised a blessing (the word is used twice in v. 3) for all who study the Book of Revelation. Ask the Lord for wisdom and insight to understand it.

Day 2   *The Uniqueness of Revelation*

U N I T   1 3

Special Features of Revelation

The Book of Revelation repeats many phrases. For example, four times (1:10; 4:2; 17:3; 21:10) John spoke of being "in the Spirit" as he received a revelation from God. John also used the phrase "them [they] that dwell upon [on] the earth" (3:10; 6:10; 11:10; 13:8, 14) as a reference to evildoers who will receive the judgment and punishment of God. As we observe these repeated phrases and their definitions, we can grasp the development and teaching of God's message in Revelation.

Repetition of Phrases

---

2. Answers: 1- prophecy, 2-letter, 3- apocalyptic material. Go back and check to be sure you underlined the three styles of literature and their characteristics.

Blocks of Material

Revelation contains blocks of material. In chapters 2–3 we find a message to the churches. In 6:1–8:6 John revealed the seal judgements, the trumpet judgments in 8:7–11:19, and the bowl judgments in chapter 16. Interspersed within these blocks of material are interludes which show pauses in God's action and create a sense of anticipation among the readers (see 10:1–11:14; 12:1–14:20).

Songs of Praise

Revelation is filled with magnificent songs of praise to God. These songs (see 4:8,11; 5:9-14; 15:3-4) extol God's person and work. They become a model for Christians to use in their own worship of God. The Book of Revelation makes much use of

Use of Numbers

numbers. Interpreters struggle to determine whether the references are to be taken as symbolic or as literal. Common numbers are seven (see 1:20), four (see 7:1), three (see 16:13), and one thousand (see 20:2-3,5).

Old Testament References

The Book of Revelation makes frequent reference to the Old Testament. John drew heavily on references to Psalms, Isaiah, Ezekiel, Zechariah, and Daniel. He never formally cited the Old Testament in a quotation, but he made frequent reference to incidents and features rooted in the Old Testament.

 List five special features of Revelation.[3]

1._____

2._____ 4._____

3._____ 5._____

The Interpretation of Revelation

Interpreters of Revelation usually choose among four approaches to understanding the book. Many use features from all of these approaches in their interpretation.

 Circle the names of the interpretative approaches to Revelation as you encounter them.

No Reference to Historical Events

Idealist interpreters view Revelation as a picture of the continuous struggle between good and evil. This system views the book as teaching general truths about God, the church, and the future victory of Christianity with no specific reference to historical events. This approach is hesitant to emphasize predictive prophecy.

Fulfilled in Early Church History

Preterist approach suggests that the teaching of Revelation was fulfilled in the days of the Roman Empire. Many who follow this approach hold Revelation to be inspired literature, but they are convinced that most of its message was fulfilled. They see the book as giving encouragement for those who faced persecution in Asia Minor in the first century, but they do not see it as having reference to future events.

Symbolic History of the Church

Continuous-historical approach relates the book to historical events. One who follows this method views the book as a forecast in symbols of the history of the church. The system often makes the Book of Revelation a prophecy dealing with the apostasy of the Roman Catholic Church from the New Testament faith. It seeks parallels between the events in Revelation and such secular events as the invasions of the Huns, the Muslims, and the Turks.

---

3. Answers: 1-The Book of Revelation contains many repeated phrases. 2-Revelation contains blocks of materials. 3- Revelation is filled with magnificent songs. 4-Revelation makes much use of numbers. 5-Revelation makes frequent references to the Old Testament.

Events at End of Time

Futurist approach is the opposite of one who is a preterist. The futurist views much of Revelation as dealing with events at the end of the world. Futurists understand that chapters 2 and 3 are referring to churches that existed in the first century. Starting in chapter 4, they feel that Revelation contains events closely connected with the return of Christ. Those who follow this approach face the challenge of understanding how the book was relevant to first-century Christians when they feel that most of its message is about events at the end of the ages.

Many modern interpreters of Revelation follow the futurist approach. Some employ insights of other approaches (such as the preterist or the idealist system) in order to make the book relevant to the first century and this century.

🌿 **Match the name of the approach to interpreting the Revelation with the correct description.[4]**

____ 1. Idealist view

____ 2. Preterist view

____ 3. Continuous-historical view

____ 4. Futurist view

A. Makes the Revelation a forecast in symbols of th history of the church.
B. Makes the Revelation a picture of the continuing struggle between good and evil.
C. Makes the Revelation, starting at Chapter 4, deal with events closely connected with the return of Christ.
D. States that the Revelation's teaching was fulfilled in the days of the Roman Empire.

MILLENNIAL VIEWS

Postmillennialism—church brings millennium
Amillennialism—no literal millennium on earth
Historical premillennialists—Christ brings millennium
Dispensational premillennialists—Christ brings millennium

Closely tied to various interpretations of Revelation are millennial views. *Millennium* means literally *one thousand years,* and it has come to symbolize the golden age predicted by the Old Testament prophets.

Postmillennialists believe the preaching of the gospel will cause life (or people) to get better and better until earth will enter a golden age. Christ will come after (or *post*) the millennium.

Amillennialists believe there is no literal reign of Christ on earth (*a millennia* means *no millennium*), but Christ's present rule over the church is the millennium. According to this view, Satan is a defeated enemy, and believers reign in life by Christ Jesus.

Historical premillennialists believe Christ will return before (*pre*) the golden age and will reign on earth with His saints.

Dispensational premillennialists (like historical premillennialists) believe Christ will return before the golden age and will reign on earth with His saints. They.

---
4. Answers: 1-B, 2-D, 3-A, 4-C.

believe God has worked with humanity in different ways during each of several dispensations (or ages). They generally believe that prophetic passages will be fulfilled more literally with two stages to Christ's return (1-a, rapture that secretly removes the church, and 2-a, later return in glory), and they believe in several judgments.

RESPONDING TO GOD'S WORD

Read Revelation 3:20. Jesus stands outside what? _____

What does the door symbolize? _____

What is Jesus doing? _____

What response does He want? _____

Day 3   *A Panoramic View of Revelation*

UNIT 13

Outline

Overview of Revelation

Theme of Revelation: A Vision of Our Conquering Christ

   I. Christ Strengthening the Churches (1:1–3:22)
   II. Christ's Judgment on Sin (4:1–16:21)
   III. Christ's Victory over Evil (17:1–21:8)
   IV. Christ's Ultimate Triumph (21:9–22:21)

Four Basic Visions

Glorified Christ (1–3)

Revelation contains four basic visions that portray God at work in the world. John opens his prophecy with a picture of the glorified Christ strengthening churches that face persecution (1:1–3:22). John saw a vision of Christ (1:12-16) that he used to encourage the seven churches of Asia as they faced persecution.

Divine Judgment (4–16)

John's second vision shows divine judgment on the world of sin (4:1–16:21). In this section John described the sequences of judgment—known as seals (6:1–8:1), trumpets (8:7–11:19), and bowls (16:2-21)—in order to show God's work in pouring out wrath and affliction on the world of sin.

Victory of Christ (17–20)

John's third vision pictured the victory of Christ over evil (17:1–21:8). In this section John saw the destruction of a secular civilization (18:1-24), the return of Christ in glorious victory (19:11-16), and the millennial reign of Christ (20:1-6).

Ultimate Triumph (21–22)

In John's final vision the apostle pictured Christ in triumph over the ages (21:9–22:5). Here John portrayed a symbolic picture of heaven with God the Father and Jesus Christ the Son shown in triumph and victory (21:22-24). This vision would inspire hope and encouragement for believers.

In a concluding section (22:6-21) John relayed to the churches warnings and promises he received from Christ.

🌿 Fill in the blanks.[5]

1. Revelation contains _____ basic _____ which portray God at work in the _____.

2. The first vision is a picture of the _____ Christ _____ churches that face _____.

3. The second vision shows _____ _____ on the world of _____.

4. The third vision pictures the _____ of Christ over _____.

5. The fourth vision pictures Christ in _____ over the _____.

6. In the concluding section John relayed to the churches _____ and _____ he received from _____.

Christ Speaks to the Churches (1–3)

John began Revelation with an introduction in 1:1-8. In verses 1-3 he included a title to the book. He designated the book as a revelation of Jesus Christ. The word *revelation* refers to an uncovering of something that man alone could not discover.

🌿 Read and compare Revelation 1:1-8 and 1 Corinthians 2:9-10 (in the margin). Mark the following statements *T* (true) or *F* (false).[6]

____ 1. Revelation is the natural result of man's inquiry into spiritual things.
____ 2. God has prepared things for His people that they could never imagine.
____ 3. God reveals truth to us through His Spirit.
____ 4. We may freely understand the things of God as His Spirit enables us.
____ 5. Jesus' greeting to John included grace and peace from the Father.

"No eye has seen, no ear has heard, no mind has conceived what God has prepared for those who love Him; but God has revealed it to us by his Spirit."

—1 Corinthians 2:9-10

The channel of disclosure of the book was from the Father to the Son and through an angel to John. The term *signified* prepares us to expect many symbols within the book. In 1:7 he outlined the theme of the book. John was reminding his readers of the return of Christ and of all events that occur in connection with that return.

In chapters 1–3 John narrated the first vision. In 1:12-16 John saw Christ in an exalted state and pictured Him with features that called attention to His majesty and power. In chapters 2 and 3 John gave a message to the seven churches of Asia. Most messages to the churches follow the general order of first describing Jesus the speaker with terms taken from the glorious appearance of Christ in 1:12-16; then a word of commendation or praise, rebuke, warning, and promise.

The church at Laodicea receives no praise. The church at Philadelphia receives no rebuke. These seven churches represent typical churches and needs from the first-century period. The words of Christ to the churches are relevant for churches in our century also. They provide vivid pictures of what God can do in judging disobedient churches and in strengthening and using committed churches.

Cities of Asia

- Ephesus
- Laodicea
- Pergamum
- Philadelphia
- Sardis
- Smyrna
- Thyatira

---

5. Answers: 1-four, visions, world, 2-glorified, strengthening, persecution, 3- divine judgment, sin, 4- victory, evil, 5-triumph, ages, 6-warnings, promises, Christ.
6. Answers: 1-F, 2-T, 3-T, 4-T, 5-T.

"Among the lampstands was someone 'like a son of man,' dressed in a robe reaching down to his feet and with a golden sash around his chest. His head and hair were white like wool, as white as snow, and his eyes were like blazing fire. His feet were like bronze glowing in a furnace, and his voice was like the sound of rushing waters. In his right hand he held seven stars, and out of his mouth came a sharp double-edged sword. His face was like the sun shining in all its brilliance."

—Revelation 1:13-16

RESPONDING TO GOD'S WORD

Read Revelation 1:13-16 in the margin. Answer the following.

1. What is Jesus trying to reveal about Himself in this vision?

_____

2. How does His majesty and triumph relate to my life today?

_____

_____

Day 4   *The Judgment of God (Rev. 4–11)*

UNIT 13

Vision of Divine Judgment (4–16)

The Great Tribulation

"Come up Here" (Rev. 4–5)

John presented his second vision in 4:1 through 16:21. In this section he outlined the three series of judgments–seals, trumpets, and bowls–that God will bring into the world as a punishment for sin.

Interpreters disagree concerning the question of the place of the church in this section of Revelation. Some interpreters feel that the call to "Come up here" (4:1) represents the rapture of the church. In this view the church is removed from the earth prior to the time of trial and affliction at the end known as the great tribulation. The church escapes the trials, afflictions, and outpouring of wrath during this time. Other interpreters feel that this section has images that suggest the church is present on earth but will not experience the wrath of God.

Check the correct ending for each of the following statements.[7]

1. In Revelation 4:1–16:21, John outlines three series of judgments God will bring into the world to
   ❑ a. destroy Satan   ❑ b. cleanse the saints.   ❑ c. punish sin
2. The call to "Come up here" is said to refer to which two of the following by various interpreters of the Revelation:
   ❑ a. John   ❑ b. An angel   ❑ c. The church

3. The time of trial and affliction at the end of time is know as
   ❑ a. the great tribulation   ❑ b. Christ's judgment   ❑ c. Moses' mourning

4. God's wrath is His
   ❑ a. vindication of His people
   ❑ b. judgment of a sinful church
   ❑ c. punishment on sin and sinners

_____

7. Answers: 1-c, 2-a, c, 3-a, 4-c.

A Picture of Majesty

This section begins with God on His heavenly throne. Chapter 4 seeks to answer the question "Who is in charge of the events of history?" John's vision teaches that the all-powerful God controls the events of history. In chapter 5 John raised the question of "Who will carry out God's will in history?" John's vision teaches that the Lamb of God, Jesus Christ, is worthy.

🌿 **Answer the following questions with a word or phrase.**[8]

　　1. Who is on the throne in chapter 4?_____

　　2. Who is in charge of the events of history?_____

　　3. Who will carry out God's will in history? _____

The Seal Judgments (6–7)

The seal judgments, extend from 6:1 through 8:1 with an interlude in 7:9-17. The seal judgments obtain their name from the wax seals used to close the scroll (*book* in 5:1 refers to scroll). This scroll contains the revelation of God's plan for the conclusion of history. As each seal is removed from the scroll another picture, usually representing a judgment, occurs. The **first four seals** represent the spirit of conquest, war, famine, and death. The opening of the **fifth seal** gives a vision of the safety of God's people in His presence. The opening of the **sixth seal** provides a vision of the coming terrible divine judgment at the conclusion of the ages.

Conquest, War, Famine, Death

Some interpreters see these seal judgments as events occurring during the great tribulation. It seems best to view them as examples of judgments that occur throughout this present age. During this age we constantly see conquest, war, famine, and death as the unfortunate results of sin. This same sequence of judgments also appears in Matthew 24:1-13. Jesus described those events as the "beginning of birth pains [or sorrows]" (Matt. 24:8). The seal judgments represent those judgments which God brings on sin and sinners in this age.

🌿 **Fill in the blanks.**[9]

　　1. The first round of judgments is called the _____ judgments.

　　2. The first four seals represent in order _____, _____,

　　　　_____, and _____.

　　3. The fifth seal shows God's people safe in _____ _____.

　　4. The sixth seal shows _____ _____ at the conclusion of the ages.

　　5. The seal judgments represent those judgments which God brings

　　　　on _____ and _____ in _____ _____.

God's People Are Protected

The interlude in chapter 7 between the sixth and seventh seals provides a picture of the sealing of God's people for protection from God's wrath during the great tribulation. Interpreters differ concerning the identity of the 144,000 in 7:1-8. Some identify them as a godly remnant of Jews whom God preserves to be on

---

8. Answers: 1-God, 2-God, 3-The Lamb of God, Jesus Christ.
9. Answers: 1-seal, 2-the spirit of conquest, war, famine, and death, 3-His presence, 4-divine judgment, 5-sin, sinners, this age.

earth when Christ returns. Others see the figure of the 144,000 Israelites as a symbol of the full number of God's people in the church. They observe that the New Testament sometimes applies Old Testament images of Israel to the church (see Gal. 3:29; 1 Pet. 2:9-10).

144,000

John seems to be designating this group of 144,000 as believing Jews, which could be construed as referring to the church (Rom. 2:28-29). John declared that they would be preserved during the coming time of trouble. The vision in 7:9-17 refers to a great multitude of Gentile believers in the church (7:9), but this time the vision pictures them at the conclusion of the time of tribulation.

The Trumpet Judgments (8–11)

Judgment During the Great Tribulation

In 8:1 John announced the opening of the **seventh seal**, and this led to silence, a dramatic pause. After a brief period of silence, a new period of judgments—the **trumpet judgments**—began (8:7–11:19). Within those judgments is another brief interlude in 10:1–11:13. Most interpreters view the trumpet judgments as taking place during the great tribulation. At the beginning of each trumpet judgment an angel stepped forward to sound a trumpet.

The **first four trumpet judgments** affect the earth or heavenly bodies. These judgments bring destruction to vegetation (8:7), oceans (8:8-9), inland waterways (8:10-11), and heavenly bodies (8:12). The **fifth and sixth trumpet judgments** afflict men with pain and torture (9:4,6,10), and with death (9:18). The **seventh trumpet judgment** (11:15-19) introduces the period of the end and resembles somewhat the sixth seal judgment (see 6:12-17).

These trumpet judgments are partial in their effects as indicated by the use of a fraction to describe the results of the judgments (see 8:7-9). We also see a similarity between these trumpets and the plagues in Egypt appearing in Exodus. The mention of the failure of men to repent in 9:21 implies that repentance is a purpose in God's bringing these judgments. God is not merely seeking to be punitive in His judgments, but He desires to bring people to repentance. God shows His long-suffering in extending to sinners an opportunity for repentance (2 Pet. 3:9).

🌿 **Mark the following statements T (true) or F (false).**[10]

_____ 1. The judgments in 8:7–11:19 are called the trumpet judgments.
_____ 2. No interpreters place the trumpet judgments during the great tribulation.
_____ 3. The first four trumpet judgments affect the earth or heavenly bodies.
_____ 4. The fifth and sixth trumpet judgments afflict man with pain only.
_____ 5. The seventh trumpet judgment introduces the period of the end.
_____ 6. The trumpet judgments are total in their effects.
_____ 7. There is a similarity between the trumpet judgments and the plagues in the Egyptian Exodus.

God's Judgment

In chapter 10 God reaffirmed His commission to John to serve as a prophet (10:11). In chapter 11 John used the symbol of the measurement of the temple to show God's protection of His own during the great tribulation. The act of measuring the temple probably symbolizes God's protection of the redeemed (see 2 Sam. 8:2). Protection does not imply that Christians will have no harm or affliction during the great tribulation. Christians will face suffering and even death (see 11:7-8). Believers are never

God Protects His Own

promised exemption from physical trials (see Acts 14:22). However, nothing can harm the believers spiritually or rob them of eternal life.

---

10. Answers: 1-T, 2-F, 3-T, 4-F, 5-T, 6-F, 7-T.

RESPONDING TO GOD'S WORD

Read Revelation 11:7-12. What do the two witnesses represent?

_____

After giving them power for ministry and using them mightily, why would God

allow them to be killed? _____

Read Revelation 2:10 (in margin). Am I willing to witness for Him, even if sacrifice or suffering result?

"Be faithful, even to the point of death, and I will give you the crown of life."

—Revelation 2:10

Day 5

Further Judgment and Blessing (Rev. 12—22)

UNIT 13

Interlude (Rev. 12–14)

Conflict Between Satan and God's People

John presented a third interlude in chapters 12—14 to give encouragement to persecuted Christians as they face opposition. The vision of the woman and the dragon (chap. 12) shows the perpetual conflict between Satan and God's people. The vision reminds believers that Christ has defeated Satan (Heb. 2:14), and commitment to Christ brings victory over Satanic temptation and harassment (12:9-12).

The Antichrist and the Beast

In chapter 13 John presented the Antichrist, the beast from the sea (13:1), as an example of the use of political power to carry out Satan's diabolical purposes (13:5-8). The second beast in the chapter, the beast from the land, is sometimes named the false prophet (16:13). He uses religious power to trick unbelievers into giving worship and obedience to Satanic influence (13:12). Believers will face an array of Satanic opposition, but John reassures them by visions of hope in chapter 14. Here he reminded his readers that God gave spiritual victory to those who endured in their commitment to Christ (14:1-5).

Match the phrases on the left with the correct matches on the right. Write the correct letters in the blanks.[11]

____ 1. Chapter 12–14

____ 2. The woman and the dragon

____ 3. The Antichrist, the beast from the sea

____ 4. The beast from the land, the false prophet

____ 5. Those to whom God gives spiritual victory

A. Those who endured in their commitment to Christ

B. Use of political power to carry out Satan's purposes

C. The third interlude

D. Use of religious power to trick unbelievers into giving worship and obedience to Satanic influence

E. Perpetual conflict between Satan and the people of God

---

11. Answers: 1-C, 2-E, 3-B, 4-D, 5-A.

The Bowl Judgments (Rev. 15–16)

Wrath of God

The final round of judgments, the bowl judgments, appear in chapter 15 through 16. In these judgments John saw angels pouring from a bowl filled with a liquid which symbolized the wrath of God. Each outpouring brought forth a new act of judgment on sin and sinners. John introduced the prelude to these judgments in chapter 15. The occurrence of the judgments is narrated in chapter 16. The first four bowl judgments follow the order of the trumpet judgments in affecting the earth, the oceans, the inland waterways, and the heavenly bodies.

Armageddon

However, these judgments are not partial (no fractions are used to describe them) but complete. These judgments affect humans at the beginning. The outpouring of the fifth bowl represents God's judgment on demonic civilization in the final times (16:10-11). The sixth bowl judgment represents a preparation for the final spiritual battle symbolized by the reference to Armageddon. The Hebrew term, *Armageddon,* signified "the mountain of Megiddo" where many famous battles in Old Testament times were fought (Judg. 5:19; 2 Kings 23:29). John used it to represent the place of final struggle between the powers of evil and God's kingdom.

The outpouring of the seventh bowl led to the fall of Babylon and the consummation of God's judgment on the world (16:17-21). The mention of the destruction of Babylon makes a natural passage into the third vision in Revelation.

Consummation of All Things (Rev. 17–20)

Vision of Christ's Victory (17–20)

From 17:1 through 21:8 John narrated a vision of consummation. In chapter 17 he explained the symbolism of Babylon, and in chapter 18 he narrated the downfall of the city. To readers in the first century this picture referred to Rome, but John also used it in reference to society organized in opposition to the will of God.

Triumphant Return of Christ

In 19:11-16 John pictured the triumphant return of Christ. He used images of glory and majesty to describe Christ (19:12-13). He named Him "King of Kings and Lord of Lords" (19:16). After narrating His appearance John pictured His triumphant victory over the forces of Satan in the occurrence of the Battle of Armageddon (19:17-21). In this incident John lauded the spiritual power of Christ in destroying the forces of Satan and his henchmen. The beast (the Antichrist from 13:1) and the false prophet (the beast from the land in 13:11) receive God's judgment and are cast into the lake of fire (19:20). The devil himself also is cast into the lake of fire in 20:10.

🌿 **Check the correct ending to each of the following statements.**[12]

1. To first century readers Babylon symbolized
   ❏ a. Rome   ❏ b. Jerusalem   ❏ c. Armageddon

2. John uses pictures of glory to describe
   ❏ a. Armageddon   ❏ b. Jesus   ❏ c. Jerusalem

Christ's Millennial Reign

In chapter 20 John narrated the Messianic triumph of Christ in His millennial reign. This chapter has received many different interpretations during the course of Christian history (see day 2 for various millennial views). Those who are amillennial feel that this chapter shows the binding of Satan to allow the spread of the gospel on earth (20:1-3) and the spiritual rest of believers with Christ in heaven (20:4-6). Amillennialists feel that these verses describe events now occurring in this age.

---

12. Answers: 1-a, 2-b.

This writer has followed a premillennial approach, which advocates that Christ's return precedes the period known as the millennnium. In this interpretation the binding of Satan represents the limiting of his power during the millennial age (20:1-3). The description in 20:4-6 shows victorious believers reigning with Christ on earth. These believers have experienced a bodily resurrection in the first resurrection, and they reign with Christ a thousand years (20:4-6). Some premillennialists view the thousand years as literal in length, and others see the thousand years as a symbol for a period in history that represents peace and victory with Jesus.

Satan Released for a Time

At the conclusion of the millennial period Satan is released to cause an additional period of chaos. He will be defeated and cast into the lake of fire (20:10). The ability of Satan to cause trouble on the earth after a period of perfect peace makes clear that the ultimate cause of sin is in the human heart and not merely in social conditions or environment. This suggests that one result of God's allowing the millennium is to show that sin is personal and not merely social in origin.

The Great White Throne

After the judgment of Satan another group of individuals is brought to stand before God in the final judgment. This is the judgment of the great white throne (20:11-15). Since believers were raised from the dead in the first resurrection (20:5), this raising of individuals must be a reference to unbelievers. Those who stand before God in this judgment ultimately are cast into the lake of fire (20:13-15). This is the second death (20:14).

Everything Made New (Rev. 21–22)

After the final destruction of Satan and the last judgment, John gave a brief statement of the beginning of the new heavens, the new earth, and the new Jerusalem in 21:1-8.

🌿 **Mark the following statements *T* (true) or *F* (false).**[13]

    ___ 1. The final judgment is called the great white throne judgment.
    ___ 2. Believers do not face this judgment.
    ___ 3. Unbelievers face this judgment.
    ___ 4. Those who face this judgment are cast into the lake of fire.

Vision of Ultimate Triumph (21–22)

The vision of the heavenly Jerusalem represents John's final vision. In this section John used earthly language to describe eternal Jerusalem. He was making a deliberate contrast between the evil city of the beast (Babylon, 17:1-18) and the heavenly city of God's dwelling.

New Jerusalem Represents Heaven

John used the term "new Jerusalem" (21:2) to refer to the place in which believers will live in a new order for eternity. The most striking feature of this new Jerusalem is its glory (21:11). The act of measuring the city and the description of its beauty (21:15-21) refer to its magnificence. The worship and service of God will be the chief joy of God's people in this new Jerusalem (22:3).

Blessings, Warnings, Invitation

In 22:6-21 John presented an epilogue consisting of warnings and promises to the church. John recorded a blessing for those who heard this prophecy and obeyed its emphases (22:7). He contrasted the destiny of the saints with the fate of the wicked (22:14-15). He also recorded Christ's invitation to the world to come and share in fellowship with Him (22:17). He delivered a solemn warning to any who might willfully distort or alter the teaching of this book (22:18-19). He concluded with an expression of longing for Jesus' return (22:20).

---

13. Answers: All four statements are true.

Come, Lord Jesus, in Majesty!

Reading through this book will promote in our lives a sober, righteous, and godly behavior, as we look for and await the return of the Lord Jesus Christ (Titus 2:12-13). Come, Lord Jesus, in majesty!

SUMMARY REVIEW

To review this unit, see if you can mentally answer the following questions. You may want to write the answers on a separate sheet of paper. Mark your level of performance on the left: circle *C* if you can answer correctly and circle *R* if you need to review.

C R 1. What is the meaning of the word *Revelation*, and how was this revelation given?

C R 2. What was God's three-fold purpose in giving Revelation?

C R 3. List and explain three views people hold about Revelation.

C R 4. What is the theme of Revelation? List the four visions.

C R 5. What symbols are used in the three series of judgments from God on the earth?

C R 6. How will history end?

C R 7. What shall Christ do after He returns?

C R 8. What thoughts are we to have about the coming of the Lord Jesus?

RESPONDING TO GOD'S WORD

Reflect back on your time in *Step by Step Through the New Testament.* You have been in this intense study of the New Testament for 13 units. What significant truth have you applied to your life?

_____

How is God going to use this knowledge in your service for Him?

_____

Record below one truth you will share with someone this week as you continue to walk with Christ.

_____

Now that you have walked through the New Testament, step into the Old Testament.

Step by Step Through the Old Testament by Waylon Bailey and Tom Hudson provides a survey of the message and important events, people, places, and themes of the Old Testament.

- Build a framework for understanding and interpreting the Old Testament.
- Gain an understanding of the biblical background needed for a lifetime of meaningful study of God's Word.
- Respond to God as He speaks to you through His Word.

Step by Step Through the Old Testament is a 13-unit course designed for a combination of individual and small-group study. Resources include a Bible study book (item 001116311) and leader guide (item 005741126, available as a free PDF download from LifeWay.com).

To obtain more information or to place an order, write to LifeWay Resources Customer Service; One LifeWay Plaza; Nashville, TN 37234; fax 615-251-5933; phone toll free 800-458-2772; email orderentry@lifeway.com; or order online at LifeWay.com.